Deleuze and Research Methodolo

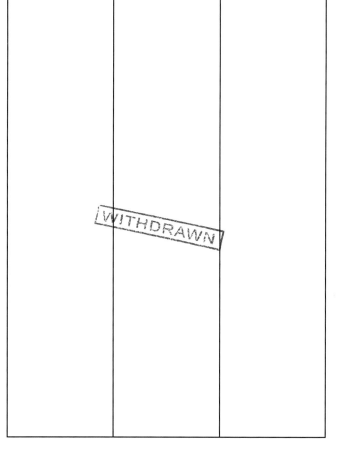

Deleuze Connections

'It is not the elements or the sets which define the multiplicity. What defines it is the AND, as something which has its place between the elements or between the sets. AND, AND, AND – stammering.'

Gilles Deleuze and Claire Parnet, *Dialogues*

General Editor
Ian Buchanan

Editorial Advisory Board

Keith Ansell-Pearson
Rosi Braidotti
Claire Colebrook
Tom Conley

Gregg Lambert
Adrian Parr
Paul Patton
Patricia Pisters

Titles Available in the Series

Ian Buchanan and Claire Colebrook (eds), *Deleuze and Feminist Theory*
Ian Buchanan and John Marks (eds), *Deleuze and Literature*
Mark Bonta and John Protevi (eds), *Deleuze and Geophilosophy*
Ian Buchanan and Marcel Swiboda (eds), *Deleuze and Music*
Ian Buchanan and Gregg Lambert (eds), *Deleuze and Space*
Martin Fuglsang and Bent Meier Sørensen (eds), *Deleuze and the Social*
Ian Buchanan and Adrian Parr (eds), *Deleuze and the Contemporary World*
Constantin V. Boundas (ed.), *Deleuze and Philosophy*
Ian Buchanan and Nicholas Thoburn (eds), *Deleuze and Politics*
Chrysanthi Nigianni and Merl Storr (eds), *Deleuze and Queer Theory*
Jeffrey A. Bell and Claire Colebrook (eds), *Deleuze and History*
Laura Cull (ed.), *Deleuze and Performance*
Mark Poster and David Savat (eds), *Deleuze and New Technology*
Simone Bignall and Paul Patton (eds), *Deleuze and the Postcolonial*
Stephen Zepke and Simon O'Sullivan (eds), *Deleuze and Contemporary Art*
Laura Guillaume and Joe Hughes (eds), *Deleuze and the Body*
Daniel W. Smith and Nathan Jun (eds), *Deleuze and Ethics*
Frida Beckman (ed.), *Deleuze and Sex*
David Martin-Jones and William Brown (eds), *Deleuze and Film*
Laurent de Sutter and Kyle McGee (eds), *Deleuze and Law*
Arun Saldanha and Jason Michael Adams (eds), *Deleuze and Race*
Rebecca Coleman and Jessica Ringrose (eds), *Deleuze and Research Methodologies*
Inna Semetsky and Diana Masny (eds), *Deleuze and Education*
Hélène Frichot and Stephen Loo (eds), *Deleuze and Architecture*

Visit the Deleuze Connections website at
www.euppublishing.com/series/delco

Deleuze and Research Methodologies

Edited by Rebecca Coleman and Jessica Ringrose

EDINBURGH
University Press

© editorial matter and organisation Rebecca Coleman and Jessica Ringrose, 2013
© the chapters their several authors

Edinburgh University Press Ltd
22 George Square, Edinburgh EH8 9LF

www.euppublishing.com

Reprinted 2014 (twice)

Typeset in 10.5/13 Adobe Sabon
by Servis Filmsetting Ltd, Stockport, Cheshire,
printed and bound in Great Britain by
CPI Group (UK) Ltd, Croydon CR0 4YY

A CIP record for this book is available from the British Library

ISBN 978 0 7486 4411 7 (hardback)
ISBN 978 0 7486 4410 0 (paperback)
ISBN 978 0 7486 4412 4 (webready PDF)
ISBN 978 0 7486 7637 8 (epub)
ISBN 978 0 7486 7638 5 (Amazon ebook)

Contents

Acknowledgements

This is a book that has been produced in-between. In-between us, in-between the contributors, and in-between the other academic and personal activities that we have been involved in. There are therefore many people connected to the book who we would like to thank. Thanks to contributors for their work and patience; we have enjoyed being in this process with you all and hope that our conversations will continue. Thanks also to Ian Buchanan for responding so positively to our book proposal, Jenny Daly and Carol MacDonald at Edinburgh University Press, and Peta Malins, Jennifer Lea and Maria Tamboukou. We had the idea for this book during the ESRC Researching Affect and Affective Communication Seminar Series (2008–10), and we would like to acknowledge the participants in that series, and in particular thank Valerie Walkerdine for organising it.

Permission to quote the poem, 'Matter 9: To Texture To Verb' by Meredith Quartermain in Chapter 9 was kindly granted by Quartermain.

Acknowledgements

Introduction: Deleuze and Research Methodologies

Rebecca Coleman and Jessica Ringrose

It is widely acknowledged that Deleuze's work is having a significant impact across different fields in the social sciences and humanities. Our aim in this book is to examine the ways in which Deleuzian thinking is inspiring *empirical research practice*. Deleuze's work has typically been viewed as 'high' theory, and as a set of ideas that work in an abstract way but which have little relevance to 'doing research'. For example, Deleuzian ideas have been explored in social, cultural and feminist theory (see for instance the other books published in the Deleuze Connections series) and in the fields of art, film and media studies (see for example Colman 2011; Munster 2006; O'Sullivan 2006). As such, there has tended to be a focus on textual modes of analysis, with the 'practical' dimensions of Deleuze's philosophy and approach to the empirical largely neglected. However, it has recently become apparent that Deleuzian inspired empirical research in the social sciences is steadily growing (see as examples Hickey-Moody and Malins 2007; Masny and Cole 2011; Ollson 2009; Potts 2004; McCormack 2007; Latham and McCormack 2009; Tamboukou 2008; Jensen and Rödje 2009). *Deleuze and Research Methodologies* draws on and contributes to this movement. At the same time, it contributes to wider shifts in social science, which indicate the need for methodologies capable of attending to the social and cultural world as mobile (Buscher, Urry and Witchger 2010), messy (Law 2004), creative (Massumi 2002), changing and open-ended (Lury and Wakeford 2012), sensory and affective (Stewart 2007; Orr 2006; Pink 2009), and that account for the performativity of method; social science methodologies not only describe the worlds they observe but (at least in part) are in involved in the invention or creation of the world (Law and Urry 2004; Barad 2007).

Taking up these concurrent trends, the book begins from the position that Deleuze's work, with its focus on becoming, affect, relationality, creativity and multiplicity, is incredibly suggestive for social science research. We argue that Deleuze's work, solo and with collaborators like Guattari and Parnet, is particularly helpful for thinking about *methodology*, because one of its key demands is to break down the false divide between theory and practice. As Deleuze maintained, 'theory is an inquiry, which is to say, a practice: a practice of the seemingly fictive world that empiricism describes; a study of the conditions of legitimacy of practices that is in fact our own' (2001a: 36). This impels researchers to re-think research processes – to pose (and re-pose) questions about the relationship between theory and methodology, the conditions under which empirical research is conducted, and its effects/affects.

The book consists of this Introduction and twelve chapters from academics working in different social science disciplines, including Sociology, Education, Geography and Cultural Studies, and whose research draw on further disciplines: Film Studies, Media Studies, Anthropology, Gender Studies, Philosophy and Early Childhood Studies. Indeed, one of the things that we think the chapters demonstrate is the necessary *interdisciplinarity* of thinking and doing that Deleuze's work suggests, where theories and ways of doing that are key to specific disciplines are thought in relation to other modes of thinking and doing – and are perhaps transformed in the process. We also see it as imperative to continue and create research conversations across different subject areas in order to break out of methodological/disciplinary 'territorialities' (as Deleuze and Guattari [1984, 1987] might term them).

The point about interdisciplinarity is important to note in terms of how the book may be put to work. Contributors were invited to think carefully about the methodological implications of Deleuze's work – in conjunction with other approaches if illuminating – for their research, and to outline in accessible ways how Deleuze's philosophy and the wealth of new conceptual languages and thinking tools that this work produces have informed their research processes. We see the book as a starting point, rather than as a comprehensive or complete collection. The book does not – cannot – include contributions from all of those working in this area, although we do discuss some of the important Deleuzian methodological arguments that are not featured in the book below. Rather, the book aims to bring some cohesion to the emerging field of Deleuzian inspired empirical research, and provide inspiration and initial guidance for those wanting to use and further develop these methodologies. The book is not a blueprint for how-to-do-Deleuzian-research though. Such a task would be impossible and unnecessary, particularly as one of the things that we think Deleuze's work encourages is the development of concepts and methodologies that are specific, relevant or appropriate to the problem at stake (Fraser 2009; Coleman 2008, 2009). However, we hope that the book will be helpful in mapping out and making clear(er) some of the ways in which the often seemingly abstract ideas of Deleuze are being and might be put to work.

Furthermore, we think that different chapters may be of interest to different readers for different reasons, and see this as part and parcel of Deleuzian-inspired research practice, where issues of multiplicity and difference, lines of flight, sense and sensation are highlighted. While the research foci and/or methodology and/or concepts of concern in different chapters may be different to those at stake in your own research, we hope that the chapters will resonate at different levels. It may be, for example, that your interest in affect takes you to some chapters rather than others, or that your ethnographic mode of working prioritises some chapters, or that your focus on young people, or images, or gender or race makes certain chapters stand out. So, while a particular contributor's focus on students, or anorexia, or elephants, or shanty towns may not be your research topic, their methodology of interviewing, or online research, or film-making may be, and/or their discussion of concepts such as desire, or the body, or (non-)representation, may be. Towards the end of the chapter we provide various 'routes through' the book – and of course these are not exhaustive. Before that, we outline a series of moves happening within social science methodologies more generally, and then make links between these shifts and the Deleuzian concepts and practices in focus in this book.

Affect, Mess, Performativity: Contemporary Methodological Issues

The research methodologies that are explored in this book include ethnography, group and individual interviewing, film-making and online research. The book also includes discussions that trouble traditional modes of analytic practice, including coding, data analysis and interpretive strategies. The chapters are thus all clearly rooted in an empirical social science tradition. Indeed, we would like to make clear at the start of the book that we see the ideas that we examine in the Introduction, and that the contributors unpack in their chapters, as firmly part of existing, but changing, social science paradigms and ways of working. The purpose of this book then, is not to propose that all social science research should be Deleuzian, nor to suggest that the chapters in this book refute, reject or completely re-work methodologies that have long been at the centre of how social science is produced. Rather, our suggestion is relatively modest: that putting to work some of Deleuze's ideas about the world and ways of studying it might help to shed light on other ways of knowing, relating to and creating the world, 'noticing' (Stewart 2007; Blackman and Venn 2010) different kinds of things that might be happening, or things that might be happening differently.

We go on to discuss how Deleuze's work might help to activate these different ways of thinking, knowing and relating to the world through the contributions in the book. But here we want to briefly outline some more general shifts occurring in social science methodologies, to place the Deleuzian inspired work within a broader set of issues. Kathleen Stewart's book *Ordinary Affects* (2007), an ethnography on the affective dimensions of everyday life, is a helpful place from which to begin, partly because it is referred to in some of the chapters, partly because its interest is in affect and the everyday, mundane or habitual, and partly because, as noted above, it brings to life a particular method of noticing the world around us.[1] Stewart's method is to start not with 'a totalized system' (2007: 1) – neoliberalism, (advanced) capitalism or globalisation – into which characteristics of the everyday can be identified and ticked off, but rather with 'the live surface' (2007: 4); the sensations, intensities and textures through which ordinary life is experienced.

Stewart's account of the everyday is thus twofold. First, she suggests that everyday life 'is' affective; 'the ordinary is a shifting assemblage' of 'things that happen' and are felt, 'in impulses, sensations, expectations, daydreams, encounters, and habits of relating', for instance (2007: 1–2). These things that happen are intensive, immanent, palpable, moving, potentials; they exceed or evade 'meaning' and 'representation' (2007: 3, 4). Second, Stewart indicates that in order to get to grips with – to attend to if not completely capture – ordinary affects, methodologies need to 'attune' to different kinds of things. For Stewart, this involves both taking in and examining the 'fractious, multiplicitous, and unpredictable' (2007: 3), and finding ways of writing and portraying the affective. She takes up a number of techniques to do this: her book is organised as 'an assemblage of disparate scenes' (2007: 5), a series of vignettes that describe scenes from everyday life in the United States (shopping in Wal-Mart, driving, news reports about crimes committed at Greyhound bus stations, domestic violence, television) and offers critical reflections on and analysis of how ethnography might grapple with affect. For example, she writes of her encounters with the worlds she explores in the third person, and reflects on how a focus on the affective changes the ways in which social science might understand important concepts, such as ideology, or the self.

How methodologies can attend to the affective and/or to 'little experiences' is central to many of the chapters in this book, as we discuss below. Here though, we pick up on Stewart's emphasis on assemblage, as it connects with other moves made in social science methodologies, for example by John Law (2004) in his work on how methods need to be reinvented in order to deal with the fluidity, multiplicity and vagueness of reality. For Law, reality is messy, and methodologies that seek to convert this mess into something smooth, coherent and precise both miss out on particular textures of life (and here Law's list of the affective or ephemeral that are often overlooked by social science bears striking similarity to Stewart's), and tends to make a mess of what it does seek to understand, because it fails to account for complexity. As such, Law argues, 'the task is to imagine methods when they no longer seek the definite, the repeatable, the more or less stable' (2004: 6). Law's book is wide-ranging, and its main focus is on developing a methodology from accounts from his own field of research, Science and Technology Studies (STS). What is of interest for this book is Law's concern with how STS understands the world as necessarily multiple and in movement: the world is 'a "generative flux" that *produces* realities' (2004: 7); there are realit*ies* rather than *a* reality. In order to seek the generative, the multiple, the changing, Law proposes method 'in [an] extended manner', a '*method assemblage*' (2004: 41). For those unfamiliar with Deleuzian terminology, 'assemblage' is a key concept that seeks to account for multiplicity and change (or becoming). Drawing on Deleuze, Law defines method assemblage as 'a tentative and hesitant unfolding, that is at most only very partially under any form of deliberate control. It needs to be understood as a verb as well as a noun' (2004: 41–2).[2]

For Law, method assemblage is 'the enactment or crafting of a bundle of ramifying relations that generates presence, manifests absence and Otherness, where it is the crafting of presence that distinguishes it as a *method* assemblage' (2004: 42). That is, method is the *crafting* of the boundaries between what is present, what is manifestly absent, and what is Othered.[3] There is no avoidance of these boundary-making practices Law argues (see also Suchman 2007), but method assemblage is an attempt to 'imagine more flexible boundaries, and different forms of presence and absence. Other possibilities can be imagined, for instance if we attend to non-coherence' (2004: 85). One of the things that an awareness of boundary-making involves is a focus on relations; indeed, Law suggests that method assemblage involves 'the making of relations' (2004: 84), so that the question for social science method-ologies becomes whether it is possible to *know* social realities: 'How might we catch some of the realities we are currently missing? Can we know them well? *Should* we know them? Is "knowing" the metaphor that we need? And if it isn't, then how might we relate to them?' (2004: 2).[4]

We return to the potential shift from 'knowing' to 'relating to' the world below. Here we want to develop the understanding of the multiplicity of the world/worlds, and the questions raised for the role of methods in not only 'catching' these multiple realities, but *making* them. The idea that methods are not only descriptive and generative but *performative* is an issue that Law discusses in the context of STS (see especially Law 2004: chapter 5), and it is also at stake in an influential article[5] written with John Urry (Law and Urry 2004), where they argue that, just as the social world that the social sciences study changes, so too do the methods through which social sciences study the world. What this suggests is that 'the social sciences work upon, and within, the social world, helping in turn to make and remake it' (2004: 392). As such, methods perform: 'they make differences; they enact realities; and they can help to bring into being what they discover': 'social reality is a relational effect produced in arrangements generated in social science' (2004: 393–4). These are significant points that shift methodology from 'epistemology (where what is known depends upon perspective) to ontology (what is known is also being *made* differently)' (2004: 397).

Crucially, to say that social science brings social worlds into being is not to argue that 'reality is arbitrary' (2004: 395), nor to imply that the social scientist is an all-powerful figure who can magically conjure up the world they imagine. Rather, taking seriously the idea that methodol-ogy is a way of relating to multiply assembled worlds suggests that social scientists are themselves entangled within the assemblages they seek to study. Researchers are thus one point of the relations within an assem-blage. An important point, undeniably; as Karen Barad (2007) amongst others encourages us to realise, researchers need to be responsible for the 'cuts' that are made in the practice of boundary-making. This move away from seeing individuals as clearly bounded subjects and towards a mapping of the relations in which researchers are always involved is key to many chapters in this book (see below). It also draws attention to the *politics* of methodology. The critical questions, as Law and Urry pose them, become, 'is it possible to imagine developing methods that strengthen particular realities while eroding others? Is it possible to imagine social science method as a *system of interference* (we draw the term from Donna Haraway) for working towards and making particular forms of the social real while eroding others?' (2004: 397).

Inventive Methods, Creative Concepts

One way to approach these questions is to see methodology as a relation between *what is* and *what might be*. In their Introduction to the book, *Inventive Methods: The Happening of the Social*, Celia Lury and Nina Wakeford define inventive methods as, in part, 'always oriented towards making a difference' (2012: 11). In this sense, to address the problems put forward by Law and Urry, social science methods may aim to make a difference by interfering in how power is understood and relayed. But Lury and Wakeford also discuss methods as 'making a difference' in terms of the relationship between the 'here' and 'now', and the 'there' and 'then'. What makes a method *inventive*, they argue, is its capacity to be both specific and 'beyond' its situation, singular and multiple, actual and virtual. 'An inventive method', they write, 'addresses a specific problem, and is adapted in use in relation to that specificity; its use may be repeated, but the method is always oriented to making a difference' (2012: 11). It is interesting to note here that difference is in relation to repetition. In methodological terms, this suggests that methods cannot simply be repeated, because in repetition there is always difference; methods are done differently, and will make a difference. In more philosophical terms, Lury and Wakeford's point can also be understood to refer to how life *is* difference; for Deleuze, 'the whole of life is difference . . . the power to think differently, to become different and to create differences' (Colebrook 2002: 13). Mapping difference, opening up spaces of and for difference, is thus a central problem for Deleuzian scholars where, methodologically, 'to repeat is to behave in a certain manner, but in relation to something unique and singular which has no equal or equivalent' (Deleuze 2001b: 1).

The development of inventive methods links with the more explicitly Deleuzian methodology that Brian Massumi explains in *Parables for the Virtual* (2002). For Massumi, drawing on Deleuze's ideas of concepts as creative, Deleuzian methodology is, or should be, inventive. For Deleuze, concepts are not representative, reflective or descriptive but are *creative*. Concepts are 'no longer "concepts of", understood by reference to their external object' (Tomlinson and Habberjam 2005: xv), but are immanent to the object at stake. Deleuze's understanding of concepts emerges through the ontology of becoming where 'to become is never to imitate, nor to "do like", nor to conform to a model' (Deleuze and Parnet 2002: 2). That is, in a Deleuzian sense, a concept is neither a pre-existing theoretical framework into which empirical material is fitted and interpreted, nor a notion that springs from empirical research (although it is probably closer to the latter). Rather, *concepts do things*. Understanding concepts as *doing* is, fundamentally, an understanding of concepts as becoming. Deleuze argues that concepts are inventive: 'Let us create extraordinary words, on condition that they be put to the most ordinary use and that the entity they designate be made to exist in the same way as the most common object' (Deleuze and Parnet 2002: 3). Indeed, Massumi argues that the invention of concepts is an essential project to ensure creative methodologies of relating to and engaging with the world(s). What these methodologies would invent are:

> concepts and connections between concepts. The first rule of thumb if you want to invent or reinvent concepts is simple: don't apply them. If you apply a concept or system of connection between concepts, it is the material you apply it to that undergoes change, much more markedly than do the concepts. The change is imposed upon the material by the concepts' systematicity and constitutes a becoming homologous of the material to the system. This is all very grim. It has less to do with 'more to the world' than 'more of the same'. It has less to do with invention than mastery and control. (Massumi 2002: 17)

Massumi's version of inventive methodology is to notice and bring about 'more to the world'. In this sense, as Law and Urry ask us to consider, thinking about methodology is thinking about social change. Lury and Wakeford argue that inventive methods 'are able to grasp the here and now in terms of somewhere else, and in doing so – *if* they can also change the problem to which they are addressed – they expand the actual, inventively' (2012: 13, reference omitted). An attention to that which has conventionally escaped or troubled social science – the virtual, the affective, the ephemeral – is thus one of the ways in which social science might expand the actual, invent and/or strengthen particular worlds. For example, as Alan Latham and Derek McCormack (2009) put it in their Deleuzian inspired work on images, 'working to hold open this potential (another word for which is the virtual) does not mean that images can do everything, but that within a given set of constraints they always have the potential to surprise us, however gently' (2009: 260). In the next section, we stay with this idea that Deleuze's work might open up potential, through introducing some of the concepts that contributors take up and develop methodologically.

Deleuze and Methodology: Multiplicity, Transcendental Empiricism and Immanence

As we have considered so far, the issue of multiplicity is currently central within the social sciences. While the discussion above makes clear that multiplicity is not only at stake for Deleuzian thinking, we think that Deleuze's work provides a particularly helpful discussion of multiplicity in terms of empiricism:

> States of things are neither unities or totalities, but *multiplicities*. It is not just that there are several states of things (each one of which would be yet another); nor that each state of things is itself multiple (which would simply be to indicate its resistance to unification). The essential thing, from the point of view of empiricism, is the noun *multiplicity*, which designates a set of lines or dimensions which are irreducible to each other. Every 'thing' is made up in this way. (Deleuze and Parnet 2002: vii)

In arguing that multiplicity refers not only to 'several states of things', nor to 'resistance to unification', Deleuze and Parnet go on to outline multiplicity in terms of relationality: 'In a multiplicity what counts are not the terms or the elements, but what there is "between", the between, a set of relations which are not separable from each other' (Deleuze and Parnet 2002: viii). 'A' multiplicity can thus be understood in terms of the assemblage, a temporary grouping of relations. The emphasis here is not so much on 'the terms or elements' that 'make up' the multiplicity/ assemblage, but rather on the relations, the 'in-between'. Moreover, Deleuze and Parnet describe these relations, these 'lines' between things, as becomings, that is, as always in process, changing, moving. The multiplicity/assemblage is temporary, then, because it is unfinished, open-ended, in excess of the actual, or containing the virtual within it. As many of the contributors detail, it is important not to confuse Deleuze's concept of becoming with an unrestricted process (see also Coleman 2009). It is not that an assemblage can become anything – and here the question of power is raised, in that a Deleuzian approach to the social is as much a mapping of what is impossible, what becomes stuck or fixed, as it is of flux and flow. Furthermore, becoming is not a process that begins from one point and ends up at another. Becoming is not a process of transforming from one thing into another; 'a line of becoming has neither beginning nor end, departure nor arrival, origin nor destination . . . A line of becoming has only a middle' (Deleuze and Guattari 1987: 293). The methodological task is thus to enter the middle, the between; to relate.

Deleuze and Parnet suggest that in order to study the relations that constitute a multiplicity a particular style of *empiricism* is required. This is an empiricism where 'the abstract does not explain but must itself be explained; and the aim is not to rediscover the eternal or the universal, but to find the conditions under which something new is produced (*creativeness*)' (Deleuze and Parnet 2002: vii). Deleuze and Parnet contrast this style of empiricism to rationalist philosophies where 'the abstract is given the task of explaining, and it is the abstract that is realised in the concrete. One starts with abstractions such as the One, the Whole, the Subject, and one looks for the process by which they are embodied in a world which they make conform to their requirements.' Empiricism, on the other hand, 'starts with . . . extracting the states of things, in such a way that non-pre-existent concepts can be extracted from them' (2002: vii).

In arguing for an empiricism through which 'non-pre-existent', creative concepts are produced from the 'states of things', Deleuze is pointing to an empiricism that becomes through immanence. That is, empiricism is a way to study the multiplicity of a thing – its relationality – through beginning from and extracting what is immanent to that thing. Immanence refers to the specificity or singularity of a thing; not to what can be made to fit into a pre-existent abstraction (neo-liberalism, capitalism, or globalisation, for example). However, as we indicated above, a focus on the 'in-itself' is not a model of isolating particular things, or aspects of things, from their relations. Deleuze's empiricism does not 'stop' with the 'in itself' but traces the lines between immanence and 'a wider series' in what Deleuze (2001a) explains as the project of 'transcendental empiricism'.

The 'transcendental' referred to in Deleuze's transcendental empiricism is not, then, an abstract, supplementary framework into which immanence can be fitted; it is not 'the transcendent' (Deleuze 2001a: 26). Instead, Deleuze describes how there 'is something wild and powerful in this transcendental empiricism' (2001a: 25):

> The life of an individual gives way to an impersonal and yet singular life that releases a pure event freed from the accidents of internal and external life, that is from the subjectivity and objectivity of what happens . . . It is a haeccity no longer of individuation but of singularisation: a life of pure immanence. (Deleuze 2001a: 28–9)

Here, what is relevant methodologically is the singularisation that Deleuze refers to – an attempt to 'capture' the 'impersonal yet singular' nature of life, that is, the relationship between the actual and the virtual, as discussed above. Colebrook explains the project of Deleuze's empiricism as 'a commitment to beginning from singular, partial or "molecular" experiences, which are then organised and extended into "molar" formations' (Colebrook 2002: 82). Transcendental empiricism thus begins with singular experiences and traces the ways in which the virtual is actualised, and may be actualised differently. In methodological terms, this is to attend to the ways in which social realities are made through methods, and might be made in other ways.

Ethics, Power and Feminist Research

Deleuze's project of transcendental empiricism is particularly important for a methodology book concerned with empirical research. In the Introduction to their edited book, *Deleuzian Encounters: Studies in Contemporary Issues* (2007), Anna Hickey-Moody and Peta Malins tie Deleuze's insistence that 'theory *is* practice' (2007: 3) to his understanding of ethics, something 'very different from a "morality", which operates as an overarching or transcendent system of prior rules and judgements. Such judgements work to close off and limit the potentiality of a situation, foreclosing its future' (Hickey-Moody and Malins 2007: 3). As is stressed in the discussion above, transcendental empiricism rejects such transcendent systems, and instead pays attention to the immanent and singular. In contrast to morality, then, what emerges instead is 'an immanent form of ethics: one which resides within (rather than above or outside) matter and practice, and which seeks to evaluate relations as they emerge, rather than judge them a-priori'. As such:

> Deleuze's approach to ethics is thus concerned with evaluating 'what we do, [and] what we say, *in relation to the ways of existing involved*', and in relation to the kinds of potentials and capacities that those ways of existing affirm. Within such an evaluation, it is not what a body 'is' that matters, but what it is capable of, and in what ways its relations with other bodies diminish or enhance those capacities. (Hickey-Moody and Malins 2007: 3, emphasis added)

One of the key ways in which the ethics of research have been explored is through an attention to how 'relations with other bodies diminish or enhance those capacities'. This issue has been key to feminist methodological approaches from a wide range of perspectives, where reflexivity about the power relations inherent to any research encounter has been encouraged (for example Stanley and Wise 1983). Indeed, several chapters pay explicit attention to gender/feminism (Blaise, Dyke, Renold and Mellor, Ringrose and Coleman), and to axes of power and inequity, including race (Jackson, Mazzei, Taylor), religion (Cole) and poverty (Grinberg), with many chapters illustrating the politicised dimensions of Deleuzian informed research methods (for example, Hickey-Moody, MacLure). The relations between researcher and researched are also highlighted through Deleuzian approaches, via an attention to affective capacities for example (Ringrose and Coleman, Dyke, Blaise, Lorimer, Renold and Mellor), and to the problem of distinguishing between the subjects and objects of research.

Indeed, for some of the contributors located in Education, Elizabeth St. Pierre's (1997; St. Pierre and Pillow, 2000) contributions to feminist poststructuralist methodologies have been particularly inspiring (Cole, Jackson, Mazzei). For example, in one article, St. Pierre discusses struggling to 'write up' her ethnography with older white women in the American town in which she grew up, because she had 'such difficulty separating myself from my participants' (1997: 178). Taking up Deleuze's concept of the fold – which as she explains 'disrupts our notion of interiority, since it defines "the inside as the operation of the outside"' (1997: 178, references omitted) – St. Pierre found that she was able to place herself *within* the research assemblage, as one of the relations *between* the different elements of the research. In thinking about how her 'own' subjectivity was folded into the subjectivities of the women in her study, St. Pierre describes how she also began to ruminate on the status of 'data', and how certain kinds of data 'were uncodable, excessive, out-of-control, out-of-category' (1997: 179). Paying attention to such 'transgressive data', St. Pierre argues, is an ethical project, in that it is concerned with responsibility, with 'theorising our own lives, examining the frames with which we read the world, and moving toward an ongoing validity of response' (1997: 186). Here, ethics is not a response that can be 'defined for all situations. Rather ... ethics is invented within each relation as researcher and respondent negotiate sense-making' (1997: 186). Perhaps this negotiation is made especially stark for those working with young children (see Blaise, Renold and Mellor, MacLure), where 'sense-making' is a process that happens 'outside' of adult understandings of (verbal and written) discourse.

Ethics also become apparent where the relations are between humans and nonhumans, whether those nonhumans are elephants, as in the case of Jamie Lorimer's chapter, or scientific or technological objects and activities such as social networking sites or websites, as with Ringrose and Coleman's and Dyke's chapters. Indeed, Law's method assemblage is developed via STS, and is involved in acknowledging and crediting 'materials other than those that are currently privileged ... as presences that reflect and help to enact reality': 'bodies, devices, theatre, apprehensions, buildings' (Law 2004: 153), to list just a few.[6] Deleuze's concept of machines is taken up by some contributors to the book (Jackson, Ringrose and Coleman) as a means to locate the 'ethical axes' of life (Bonta and Protevi 2004), including the agency or enactment of the non-human. Other contributors theorise materiality as a way of researching the micropolitics of what is significant in a research encounter (Blaise, Dyke, Grinberg, Renold and Mellor, Taylor).

Indeed, re-thinking spatial relations through Deleuzian concepts is one of the ways educational researchers in particular have explored power relations in pedagogical domains through framings like micropolitics that allow them to investigate lines of connection and rupture in relation to territories. In the important educational text *Working the Ruins*, St. Pierre used nomadic analysis and the idea of a becoming a 'nomadic ethnographer' to explore the contours of smooth (fluid and open) and striated (overcoded and closed) spaces in her writing, and to consider her affective relationship to her fieldwork geographies and her 'armchair ethnography' musings (St. Pierre and Pillow 2000: 264). In the same volume, Alverman uses the concepts of rhizoanalysis (see also Masny 2010) to outline processes of mappings that can help us understand connections, linkages and offshoots in data in new ways. These ideas of nomadic analyses are taken up in Cole's chapter, and the mapping of power relations in online spaces in Ringrose and Coleman's, whilst the concept of the rhizome is touched upon by Mazzei in thinking about becoming, and by Grinberg in thinking about control and flight.

How Might This Book Work? Or, Making Connections Across the Book

In our discussion of Deleuze's work so far, it should be apparent that it is difficult to separate out completely different concepts. As noted, Deleuze and Parnet describe the concept in empiricism as a 'being-multiple' (2002: viii). One of the implications of a Deleuzian focus on multiplicity, relationality and assemblage, then, is that concepts change, they connect, are in relation to each other. It might be helpful to think about this idea of the multiplicity of the concept via the concepts of becoming, assemblage and immanence discussed above. While in Deleuzian terms, all of these concepts refer to something quite specific, at the same time they are connected to each other; they make sense through their relations with each other. Deleuzian concepts take us to other concepts, they encourage us to make maps of connections, and to take care in the connections (and cuts) that we make: the ethics of transcendental empiricism indicate that it is crucial to consider how concepts fit together, or not. This is perhaps especially significant when connecting Deleuzian concepts with other theories. While we are in no way arguing that researchers should only take up Deleuzian ways of thinking and working, we do think it is important to examine how we do method, given that theory is practice.

In this sense, for us to provide a simple or clear-cut explanation of the specific concept that each chapter takes up and puts to work is a difficult, if not impossible, task. Each chapter here is animated by a number of different Deleuzian concepts, and each makes its own maps between these different concepts, in some cases making different maps even when the concepts might appear to be the same (there is difference in repetition). Rather than being daunted by the multiplicity opened up by a Deleuzian approach to thinking about and doing research, we would encourage readers to go with this kind of 'nomadic thinking' (Braidotti 1994; St. Pierre 2000), to take up the chapters and concepts that resonate with you. Indeed, in his Translator's Foreword to Deleuze and Guattari's *A Thousand Plateaus* (1987), Massumi argues that the book is 'conceived as an open system. It does not pretend to have the final word' (1987: xiv). As an open system, Massumi describes the book as more akin to a record, and suggests that the book be 'played':

> When you buy a record, there are always cuts that leave you cold. You skip them. You don't approach a record as a closed book that you have to take or leave. Other cuts you may listen to over and over again. They follow you. You find yourself humming them under your breath as you go about your daily business. (1987: xiv)

Likewise we anticipate 'readers' 'skipping' some chapters and finding that other chapters 'follow' them around, become part of the 'daily business' of doing research. Moreover, we would suggest that readers go to these chapters not to find final, settled definitions of Deleuzian concepts, nor to discover a blueprint of 'how to do Deleuzian empirical research'. Rather, the chapters might become part of your 'own' research assemblages. It is in this spirit that we offer a mapping of the different chapters in the book. We suggest three mappings (there may be more) and have divided the chapters into clusters of *concepts*, of *research methodologies* and of *substantive research focus*, the first of which is the most detailed, as it also provides broader outlines of the chapters.

Concepts

While each contributor defines the specific concepts that they take from Deleuze and his collaborators, and outlines the ways in which they take them up in their own research, there are a few concepts that appear across many of the chapters that we therefore want to introduce in a little more detail. These are: becoming; the molecular and molar; affect; machines; and desire. Chapters by Alecia Jackson, Lisa Mazzei, Maggie MacLure, David Cole, Emma Renold and David Mellor and Carol Taylor all, in different ways, work with a Deleuzian ontology of *becoming*. Above, we have introduced becoming as a conviction that worlds are always in process, changing and transforming. Contributors put to work this evocation in various ways. For example, in Jackson's chapter becoming is a means to theorise data excerpts from her research with Cassandra, a black, female American academic. Jackson argues that becoming is an ethical problem of 'how to live more fully', and explores both how Cassandra's becoming is a struggle between molar and molecular forces (see below), and how data itself may be understood as becoming, as a process of machinic connections. Similar issues are also at stake in Mazzei's chapter, on white American teachers, which explores silence as a becoming, a racialised desire for privilege, and Cole's chapter reflects on a government sponsored project on the voices that shape the perspectives of young Muslims in Sydney. Cole's chapter makes a specific connection between becoming and nomadic analysis, arguing that a focus on the nomadic enables researchers to attend to the 'in-between', that (person, body, data, experience) which might not easily fit into existing social science paradigms, including those specified by research funders.

As indicated, nomadic thinking is a way of attending to what Deleuze terms 'molecular becoming'. This concept is intended to highlight that becoming is about the in-between, the middle. It is an explicit attempt by Deleuze to disrupt boundaries; the binary oppositions (between subject/object, man/woman, black/white and so on) that have governed Western philosophy. The *molecularity* of becoming is contrasted to the *molarity* of regimes of power, where becoming is fixed or fitted into pre-existing categories. The molar is thus a form of judgement that 'territorialises' the flow of becoming. As we have argued so far, a Deleuzian approach to becoming is concerned with these molar *and* molecular processes of territorialisation. Indeed, in her chapter, Silvia Grinberg examines the ways in which a Deleuzian take on 'control society' resonates with governmentality research. She argues that elaborating processes of both the molar ('the dominant') and the molecular ('the little cracks' or 'imperceptible ruptures') shifts researchers' attention from the pathologising, individualising force of surveillance and judgement, to recognition of the 'aspirations that escape nihilism'.

Mindy Blaise's chapter is also interested in the tensions between the molar and molecular. Through a focus on the 'the small, everyday encounters . . . significant to the processes of change', Blaise shows how the molar and molecular, macro and micro, work together. For example, in a detailed exploration of a research encounter where early years school children become fascinated with one of her earrings, Blaise considers how a methodological attention to embodied, small instances that might provide interruptions to research encounters re-works ideas about the role and position of (adult women bodies) researchers in their relations with research participants (child girl bodies). Blaise's concentration on a moment of research that was disruptive in some way is also a concern of other chapters (see for example Cole, who focuses on an affective moment of anger). MacLure's chapter is interested in data that does not 'fit' into traditional modes of research analysis. In a discussion of coding – the exercise through which social science categorises data – MacLure argues that a Deleuzian process of coding may disrupt these categorisations, and 'allow . . . for something other, singular, quick and ineffable to irrupt the space of analysis'. In so doing, she questions the speed at which social science can attempt to convert research encounters into something meaningful, and proposes a method of coding that allows us to sit with data that is hard to categorise, and to account for the affective resonances of data that stands out, or 'glows'. For her, this is 'an ethical refusal to take the easy exit to quick judgement, free-floating empathy, or illusions of data speaking for itself'. An ethical refusal of 'quick judgement' is also at the core of Sarah Dyke's chapter, which resists medical and common sense diagnoses of anorexia and instead takes up Deleuze's concepts of the event, the virtual and the actual in an ethnography of living with anorexia. Dyke's research, which encompasses both online and offline elements, opens up a 'different methodological space in which we might consider the "research problem"' (i.e. where researchers might 'look for' experiences of anorexia), and of the potential of 'living differently' with anorexia (when it is understood as neither 'lifestyle choice' nor mental or physical 'illness').

Renold and Mellor's and Taylor's chapters focus on becoming in relation to concepts of *affect* and sensation. Both are interested in how a focus on the affective might be a means of tracing how the becomings of nursery-age children and students in higher education are channelled in particular ways (via gender and sexuality for Renold and Mellor, and via educational trajectories and race for Taylor). Both chapters engage visual methods in order to research affect. Renold and Mellor film the action in a nursery, and argue that this visual method extended their focus on the material and sensory; indeed, they argue that through this attention to the sensory, traditional gender roles are seen – and heard – to be both reinforced and ruptured, processes that may have been missed if the focus of the ethnography were only on what becomes visible through sight or discourse. Film is also employed in Taylor's research, which develops Deleuze's work on cinema and the materiality and affectivity of images in relation to user-generated videos. Taylor focuses on faciality and the close-up, and the intensive temporality of film, arguing that Deleuze's understanding of images as material highlights how film is a particularly helpful method to focus on intensive experience.

Taylor's interest is in how a Deleuzian methodology develops a non-representational understanding of images. This is also the focus of Jamie Lorimer's chapter where he turns to recent non-representational theories of images, developed in cultural geography in particular, to witness and evoke the behaviours of elephants and their various interactions with humans. Via both making and analysing films of elephants, Lorimer draws attention to the various affective logics that come to characterise how humans understand and relate to elephants, and to ways in which 'moving imagery' methodologies might 'open thinking spaces for an affective micropolitics of curiosity in which we remain unsure as to what bodies and images might yet become'. Anna Hickey-Moody's chapter also takes up the methodological implications of Deleuze's work on affect. Hickey-Moody is particularly concerned to develop Deleuze's Spinozian concept of affect as a research methodology, because she argues that affect draws attention to what moves us, and thus to what might be registered as change. She outlines her concept of 'affective pedagogy', the idea 'that aesthetics teach us by changing how we feel', and considers ways in which 'this awareness can be brought into research'.

In their chapter, Ringrose and Coleman also develop Spinoza's definition of affect in terms of bodies – 'a body affects other bodies, or is affected by other bodies' (Deleuze 1992: 625). Reflecting on various research projects with young women and men on topics such as sexting, sexualisation and images, the chapter is particularly interested in how relations of affect are constituted and experienced through looking. Of relevance to this chapter is also Deleuze and Guattari's (1984, 1987) concept of the *desiring machine*. Here, the machine is a means of thinking about the research assemblage, as that which makes connections between different elements within a particular grouping. The chapter maps out these 'affective assemblages' in space/time articulating the 'geophilosophical' importance of Deleuze and Guattari's work. Jackson takes up the concept of the machine as well, and argues that an understanding of data excerpts as machinic shifts the focus of methodology away from asking how data can accurately represent an encounter, towards a mapping of how different elements come to be 'plugged in to' each other. Mazzei is also interested in this concept of the desiring machine, arguing that 'to think with Deleuze is to consider the forces of desire that are acting through and with our research participants and to make sense of what results from such interaction'. Across these chapters, in line with Deleuze and Guattari's refusal of certain psychoanalytic definitions, desire is not *lack*, but is reconceived as a *productive* force through which things come together and become (for more on Deleuzian desire and qualitative research, see Jackson and Mazzei 2012).

Methodologies and Methodological Process

While the clustering of concepts in particular chapters is one way of mapping the book, perhaps readers will also or instead be coming to this book because of an interest in a specific research methodology. There are a wide range of qualitative research methodologies explored in this collection, including discussions on interviewing, ethnography and visual methodology. There is also exploration and troubling of methodological processes such as data analysis, coding, categorisation, thematisation and interpretation. Again, while it is impossible to separate out completely these different foci – all of the chapters deal in some way with data analysis for example – we would suggest a mapping of methodological foci of the chapters along the following lines:

Ethnography
Blaise; Dyke; Grinberg; Lorimer; Renold and Mellor

Interviewing
Cole; Dyke; MacLure; Mazzei; Ringrose and Coleman; Taylor; Jackson

Visual and/or sensory methods
Hickey-Moody; Lorimer; Renold and Mellor; Ringrose and Coleman; Taylor

Online methods
Dyke; Ringrose and Coleman

Data collection and analysis
Hickey-Moody; MacLure

Research Focus

As we have mentioned at various points, many of the contributors come from the discipline of Education. We think there are a number of different reasons for this (including, of course, our own research assemblages, where we have both taken up Deleuze's work in research with young people). In relation to this point, we would particularly like to stress again the instability of the divide between theory and practice that Deleuze encourages us to notice, and to suggest that the distinction between theory and practice does not hold for those already working in an interdisciplinary and practitioner-based field of Education. Indeed, it may also mean that academics within Education are ideally placed to reflect on the significance of Deleuze's work for interdisciplinary, empirical research at the interface of theory and (policy, professional, pedagogical and institutional) practice. We would also like to point here to the already burgeoning field of *empirical* and *methodological* Deleuzian-inspired work in Education; indeed, several of the key methodological texts we have referred to so far come from those working in Education, including work by St. Pierre, Jackson and Mazzei, Hickey-Moody and Malins. As such, many of the substantive research foci of the chapters are on those associated with Education (children, young people, students, teachers, schools, universities, institutional management, etc.), but we would also like to suggest other kinds of mapping of research interests:

Pedagogical institutions
Grinberg; Jackson; Mazzei; Taylor

Children and young people
Blaise; Cole; Grinberg; MacLure; Renold and Mellor; Ringrose and Coleman

The body/sensory
Blaise; Dyke; Hickey-Moody; Lorimer; MacLure; Renold and Mellor; Ringrose and Coleman

Humans/nonhumans
Lorimer; Renold and Mellor

Gender
Blaise; Dyke; Renold and Mellor; Ringrose and Coleman

Race/ethnicity
Cole; Mazzei; Taylor

Images/vision
Lorimer; Renold and Mellor; Ringrose and Coleman; Taylor

Conclusion: Wonder

In suggesting these mappings, outlining some of what we consider to be key Deleuzian concepts, and making connections between Deleuze's work and other moves in social science methodologies, what we have tried to do in this Introduction is assemble together some starting points via which readers might want to explore further the implications of Deleuze's philosophy for their own research practice. Our aim in this book, then, is to suggest that Deleuze's work might indicate ways in which social worlds can be noticed, assembled and made. Indeed, to return to Latham and McCormack's point, discussed above, Deleuzian methodologies might enable the world to surprise us, however gently. In her chapter in this book, MacLure writes of something similar when she argues that what might emerge from the 'languorous pleasure' of coding is 'wonder', that which 'confounds boundaries' and 'opens and connects'. This book, then, is an attempt to think about the ways in which Deleuze's work might maintain and perhaps expand the wider social science project to open up the world, to make the world 'glow'.

Notes

1. This is not to suggest that Stewart's is the only example of work that does this. See for example Patricia Clough's fascinating ethnography of Corona, Queens (Clough 2010a, 2010b), that, drawing on a Deleuzian way of thinking, also re-works forms of academic writing and performance.
2. To define method assemblage, Law discusses the translation of the French word 'agencement' into the English term 'assemblage'. The French word has no literal or single equivalent in English, and Law emphasises that Deleuze's sense of assemblage refers both to arrangement and activity or action.
3. On craft as a social science method, see also Back (2007), Lyon and Back (2012).
4. It is worth noting here that Deleuze's work problematises the notion of metaphor, as metaphor works through a representational model, where something stands in for something else. As we discuss below, Deleuzian thinking instead seeks to emphasise immanence, the 'in itself'.
5. See for example, Fraser (2009).
6. A more sustained attempt to explicate the relations between Deleuze's work and STS can be found in Casper Bruun Jensen and Kjetil Rödje's book, *Deleuzian Intersections: Science, Technology, Anthropology* (2009), and we would like to flag up the potential that we see in making connections between these two fields, perhaps especially around the issue of methodology.

References

Back, L. (2007), *The Art of Listening*, Oxford: Berg.
Barad, K. (2007), *Meeting the Universe Halfway: Quantum Physics and the*

Entanglement of Matter and Meaning, Durham, NC: Duke University Press.

Blackman, L. and C. Venn (2010), 'Affect', *Body and Society*, 16(1): 7–28.

Bonta, M. and J. Protevi (2004), *Deleuze and Geophilosophy: A Guide and Glossary*, Edinburgh: Edinburgh University Press.

Braidotti, R. (1994), *Nomadic Subjects: Embodiment and Sexual Difference in Contemporary Feminist Theory*, New York: Columbia University Press.

Büscher, M., J. Urry and K. Witchger (eds) (2010), *Mobile Methods*, London: Routledge.

Clough, P. T. (2010a), 'Scenes of Secrecy/Scales of Hope', *Qualitative Inquiry*, 16(9): 691–6.

Clough, P. T. (2010b), 'Praying and Playing to the Beat of a Child's Metronome', *Subjectivity*, 3: 349–65.

Colebrook, C. (2002), *Gilles Deleuze*, London: Routledge.

Coleman, R. (2008), 'A Method of Intuition: Becoming, Relationality, Ethics', *History of the Human Sciences*, 21(4): 102–21.

Coleman, R. (2009), *The Becoming of Bodies: Girls, Images, Experience*, Manchester: Manchester University Press.

Coleman, R. (2012), *Transforming Images: Screens, Affect, Futures*, London: Routledge.

Colman, F. (2011), *Deleuze and Cinema*, Oxford: Berg.

Deleuze, G. (1992), 'Ethology: Spinoza and Us' in J. Crary and S. Kwinter (eds), *Incorporations*, New York: Zone, pp. 625–33.

Deleuze, G. (2001a), 'Immanence: A Life' in *Pure Immanence: Essays on A Life*, trans. A. Boyman, New York: Zone, pp. 25–33.

Deleuze, G. (2001b), *Difference and Repetition*, trans. P. Patton, London and New York: Continuum.

Deleuze, G. and C. Parnet (2002), *Dialogues II*, trans. H. Tomlinson and B. Habberjam, London: Continuum.

Deleuze, G. and F. Guattari (1984), *Anti-Oedipus: Capitalism and Schizophrenia*, trans. R. Hurley, M. Seem and H. R. Lane, London: Athlone.

Deleuze, G. and F. Guattari (1987), *A Thousand Plateaus: Capitalism and Schizophrenia*, trans. B. Massumi, London: Athlone.

Fraser, M. (2009), 'Experiencing Sociology', *European Journal of Social Theory*, 12(1): 63–81.

Hickey-Moody, A. and P. Malins (eds) (2007), *Deleuzian Encounters: Studies in Contemporary Social Issues*, Basingstoke: Palgrave Macmillan.

Jackson, A. Y. and L. Mazzei (2012), *Thinking with Theory in Qualitative Research*, London and New York: Routledge.

Jensen, C. B. and K. Rödje (2009), *Deleuzian Intersections: Science, Technology, Anthropology*, New York and Oxford: Berghahn Books.

Latham, A. and D. McCormack (2009), 'Thinking with Images in Non-Representational Cities: Vignettes from Berlin', *Area*, 41(3): 252–62.

Law, J. (2004), *After Method: Mess in Social Science Research*, London and New York: Routledge.

Law, J. and J. Urry (2004), 'Enacting the Social', *Economy and Society*, 33(3): 390–410.

Lury, C. and N. Wakeford (eds) (2012), *Inventive Methods: The Happening of the Social*, London: Routledge.

Lyon, D. and L. Back (2012), 'Fishmongers in a Global Economy: Craft and social relations on a London market', *Sociological Research Online*, 17(2): 23.

McCormack, D. (2007), 'Molecular Affects in Human Geography', *Environment and Planning A*, 39(2): 359–77.

Masny, D. (2010), 'Rhizoanalysis: Nomadic pathways in reading, reading the world and self' <http://www.litteratiesmultiples-multipleliteracies.ca/dmasny/presentations.htm> (accessed 16 June 2012).

Masny, D. and D. R. Cole (2011), 'Education and the Politics of Becoming', *Discourse: Studies in the Cultural Politics of Education*, London: Routledge.

Massumi, B. (1987), 'Translator's Foreword: The Pleasures of Philosophy', in G. Deleuze and F. Guattari (1987), *A Thousand Plateaus: Capitalism and Schizophrenia*, London and New York: Athlone Press.

Massumi, B. (2002), *Parables for the Virtual: Movement, Affect, Sensation*, Durham, NC: Duke University Press.

Munster, A. (2006), *Materializing New Media: Embodiment in Information Aesthetics*, Lebanon, NH: University Press of New England.

Olsson, L. M. (2009), *Movement and Experimentation in Young Children's Learning: Deleuze and Guattari in Early Childhood Education*, New York: Routledge.

Orr, J. (2006), *Panic Dairies: A Genealogy of Panic Disorder*, Durham, NC: Duke University Press.

O'Sullivan, S. (2006), *Art Encounters Deleuze and Guattari: Thought Beyond Representation*, Basingstoke: Palgrave Macmillan.

Pink, S. (2009), *Doing Sensory Ethnography*, London: Sage.

Potts, A. (2004), 'Deleuze on Viagra (Or, What Can a "Viagra-Body" Do?)', *Body and Society*, 10(1): 17–36.

Ringrose, J. (2011), 'Beyond Discourse? Using Deleuze and Guattari's schizoanalysis to explore affective assemblages, heterosexually striated space, and lines of flight online and at school', *Educational Philosophy and Theory*, 43(6): 598–618.

St. Pierre, E. (1997), 'Methodology in the Fold and the Irruption of Transgressive Data', *International Journal of Qualitative Studies in Education*, 10(2): 175–89.

St. Pierre, E. (2000), 'Nomadic Inquiry in the Smooth Spaces of the Field: A Preface' in E. St. Pierre and W. Pillow (eds), *Working the Ruins: Feminist Poststructural Theory and Methods in Education*, London: Routledge.

St. Pierre, E. and W. Pillow (2000), *Working the Ruins: Feminist Poststructural Theory and Methods in Education*, London: Routledge.

Stanley, L. and S. Wise (eds) (1983), *Breaking Out: Feminist Consciousness and Feminist Research*, London and Boston: Routledge and Kegan Paul.

Stewart, K. (2007), *Ordinary Affects*, Durham, NC: Duke University Press.

Suchman, L. (2007), *Human-Machine Reconfigurations*, Cambridge: Cambridge University Press.

Tamboukou, M. (2008), 'Machinic Assemblages: Women, art education and space', *Discourse*, 29 (3): 359–75.

Tomlinson, H. and B. Habberjam (2002), 'Translators' Introduction' in G. Deleuze and C. Parnet, *Dialogues II*, London: Continuum.

Chapter 1

Deleuze and Guattari in the Nursery: Towards an Ethnographic Multi-Sensory Mapping of Gendered Bodies and Becomings

Emma Renold and David Mellor

The work of Deleuze and Guattari is becoming increasingly popular among researchers working with young children in early years settings. Deleuzo-Guattarian theories have been developed into a range of methodological approaches for working with young children because they offer approaches and understandings to their everyday worlds in ways that 'traditional' methods often seem unable to access. At a fundamental level, this is because such methods depend on the creation of some form of text, captured through voice recordings and observations, which can then be discursively analysed. In such an ethnographic approach, researchers blend observations and participants' accounts in order to construct rich descriptions of the social setting they are exploring. Many go further and ask participants to reflect on the texts and observations that are created by or about them in a double-movement attuned to both ethics and the quality of their developing categorisations and analyses. Some of these approaches are particularly challenging when participants have a limited vocabulary (or simply do not talk), do not read or write, and (to adult eyes) shift constantly through phases and spaces of movement in ways that do not seem to display a 'social order' as commonly understood through sociological analysis.

The specific project we discuss in this chapter is a multi-sensory micro-ethnography exploring how children are 'doing gender' in the social, material and cultural world of the nursery. We used a range of multi-media technologies, including audio digital recorders and camcorders, and more traditional technologies, such as field notes and drawings. The research was carried out over a five-month period in one state-funded nursery with a wide demographic of 'working-class' children and their families in South Wales, UK.[1] The child participants included seventeen boys and eight girls aged three to four years. While children participated in a range of activities, from guided tours around the nursery space through to mini video-diaries (e.g., talking into the camera about an event or activity), much of the data generated was classic ethnographic participant observation, capturing the ordinary everyday happenings, textures and contours of nursery life, but paying particular attention to the complexities of affect and the different modalities of the senses (see Atkinson, Housley and Delamont 2008; Pink 2009; 2011).

Like other ethnographers, particularly those researching gender politics in early years settings, we have turned to Deleuze and Guattari and tasked them to provide us with an ontological framework that reflects the dynamic realities of young socialities and subjectivities. The ways in which 'gender' works on, in and across bodies and things (e.g., cultural objects) is particularly heightened in the nursery, as are the ways in which norms of gender appear both fixed and fluid simultaneously, and much more so than in the later primary years (Mellor forthcoming; Renold 2005). As we show in this chapter, our approach involved us developing a cache of practical methods for gathering data, which we could blend with an analytic repertoire that 'saw' beyond the linguistic and textual boundaries of our previous ethnographic approaches, into a multi-sensory world. This included attending to, for example, the auditory: the sounds and silences of the nursery space. It also meant being aware of bodies as being more than the receptacles of subjectivity, of looking to movement across and through the surfaces of children's bodies. Consequently, with subjectivity moving beyond the boundaries of the individual body, we had to think about how to research subjects extending into things and objects, and to work out what this might mean for our conceptualisation of gender/sex/uality.

Our chapter continues by foregrounding the materialities of the body and, in particular, the 'doingness' of subjectivity as a complex affective assemblage of other bodies and things. Key concepts of becoming, materiality and multiplicity are explored in relation to researching the 'doing' and 'being' of young gendered subjectivities and in ways which can attend to both supple molecular and rigid molar segmentarities that make up the 'conditions of possibility' (Foucault 1978) of 'what a body can do' (see also Coleman 2009; Renold and Ringrose 2011). From here, we outline our creation of a research environment for the generation of multi-sensory data in the mapping of situated body/object/sound assemblages. This section explores the 'fit' between the ethnographic methodologies and Deleuze and Guattari's (1987) notion of 'transcendental empiricism'. Much of this involves attending to the generation of data and analysis on complex and shifting socialities and subjectivities in the ordinary and everyday world of nursery life. From an overview of the research project, we then offer three affective encounters or events that foreground sound, body and object. Each mode of analysis/method is artificially separated out for the purposes of foregrounding the affordances of each, whilst simultaneously showing their inter-relationality. The chapter concludes by raising questions, caveats, challenges and opportunities for bringing Deleuzo-Guattarian ideas to the social world of gender/sexual relational becomings in the nursery.

Becomings, Materiality and Multiplicity in Researching the Early Years

Like other researchers working with young children we want to think critically about being and growing in the early stages of life, and to go beyond the discursive, normalising and regulating practices of developmentalism (Walkerdine 1993) where universalised and thus highly classed, raced, gendered, sexualised and age-appropriate notions of 'growing up naturally' abound (Walkerdine 1993; Burman 2008). Rather, we take up and tune into 'postdevelopmental' perspectives which question and deconstruct these developmentalist hegemonies. That said, however, postdevelopmental approaches are not a wholesale rejection of development. Children in the first years of life do develop. As we alluded to above, they are 'becoming' as they stumble around and into the architecture of the social world (its materialities, temporalities, practices, identities and so on) in a pathway of navigation – of subjectification – that will become evermore crystalised as they traverse the life course. This position reflects a number of key developments in sociological theory through recent years. From a performative perspective, the becomingness of identity allows us to understand the everyday doing of gender, through ongoing conscious and unconscious repetitive acts (Butler 1990, 2005) where gender performances become psychically and corporeally inscribed on individuals over time. Of course, both these perspectives are subject-centred in so far as subjectivity is theorised at the level of individual bodies. We wish to go further than this. Taking inspiration from a Deleuzo-Guattarian notion of becoming, subjectivity is extended into a range of different 'universes' (see Guattari 1992), beyond the individual and towards a collective and connected affective assemblage of other bodies and things. This more opened out view of subjectivity has been taken up in different ways by researchers (see Blackman et al. 2008), including those researching subjectivity in early years settings (Olsson 2009; MacNaughton 2005; Mazzei 2010a, 2010b; Davies 2010; Taylor, Pacini-Ketchabaw and Blaise this collection).

What these emerging literatures offer is a view of early childhoods as uniquely constituted through complex processes of emergence and subjectification. Dominant systems of power remain; they are the mechanics which provide the 'conditions of possibility' for certain subjectivities to emerge, while others are less or not possible. Here then, are the supple 'molecular' and rigid 'molar' segmentarities, the nested forces through and along which every individual's subjectivity is organised (Deleuze and Guattari 1987; also see Bogard 1998). In early childhood these segmentarities can be seen as the deeply embedded molar level of sexed subjects, where gender circulates in a multiplicity of molecular ways, through and across their bodies, in objects, and as we explore below, in sound. So the conditions of possibility in the nursery are fundamentally material and sensorial, where the 'relational field' is not just constituted by corporeal subjects, but also by objects and a multiplicity of senses of all kinds. In this way, from a methodological point of view, we can view our research subjects as 'points of extension' around which assemblages form in more or less rigid ways, depending on their molarity or molecularity.

The research methods required for capturing this very different view of the world are troublesome – indeed, it is fair to say that we are looking for troublesome methods in two ways. Firstly, they trouble the ontology of the social, because selves – while not entirely erased – are, and can be, extended in all manner of ways. We wish to follow Foucault's (2000: 241) commitment to finding ways of making the subject 'no longer itself', where selves are simultaneously singular and plural (Davies 2010). Secondly, they are methodologically troubling because, as we noted in the introduction, the methods commonly employed in social science research aim to capture the experiences of bounded subjects in relation to other such bounded subjects. To introduce fluidity between subjects in a manner that is not simply about their relations but at the level of their very ontology opens up many difficult questions. As Deleuze notes: 'This self, therefore, is by no means simple: it is not enough to relativize or pluralize the self, all the while retaining for it a simple attenuated form' (Deleuze 1994a: 78). Of course, these are questions around the nature of subjectivity, agency, power, the human, the social and matter that cannot be addressed here (see Blackman and Venn 2010). Rather we seek to frame some of them.

Our starting point is materiality: like Deleuze, we want to get to the point where the social world is 'becoming all the more earthy' (Deleuze 1992: 293), where stuff is not just the adornments of selves but the very constituent parts of subjectivities. Thinking with Deleuzian notions of intensities and flows, Grosz (1994) has emphasised the importance of the complex materialities of the body and critiqued some postmodern writing for effectively turning the body into text. Indeed, Deleuze and Guattari do not render or convert all of reality into the textual, but seek to 'situate material signs within the substrata of matter' (Bogue, cited in Land 2006: 118) and consider a transversal subjectivity (Guattari 1992: 6). For example, in early years settings, children's bodies are not just inscribed by external societal or semiotic forces; children themselves participate in the material production of themselves and others as 'doing bodies' (Rossholt 2010). Thus, where there are no or very few words in a situation, we can focus on other practices, such as the material, affective and discursive practices of touch, that are embodied in body/place/object assemblages. In this way, movement and touch become important ways of being in the world. The Deleuzo-Guattarian imperative is to open up the social field to constant movement and to processual creativity. While there are dangers in, and objections to, pursuing these lines of argument in particular ways – from the anarcho desire of the rhizome to the disappearance of the subject – Deleuze and Guattari have always emphasised the importance of keeping hold of how subjectivity is embedded in and stratified by social, political and economic contexts (Guattari 1992, Chapter 1). For example, in relation to the anarcho desire of the rhizome, they state how 'wildy destratifying' can 'throw the strata into demented or suicidal collapse, which brings them back down on us heavier than ever' (Deleuze and Guattari 1987: 160–1). These dangers notwithstanding, like many who have dipped into the Deleuzo-Guattarian oeuvre and other post-humanist or post-representational ways of 'noticing' the move beyond language and sight (Stewart 2007), their work inspires the methodological imagination. It has the capacity to offer up new ways of seeing, feeling, connecting and engaging with complex socialities in ways that can lead to new questions and insights into new and old substantive and political concerns. In relation to our own research, this involved attending to frequently passed over pleasures, powers and dangers of everyday scenes in the nursery, as we set out below.

Deleuze and Ethnography: Creating a Research Environment for the Mapping of Multi-sensory Assemblages

Modes of attending to scenes and events spawn socialities, identities, dream worlds, bodily states and public feelings of all kinds. None of this is simply 'good' or 'bad' but always, first, both powerful and mixed. (Stewart 2007:10)

Methodologically, Deleuze and Guattari push us to attend to a specific kind of empiricism, a wild empiricism that can see and capture the unstableness of everyday life. This involves creating a research environment that enables the mapping of new conditions of possibility, which, as Stewart alludes to above, involves some complex mixing of a range of affects, of the molar and the molecular, of re- and de-territorialisations, as they surge, rub and make connections across and through bodies and things. Ethnography is one such method that enables a mapping capable of capturing the 'awkward, messy, unequal, unstable, surprising and creative qualities of encounters and interconnection across difference' (Stewart 2007: 128). In relation to the research project this chapter draws upon, we were interested in mapping the effects of the often insurmountable, highly regulated and stratified difference of gender. Indeed, one of the key aims of the project was to explore theories and methodologies which assisted us in analysing the micro-socialities and affective economies of young nursery school children. In particular, this involved capturing the often overlooked (because of the visibility of physical violence, Brown 2011) or undermined (through developmental discourses of 'play') 'normative cruelties of gender' (Renold and Ringrose 2008).

Deleuze and Guattari's notion of transcendental empiricism departs significantly from the classical epistemological definition of empiricism. As Olsson argues, their transcendental empiricism 'no longer treats thought as the great organizer of sensation'; rather, it 'concerns a certain devaluation of consciousness's capacity and aspirations to account for the world' in ways that rupture the capacity of consciousness to account for experience (Olsson 2009: 94). Foregrounding a transcendental field where consciousness is detached from the essentialised thinking subject, and thus from embodied experience, is almost a necessity in the field of early years research. Here, language often takes a back seat and articulation emerges primarily as a multi-sensorial bodily experience; just like Deleuze and Guattari's 'plane of immanence' (1994: 36), there are 'only different speeds and slowness and forces and bodies encountering each other' (Olsson 2009: 95). What follows in the three 'events' re-presented below are reconstructed tracings of body-object-sound assemblages, artificially pulled apart for the purposes of a chapter on methodology, yet in ways that show their inter-connectedness and relationality. In so doing, we hope to open up and share some complex gender/sexual assemblages and 'the leakages and lines of flights that are already there' (Dahlberg and Bloch 2006: 115, cited in Olsson 2009), but often missed, lost, silenced, or blocked in the researching of gender and power for very young children. We begin by foregrounding sound.

The Sonic Environment of the Heterosexual Matrix: Noise, Silence and Sound With(out) the Subject

Underneath the large noisy events lie the small events of silence . . . (Deleuze 1994a: 163, cited in Olsson 2009: 120)

This continuum of sound fills both what is in the frame (the visual image) and the out-of-field, that sound which has no relation to the visual image presented in that moment. (Mazzei 2010: 514)

The significance of sound within social science research is becoming increasingly foregrounded, most notably in projects that attend to multi-modal (Hurdley and Dicks 2011, Dicks et al. 2011) and performative modes of hearing (Bull and Back 2003; Back 2007; Erlman 2004; Henriques 2011). Through processes of recording, listening and playing back to listen again, the everyday cacophony of gender and sexuality, where voices and sounds break free from embodied subjects, takes centre stage, including even those sounds 'out of field'. Indeed, we identified a range of multi-layered gendered/sex/ualised aural tectonics from singular sounds to regular refrains and anthems, some foregrounded ('in field'), some backgrounded ('out of field'). A brief example of the latter was the repetitive banging on the roof of the 'Wendy house' (a small wooden shed-like house) accompanied by a group of children singing 'Bob the builder, can we fix it?' (the theme tune to a children's cartoon). These sounds, while audio recorded via the camcorder, are not immediately observed by Emma, the researcher, who was filming a scene of doll play in a different section of the nursery. What 'sounds like' an anthem of normative working-class masculinity (see Marsh 2010) is subverted, however, when body, object and sound come together. While the boys usually dominated the construction area, it was Tina, at the top of the ladder, in hard hat and hammer, who was 'fixing it' – banging away at the roof producing the sounds of gender which simultaneously rupture (e.g., girl as builder and noise-maker) and regulate (e.g., boy as noise-maker and builder) the normative when the visual image is in and out of field.

A notable example of more routine refrains was the clip-clopping of heels and the swishing of princess-dresses. This daily acoustic seemed to release both molar and molecular sonic lines of gender/sex/uality into the visual space in ways that at once territorialised (as the 'princess girls' clip clop around the nursery in their rustling dresses); deterritorialised (as one boy, Tommy, slips on a princess dress); and re-territorialised (fully dressed, Tommy declares, 'I'm a homo' and, roaring loudly, chases a group of girls, who are screaming with laughter, around the nursery floor). Although it may be useful, methodologically, to attend to sound without a subject (see Mazzei 2010), for us it seemed only by attending to the multi-sensory assemblage of bodies and movement, vision and sound (see Pink 2009) did we come to hear the fixity (molar harmonies) and flux (discordant molecularities) of how gender/sex/uality flows in and through this multi-sensory 'heterosexual matrix' (Butler 1990).

In terms of our developing argument, it is the imbrication of body, movement and sound in Tracey's high pitched sirens ('TY-LER, TY-LER, TY-LER'), that we want to focus on more closely. We begin with the field-note extract below, presenting an expanded analytic memo written after the end of a group analysis session:

Extract 1
David and I have been spending an afternoon watching a range of selected video footage generated over the course of the project. In many of the episodes, we have heard the siren of Tracey's voice as she calls out, 'TY-LER' over and over. We reflect on this. Sometimes his name is echoing in the background when the camera is focused on something else. At other times, we notice that just after these callings, the camera searches for, or pans directly over to Tyler. This focusing on Tyler and Tracey sparks a debate between us about their relationship to each other, as boyfriend and girlfriend, as the alpha-girl and alpha-boy of the nursery. But in the playing back and watching again, we also notice that wherever Tyler is, 'best friend' Sophie isn't far behind. It's almost as if the sound draws us to Sophie – makes her visible, enables her presence (both in the field, and in our analysis this afternoon). The vocality of Tracey also brings Sophie's silence to the foreground. We talk at length about the relationship between sound, image and body and how we are learning, through our methodology, about the sounds of relationship cultures of boys and girls in the nursery – especially regarding the 'friendship' dyad of Sophie and Tyler.

As this field note goes some way to illustrate, Tracey's constant calling operated to direct our aural senses, and then our visual gaze, to the physical bodies of Tracey and Tyler. Indeed, Tracey's siren was one of the first instances where we became alerted to the sonic dimensions of the 'heterosexual matrix' where affects literally resonated and lingered over time. We generated many observations and recordings of how Tyler and Tracey played as boyfriend-husband/girlfriend-wife in a range of scenarios and settings. These could be what Deleuze and Guattari might refer to as 'noisy events'; that is, easily recognisable molar representations of sedimented hetero-gendered power relations. However, it is the sound of inter-action between Tyler and Sophie that we focus on here because we were so frequently drawn to Sophie's physical presence through the constant calling of 'Tyler' by other children and staff. Indeed, where Tyler was, Sophie was too – silent, in the shadows, but always in proximity to him (e.g., sitting next to him, opposite him, running behind him). The ways in which the physicality of Sophie came into view through sound, and significantly through (the sound of) 'Tyler', speaks volumes to our methodological and theoretical journey of how to attend to scenes that 'spawn mixed and powerful socialities . . . and bodily states' (Stewart 2007: 10). Indeed, our attention to sound and the hearing of bodies intensified our findings of both the silence of bodies (in this case a girl-body), the unspoken (including bodies without voice) and, as we outline below, the ways in which bodies (through sound and movement) flowed through, and bonded with others, enabling and restricting the capacity of bodies/subjects to act, to 'become'.

Movement and Stasis: Relational Subjects, Bodily In/capacities and Stolen Becomings

> The body hums along, rages up, or deflates. It goes with the flow, meets resistance, gets attacked, or finds itself caught up in something it can't get out of. (Stewart 2007: 75)

> The girl's becoming is stolen first, in order to impose a history, or prehistory, upon her. The boy's turn comes next, but it is by using the girl as an example, by pointing to the girl as the object of his desire, that . . . [a] dominant history is fabricated for him too. (Deleuze and Guattari 1987: 276)

Tyler is wearing the wizard cloak, and enters the giant's castle. Sophie, carrying a wand with a butterfly on the end of it, follows him. Tyler doesn't acknowledge Sophie and she sits on the bench. She then moves to sit on the red rail as Tyler sits on the other side of the bench. Tyler then sits next to Sophie on the red rail and then gives her a blue coat-hanger to hold.

Extract 2
Tyler: (getting up) You stay here.
Sophie gets up.
Tyler: (pointing to where Sophie was sitting) No. You stay there.
Sophie sits back down.
Tyler: (looking into the camera, not at Sophie) Sorry, I have to go.
            (He then leaves the giant's castle.)

0:00:52
Sophie sits on the red rail and looks in the direction in which Tyler has gone. She is still holding on to the blue coat hanger that Tyler gave her.

0:01:24
Sophie is still looking across the nursery at Tyler. She has been sitting like this since he left. The camera pans around and shows Tyler, who is sitting at the snack table eating, with Jon and some other children.

0:01:36
The camera goes back to Sophie, who is still looking at Tyler. She hasn't moved
...

DM: Are you playing with Tyler?

0:02:10
Sophie glances over at Tyler, then back at David (researcher) and nods.
DM: What game are you playing?
She looks over at Tyler, back at David and displays her upturned palm.
DM: Don't know?
She nods and smiles.
DM: Where's Tyler now?
Sophie: (Looks over to where Tyler is sitting and coughs.) He's eating his snack.
DM: He's eating his snack. Did you not want a snack?
She shakes her head.
DM: No. Are you waiting for him?

0:02:23
She nods her head and then goes back to staring at Tyler.
The camera shows Tyler still sitting at the snack table, talking with the boys. He glances over in Sophie's direction, but it isn't clear if he is looking at her or not.

0:04:02
Lucas enters the giant's castle and sits down on the bench. Sophie glances at him, but doesn't move; instead she continues to focus on Tyler.

0:04:14
Lucas leaves the giant's castle. Sophie continues to sit on the red rail. She has now put the wand on the floor, and is hanging onto one of the blue coat hangers from the red rail she is sitting on. She continues looking at Tyler for another 2 minutes. Eventually, Tyler runs across the nursery and into the giant's castle. He picks up the wand, gives it to Sophie and says, 'Hold that'. Sophie stands up and takes the wand from Tyler. He then stands still for a couple of seconds, swaying his cloak around him, then walks around the walls of the giant's castle. Sophie stands still and watches him. He then walks over towards the exit of the giant's castle and looks at the pictures on the wall. Sophie turns in his direction, but continues to look at the wand.

As we alluded to in the previous section, our ethnographic gaze became increasingly focused on how Sophie's body was almost always in the shadow of her 'best friend' Tyler. While early field notes note the possible rupturing of the young heterosexual matrix in so far as their union wasn't sucked up into the dominant boyfriend-girlfriend discourse (e.g., like Tracey and Tyler, Bella and Tyler), their inseparability and 'transversal subjectivity' (Guattari 1992) darkened as we located footage after footage of Sophie's increasing incapacity to act, to move, or to speak without Tyler in close proximity. We began to see how this trans-subjectivity was rendering Sophie's body vulnerable and open to invasion and territorialisation. Very much like Deleuze and Guattari's empty body without organs (BwO), we seemed to be witnessing a body that was 'disconnecting from others . . . so that it closes in on itself, unable to transmit its intensities differently, stuck in repetition' and 'where all forms of openness are smothered' (Grosz 1994: 171).

The audio-visual transcript above illustrates this stuckness, and the ways in which Tyler almost holds Sophie's 'agency' – her bodily capacity to act (both in voice/sound and in movement). She seems to become his 'object': from 'some*body*' to 'some*thing*' to play with as he sits her amongst the coats in the dressing up corner, gives her a coat hanger to hold, demands she 'stay there' and then returns some six minutes later to enliven the 'game'/her body again. This very literal movement from subject to object was something we witnessed many times over during our fieldwork. Whether in proximity or at a distance, our methodology enabled a mapping of the darker side of how bodies are always 'becoming' in relation to other bodies and affecting how the body is permeable to the influence (and imposition) of others, with porous borders and boundaries. Indeed, while Sophie appeared to move freely around the nursery space, always at the centre of the action, this movement, her agency (her becoming) was caught up in a wider web of what sociologists might call 'unequal power relations' and what Deleuze would call molar sedimented lines or strata. There is no space here to explore the wider implications of how girls/women often operate as the empty vessels of men's becomings ('their machinic conditions'). However, the 'stolen becoming' of the girl body, the way she shadows/flows into his body/movement and the way he territorialises her body/movement, requires an analysis that becomes possible through the methodological and theoretical steps we have identified so far.

In the final extract below, we emphasise further how movement and stasis, the molar and molecular, are always operating in a dynamic relation to each other. Here we explore how bodies are sites of struggles, forces and intensities that are territorialised and reterritorialised in micro-processes of regulation and rupture (Renold and Ringrose 2008). And it is the assemblage of bodies and things in the micro-social world of doll play that we further map to show how the blockages and flows of agency/desire between overly coded gendered bodies and objects differently enable and restrict the capacity of bodies/subjects to act.

The Power of Things: When Barbie-Sophie Meets Action-Man-Tyler, or, When Objects Meet Subjects

> Bodies enhance their power in or as a heterogeneous assemblage. What this suggests for the concept of agency is that the efficacy or effectivity to which that term has traditionally referred becomes distributed across an ontologically heterogeneous field, rather than being a capacity located in a human body or in a collective produced (only) by human efforts . . . assemblages are ad hoc groupings of diverse elements of vibrant materials of all sorts. (Bennett 2010: 21)

Extract 3
Sophie and Tyler are sat opposite each other on a soft mat, in the outside play area. The camera is filming from a distance but remains close enough to capture their talk. Sophie is sat with legs tucked under her. Tyler is squatting. The camera enters the scene as Tyler is turning an Action Man doll over and over. Sophie clutches her Action Man under the arms so that he is standing upright. The Action Man dolls face each other. 'Fight again yeah', says Tyler to Sophie. 'Yeah', says Sophie. She pushes her Action Man into Tyler's Action Man and he spins the Action Man again. 'Fight again, fight again, yeah . . . fight again'. Sophie looks over at Becky who is holding princess Barbie, and pulls her Action Man away. 'What you doin?' says Tyler, 'it's better have a fighting man, eh?' Sophie puts her Action Man down by her side. Tyler picks up another Barbie. He pushes the two dolls together, their faces touching, and then throws the Barbie into the doll box. Gesturing with the Action Man he says again, 'Get the man . . . get the man'. Sophie shakes her head. 'You have to . . . you have to'. She shakes her head again. Tyler picks up her Action Man and thrusts it into her hands, saying 'get it, get . . . it'. She doesn't move. 'You have to . . . you have to'. He is now holding and gesturing with two Action Men and shouts, 'YOU HAVE TO< YOU HAVE TO'. Sophie shakes her head, and raises her shoulders up and down. He reaches into the doll box, 'you want this? you want a girl?' 'Yeah', says Sophie, smiling. She takes the princess Barbie. She looks at the doll, they face each other, and she turns the doll around to face Tyler's Action Man. 'Let's have a fight', Tyler says, as Action Man does a somersault. 'Yes' says Sophie. She holds Princess Barbie's legs with two hands and Barbie head-butts Action Man, sending him spinning to the

ground. She hits him again, and again and again. By the end of this episode of play, the two Action Men are killed many times over.

In her book, *Vibrant Matter* (2010), Jane Bennett powerfully draws attention to the ways in which bodies and things come together in complex affective heterogeneous circuits. She shows us the ways these circuits can rupture the reproduction of all sorts of 'social habits, requirements and regulations' (Grosz 2004: 181) and produce 'group-ings of all sorts of diverse elements' (Bennett 2010: 21) in ways that produce a range of unanticipated connections, relays and 'lines of flight'. Methodologically, we found our sustained ethnographic multi-sensory mapping enabled a really productive engagement with this way of seeing/thinking/hearing. For example, if the first visual/audio transcript was not explored in relation to the web of lines and relations that our longitudinal and sensory ethnographic focus produced, we may have closed off a particular analytic trail. Consider, for example, the molecu-lar movement of Sophie finally resisting Tyler's attempts to play fight with the Action Man and holding out until she is given the Barbie to play with. This scene could be viewed as Sophie being caught up in and desir-ing the sedimented molar lines of young heteronormativity, where her 'femininity' aligns with, extends and smoothly flows into the objects she plays with. However, an historical tracing of molar and molecular flows of gender and power suggests that something different is happening in the assemblage of Tyler-Sophie-Barbie-Action-Man.

Indeed, we have chosen to re-present both 'events' here because they were one of the few scenes we recorded of Sophie refusing to be drawn into play, of resisting Tyler's Rules, of 'raging' not 'deflating'. Indeed, after 'fighting' and 'fighting again', Sophie not only holds out, but repeatedly shakes her head, over and over, gesturing strongly that she does not want to play any more with the Action Man that Tyler repeatedly attempts to put her way ('get it, get it', 'you have to, you have to'). Since Sophie is not content in this moment (at least) to play *for* him, to (dis)embody and become his play-*thing*, Tyler then seems to reluctantly concede and picks up the Barbie. So, here, we have a very interesting simultaneous regulation and rupture of molar lines, through the molecularity of one very brief four-minute episode of play. It could be that Sophie connects with the flows of the molar power of heteronor-mative femininity in ways that simultaneously rupture the molar lines, as she shifts from inactive object to agentic subject in the Sophie-Barbie assemblage. We then see a further rupture, as Sophie-Barbie repeatedly hits back at Action Man-Tyler. This movement, this assemblage of things and bodies, is pivotal here – made meaningful, given the previous connections and incapacities of Sophie's relations with Tyler. As we draw out further below, our engagement with Deleuzo-Guattarian ideas has enabled us to capture (in this case) a micro-mapping of how the subject-in-object-in-subject dynamic operates in unexpected and heterogeneous ways enabling 'bodies to enhance their power' (Bennett 2010: 21).

Conclusion

> The ordinary throws itself together out of forms, flows, powers, pleasures, encounters, distractions, drudgery, denials, practical solutions, shape-shifting forms of violence, daydreams and opportunities lost or found. (Stewart 2007: 29)

Ethnography is often about making the familiar strange and coming to know, through sustained engagement, the who, where and how of ordinary everyday human interactions, socialities and cultures. The focus of this chapter has been to illustrate the ordinary everyday affects that circulate across and through bodies, objects, sounds, in the moment and over time, with the political goal of coming to know, through a multi-sensory mapping of these assemblages, the molar and molecular flows of power in the making of young gendered bodies, becomings and relations.

Central to our analysis has been thinking through what it means ethnographically and as poststructural sociologists to map and explore heterogeneous relations of becoming, where the 'human' is always already more and other than itself (Land 2006). Not only does this provide us with ways of re-animating a range of key sociological categories (e.g., gender, power, agency, age), but it demands a reconceptualisation of the subject, as a site of immanence and flows. This is an expanded subject produced always 'in relation' to other bodies and things. Indeed, it is a mapping of the 'ethics of relationality' (Braidotti 2006) that has perhaps enabled a different way of 'seeing' the flows of power regarding how the subject extends into others, including nonhuman and material others (see also Renold and Ringrose 2011).

For the purposes of this chapter, we have tried to illustrate how a multi-sensory mapping of objects-sounds-bodies has enabled us to grasp these complex relationalities. We illustrated how 'noisy events' and paying attention to sound can shift the researcher's gaze and analytic focus (e.g., how sound drew our attention to Sophie). We also explored how the generation of multi-modal data helped us to see and analyse a range of trans-object-subjectivities (e.g., how the Sophie-Barbie assemblage seemed to create a 'line of flight' through which her body was enlivened to act in ways which ruptured old [molar] social habits and connections in previous assemblages and in blocked becomings). Indeed, we hope we have shown that we are not mobilising the idea of 'the senses' from a purely phenomenological standpoint. Rather, we have been exploring the idea of 'sense' in two interconnected ways. On the one hand, as an expanded epistemology of the social world – one that is open to the multiple events, actions and relations of bodies and objects as experienced through the oral and aural, sight, touch, taste and emotion. On the other hand, we have come to research 'sense' from a more Deleuzo-Guattarian perspective that is open to the paradoxes and multiplicities within each becoming, event, and throughout nature (Deleuze 1994a; 1994b); or, put another way, we have been looking for/at how 'there is neither one nor multiple' but rather 'multiplicity' (Deleuze 1999: 13; see also Guattari 1992). This multiplicity is at the heart of Deleuze and Guattari's philosophy, and this notion of the always already multiple has been central not only to our reconfiguration of the subject in assemblage, but also to our methodology, in terms of our sustained engagement over time in mapping these multiplicities (e.g., in our progressive analysis and indeed in the different modes of data generation from sound and moving image to touch and affect).

As in previous work (Renold and Ringrose 2008, 2011), we have been careful to attend to the molar *and* molecular lines through which bodies are becoming. In this chapter, we have been exploring the ruptures and regulations of the young heterosexual matrix and the flows of power that inflate and deflate the girl and boy body. Moreover, while we have been mapping multiplicities, jumps and surprises that rupture the molar in the process of becoming, as Grosz argues, 'these becomings are not simply a matter of choice, not simply a decision, but always involve a substantial remaking of the subject, a major risk to the subject's integration and social functioning' (1994: 174). We have mapped some of these risks through the case study of Sophie's becomings. We will continue to do so in future substantive papers and in ways that pay closer attention to embedding these embodied becomings in place and time (see Renold and Ivinson 2012; Walkerdine and Jimenez 2012).

Indeed, this movement between the molecular and the molar is essential to keep hold of. And it is the mapping of these molecular and molar lines vis-à-vis our longitudinal focus that demonstrates the importance of keeping hold of the kind of wildness and 'pivots of unpredictability' where 'trajectories, connections, and future relations remain unpredictable' (Grosz 1993:174) – in ways that continue to make the familiar strange and remain true to Deleuze and Guattari's own desire to critique and analyse the ways in which the empirical 'constitutively veils its own conditions of production' (Welchman 2009: 50). Indeed, it has been the 'being there', the ongoing watching, listening and playing back again, that has enabled us to keep focused on the middles of becomings (not the roots, causes or fixed trajectories), and that has made it possible for us to attempt to avoid the seductive dualisms which can push and pull us into nominating and fixing affects as good or bad, violent or not violent, masculine or feminine, passive or active, subjective or objective. Taking Deleuze and Guattari into the nursery, then, has afforded us a way of mapping, seeing and attending to events (things, feelings, sounds, bodies) and has enabled a textured multi-sensory way of knowing, but always in ways that are 'saturated with affect's lines of promise and threat' (Stewart 2007: 129).

Note

1. The research team included Chantelle Haughton (University of Glamorgan), David Mellor (Bristol University) and Emma Renold (Cardiff University). The project was funded by the Welsh Education Research Network (HEFCW).

References

Atkinson, P., W. Housley and S. Delamont (2008), *Contours of Culture: Complex Ethnography and the Ethnography of Complexity*, Walnut Creek, CA: AltaMira Press.
Back, L. (2007), *The Art of Listening*, Oxford: Berg.
Bennett, J. (2010), *Vibrant Matter*, Durham, NC: Duke University Press.
Blackman, L., J. Cromby, D. Hook, D. Papadopolous and V. Walkerdine (2008), 'Creating Subjectivities', *Subjectivity*, 1(1): 1–27.
Blackman, L. and C. Venn (2010), 'Affect', *Body and Society*, 16(1): 7–28.
Blaise, M. (2005), *Playing It Straight: Uncovering Gender Discourses in the Early Childhood Classroom*, New York and Abingdon: Routledge.
Bogard, W. (1998), 'Sense and Segmentarity: Some markers of a Deleuzian-Guattarian sociology', *Sociological Theory*, 16(1): 52–74.
Bonta, M. and J. Protevi (2004), *Deleuze and Geophilosophy: A Guide and Glossary*, Edinburgh: Edinburgh University Press.
Braidotti, R. (2006), *Transpositions: On Nomadic Ethics*, Cambridge: Polity Press.
Brown, J. (2011), 'Understanding Dimensions of "Peer Violence" in Preschool Setting: An exploration of key issues and questions' in C. Barter and D. Berridge (eds), *Children Behaving Badly? Peer Violence Between Children and Young People*, Chichester: Wiley-Blackwell, pp. 21–32.
Bull, R. and L. Back (2003), *The Auditory Culture Reader*, Oxford: Berg.

Burman, E. (2008), *Developments: Child, Image, Nation*, London: Brunner-Routledge.

Butler, J. (1990), *Gender Trouble*, London: Routledge.

Butler, J. (2005), *Undoing Gender*, London: Routledge.

Coleman, R. (2009), *The Becoming of Bodies: Girls, Images, Experience*, Manchester: Manchester University Press.

Dahlberg, G. and M. Bloch (2006), 'Is the Power to See and Visualise Always the Power to Control?' in T. Popkewitsz et al., '*The Future is Not What it Appears to be*': *Pedagogy, Genealogy and Political Epistemology. In Honour and Memory of Kenneth Hultqvist*, Stockholm: HLS Förlag.

Davies, B. (2010), 'The implications for qualitative research methodology of the struggle between the individualized subject of phenomenology and the emergent multiplicities of the poststructuralist ~~subject~~: the problem of agency', *Reconceptualising Educational Research Methodology*, 1(1): 54–68.

Deleuze, G. (1992), 'Mediators', in J. Crary and S. Kwinter (eds), *Incorporations*, New York: Zone Books.

Deleuze, G. (1994a), *Difference and Repetition*, trans. P. Patton, New York: Columbia University Press.

Deleuze, G. (1994b), *The Logic of Sense*, trans. M. Lester with C. Stivale, London: Continuum.

Deleuze, G. (1999), *Foucault*, trans. S. Hand, London: Continuum.

Deleuze, G. and F. Guattari (1984), *Anti-Oedipus*, trans. R. Hurley, M. Seem and H. R. Lane, London: Athlone Press.

Deleuze, G. and F. Guattari (1987), *A Thousand Plateaus*, trans. B. Massumi, London: Athlone Press.

Deleuze, G. and F. Guattari (1994), *What is Philosophy?* trans. H. Tomlinson and G. Burchell, London: Verso.

Dicks, B., R. Flewitt, L. Lancaster and K. Pahl (2011), 'Multimodality and Ethnography: Working at the intersection', *Qualitative Research*, 11(3): 227–38.

Erlmann, V. (ed.) (2004), *Hearing Cultures: Essays on Sound, Listening and Modernity*, Oxford: Berg.

Foucault, M. (1978), *The History of Sexuality, Volume I*, trans. R. Hurley, New York: Pantheon.

Foucault, M. (2000), 'An Interview with Michel Foucault' in *Power: The Essential Works of Michel Foucault Vol. 3*, London: Penguin.

Gilbert, J. (2009), 'Deleuzian Politics? A survey and some suggestions', *New Formations*, 68(1): 10–33

Grosz, E. (1994), *Volatile Bodies: Toward a Corporeal Feminism*, Bloomington and Indianapolis: Indiana University Press.

Guattari, F. (1992), *Chaosmosis: An Ethico-Aesthetic Paradigm*, Sydney: Power Publications.

Henriques, J. (2011), *Sonic Bodies: Reggae Sound Systems, Performance Techniques and Ways of Knowing*, London: Continuum.

Hultman, K. and H. L. Taguchi (2010), 'Challenging Anthropocentric Analysis of Visual Data: A relational materialist methodological approach to educational research', *International Journal of Qualitative Studies in Education*, 23(5): 525–42.

Hurdley, R. and B. Dicks (2011), 'In-between Practice: Working in the "third space" of sensory and multimodal ethnography', *Qualitative Research*, 11(3): 277–92.

Jackson, A. Y. (2010), 'Deleuze and the Girl', *International Journal of Qualitative Studies in Education*, 23(5): 579–87

Land, C. (2006), 'Becoming Cyborg: Changing the subject of the social?' in M. Fuglsang and B. M. Sørensen (eds), *Deleuze and the Social*, Edinburgh: Edinburgh University Press.

MacLure, M., R. Holmes, C. MacRae and L. Jones (2010), 'Animating Classroom Ethnography: Overcoming video-fear', *International Journal of Qualitative Studies in Education*, 23(5): 543–56.

MacNaughton, G. (2005), *Doing Foucault in Early Childhood Studies: Applying Poststructuralist Ideas*, New York and Abingdon: Routledge.

Marsh, J. (2010), 'New Literacies, Old Identities: Young girls' experiences of digital literacy at home and school' in C. Jackson, C. Paechter and E. Reynolds (eds), *Girls and Education 3–16: Continuing Concerns, New Agendas*, Buckingham: Open University Press, pp. 197–219.

Mazzei, L. A. (2010), 'Thinking Data with Deleuze', *International Journal of Qualitative Studies in Education*, 23(5): 511–23.

Mazzei, L. A. and K. McCoy (2010), 'Thinking with Deleuze in Qualitative Research', *International Journal of Qualitative Studies in Education*, 23(5): 503–9.

Mellor, D. (forthcoming), *Transitions from Childhood to Youth: Researching the Social Pathways from Child to Teenager*, Basingstoke: Palgrave.

Olsson, L. M. (2009), *Movement and Experimentation in Young Children's Learning: Deleuze and Guattari in early childhood education*, Abingdon and New York: Routledge.

Parviainen, J. (2011), 'Seeing Sound, Hearing Movement: Multimodal expression and haptic illusions in the virtual sonic environment' in D. Peters, G. Eckel and Dorschel (eds), *Bodily Expression in Electronic Music: Perspectives on a Reclaimed Performativity*, New York and London: Routledge.

Pink, S. (2009), *Doing Sensory Ethnography*, London: Sage.

Pink, S. (2011), 'Multi-modality and Multi-sensoriality and Ethnographic Knowing: Or, can social semiotics be reconciled with the phenomenology of perception and knowing in practice', *Qualitative Research*, 11(3): 261–76.

Renold, E. (2005), *Girls, Boys and Junior Sexualities*, Routledge: London.

Renold, E. (2008), 'Queering Masculinity: Re-theorising contemporary tomboyism in the schizoid space of innocent/heterosexualized young femininities', *Girlhood Studies*, 1(2): 129–51.

Renold, E. and G. Ivinson (2012), 'Sexual Assemblages: Girls, bodies and sexual becomings in a semi-rural post-industrial locale', paper presented at Open University seminar, 'Studying Gender and Sexuality Psychosocially', 15 May 2012.

Renold, E. and J. Ringrose (2008), 'Regulation and Rupture: Mapping tween and teenage girls' "resistance" to the heterosexual matrix', *Feminist Theory: An International Interdisciplinary Journal*, 9(3): 335–60.

Renold, E. and J. Ringrose (2011), 'Schizoid Subjectivities: Re-theorising teen-girls' sexual cultures in an era of sexualisation', *Journal of Sociology*, 47(4): 389–409.

Robinson, K. H. and C. Jones Diaz (2006), *Diversity and Difference in Early Childhood Education: Issues for Theory and Practice*, Maidenhead: Open University Press.

Rossholt, N. (2010), 'Food as Touch/Touching the Food: The body in-place and out-of-place in preschool', *Educational Philosophy and Theory* <doi: 10.1111/j.1469–5812.2010.00677.x> (accessed 10 February 2012).

Sellers, M. (2010), 'Re(con)ceiving Young Children's Curricular Performativity', *International Journal of Qualitative Studies in Education*, 23(5): 557–77.

Stewart, K. (2007), *Ordinary Affects*, Durham, NC: Duke University Press.

Walkerdine, V. (1993), 'Beyond Developmentalism?', *Theory and Psychology*, 3: 451–69

Walkerdine, V. and L. Jimenez (2012), *Gender, Work and Community After*

De-Industrialisation: A Psycho-social Approach to Affect, London and New York: Routledge.

Welchman, A. (2009), 'Deleuze's Post-Critical Metaphysics', *Symposium: Canadian Journal of Continental Philosophy*, 13(2): 25–54.

Chapter 2

Mobile Sections and Flowing Matter in Participant-Generated Video: Exploring a Deleuzian Approach to Visual Sociology

Carol A. Taylor

This chapter focuses on Deleuze's *Cinema 1: The Movement-Image* (2005a) and *Cinema 2: The Time-Image* (2005b). At the heart of the chapter is the question 'how can Deleuze's philosophy contribute to visual sociology?' To answer this question the chapter draws on empirical data from two education research projects in which doctoral and undergraduate students employed video as a creative medium for self-expression, as a method for constructing visual meanings about their educational identities, and for producing multi-dimensional reflexive narratives. In bringing together empirical materials, philosophical concepts and sociological ideas the chapter draws out from Deleuze's writings on cinema some elements of a new conceptual language with which to consider visual data.

The chapter has three related aims. First, to introduce Deleuze's writings on cinema to those readers unfamiliar with these texts; second, to explain some key concepts from Deleuze which may contribute to visual sociology; and third, to demonstrate how Deleuzian concepts can have empirical purchase in understanding the visual study of subjectivity, time and change through instances from higher education. The chapter exemplifies Deleuze's view that concepts are 'intensities' which can be 'put to work' in the examination of a problem and situates Deleuze's philosophical interventions in cinema as a 'materialist encounter'.

Theoretical Assemblage: Concept Creation 'Alongside' Cinema

There are two statements in *Cinema 2: The Time-Image* which take us to the heart of Deleuze's philosophical practice. The first is 'the usefulness of theory in the cinema', which appears as the final entry in the contents page for *Cinema 2*. The notion that theory is to be assessed according to its 'usefulness' exemplifies Deleuze's view of philosophy as 'a practice of concepts', as a means to think the creation of concepts which can be 'put to work' in the examination of a problem. For Deleuze, concepts are 'intensities' which 'work or don't' (Deleuze and Parnet 1987: 10). Cinema – as a particular visual medium deriving from a particular technology which provides a particular viewing experience – has generated philosophical concepts which can be 'put to work' to explore matter, movement, perceptions, actions and affections. The *Cinema* books, then, exemplify Deleuze's practice of philosophy as a form of concept-testing. Deleuze acknowledges this in his statement that the cinema books provide 'a theory of cinema [which] is not "about" cinema, but about the concepts that cinema gives rise to and which are themselves related to other concepts corresponding to other practices' (2005b: 268). As Tomlinson and Habberjam put it, Deleuze 'is engaged in the work of concept creation "alongside" the cinema' (2005: xvi). This philosophical act of 'thinking with cinema' clearly differentiates him from cinema historians and theorists (Nelmes 2011), analysts of cinematic style and form (Bordwell and Thompson 2010), genre studies (Altman 1999), and theorists of the cinematic experience and viewer engagement (Block 2010). While their concerns are to explicate *cinematic* forms, texts and contexts, Deleuze's focus on the *concepts* which cinema 'gives rise to' draws a line of flight to 'other' philosophical concerns, purposes and practices.

The second relevant statement is Deleuze's comment that 'theory too is something which is made, no less than its object' (2005b: 268). For Deleuze, theory is 'made' though its assemblage of heterogeneous concepts, materials, sources, examples and illustrations. So, the *Cinema* books combine a vast knowledge of film histories, styles, genres, directors, films and film sequences, with aspects of Peirce's semiology, Bergson's philosophy of matter and time, and reflections from a multitude of film-makers on their filmic practices. These resources are then used in a distinctly Deleuzian way: they are not simply adopted or adapted but are transformed through a creative appropriation ('we borrowed from Peirce a certain number of terms whilst changing their meaning' [Deleuze 2005b: 31]). This act of making theory by connecting ideas into a new theoretical or 'machinic' assemblage, and of using theory to develop a new way of thinking (a 'line of flight') about cinematic and 'other practices', is an illustration of Deleuze and Guattari's rhizomatic thinking – a form of thinking which is acentred, connective, heterogeneous, non-hierarchical and multiple (see Deleuze and Guattari 1987). Such rhizomatic thinking means that Deleuze's *Cinema* books generate 'a whole new vocabulary and terminology to describe the ethical and philosophical implications of the dynamic composition and perennial movement of film' (Girgus 2007: 91).

Deleuze's approach of 'thinking with cinema' is akin to the one I take in this chapter. I appropriate some of Deleuze's cinema concepts in order to see what practical use I can make of them in relation to participant-generated video, and what insights they may disclose as part of a theoretical assemblage. I now turn to the encounter between Deleuze's *Cinema* books and visual sociology.

Visual Sociology, Visual Methodologies and Deleuze's Cinema-Philosophy

The recent upsurge in academic publications about visual sociology, visual methodologies, and visual research methods (Pauwels 2010; Pink 2007; Rose 2007; Spencer 2011), the establishment and growth of the International Visual Sociology Association, and the increasing number of dedicated journals and special editions devoted to visuality, provides clear evidence of a growing interest in the visual in sociological understandings. Visual sociologists now work with photographs, video, advertising images, newsreels, feature films, documentaries, graphic novels, maps and charts. Paradoxically, this growth of interest in the visual has not has been sufficient to mitigate what Grady (2001) calls the ongoing 'marginalization' of visual sociology; and it is still largely the case, according to Pauwels, that 'most social scientists are completely unaware of [the] existence or potential' of visual methods (2010: 546). These opposing pulls indicate the existence of some key tensions within sociology as a disciplinary field.

Visual sociology aims to explore and understand shifts towards greater 'ocularcentrism' in contemporary culture, many of which centre on changes in social activity relating to, and use of, television, film, new media and mobile technologies (Jay 1993; Jenks 1995; Taylor and Saarinen 1994). In efforts to step 'beyond text, towards other ways of conveying . . . the saturation of the visual and symbolic in our contemporary culture' (Atkinson and Beer 2010: 538), contemporary sociology is developing new interdisciplinary theorisations – as well as 'borrowing' from other established visual disciplines – and it is perhaps this broadening of the discipline which gives rise to some of the tensions noted above. As Pauwels notes, visual sociology 'is not really a specialised field of sociology . . . but a cross-cutting field of inquiry, a way of doing and thinking that influences the whole process of researching'

(2010: 559). From this perspective, Deleuze's entry into an interdisciplinary visual sociology is timely, and there are at least four consonances between a Deleuzian view of images and that of an interdisciplinary visual sociology. The first is the view that the image is not simply a reflection of a pre-existing 'reality' but a cultural artefact constructed in relation to social norms, values, contexts and processes, as well as possessing specific histories of production, reception and viewing. Second, that representational practices and modes of representation themselves constitute valid objects of inquiry. Third, that processes of viewing and reception need to be considered in understanding and interpreting visual materials – a point which, as I explain later, is crucial to Deleuze's cinema-inspired philosophical approach to the image. Fourth, and finally, that reflexivity concerning the conditions of knowledge production is a necessary consideration within contemporary research practice chimes with Deleuze's view that the philosophical analysis of cinema works to 'rouse the thinker in us'.

In the discussion which follows I use Deleuze's cinema-philosophy to think though some findings from two recent empirical research projects which enabled students to use video as a creative medium to express their identities and becomings during their educational journeys. In the first project, the videonarratives project, doctoral students' filmed individual videonarratives which focused on critical incidents from their research journeys as a means to enhance reflexivity and broaden their practical research skills (Taylor 2011; Taylor et al. 2011). In the second project, the Student Transitions and Experiences Project (STEP), undergraduates on an Education Studies degree used video to record and reflect on their transition to university and their experiences during the first two years of their degree studies. As I discuss later, the data from the projects provides working examples of ways in which Deleuze's concepts may be used to interpret and understand research findings. The purpose in doing this is to make more concrete what a Deleuzian theorisation of the visual may offer to education research specifically and visual sociology and social science research more broadly. But first, a brief introduction to the use of visual methodologies in education is necessary.

Just as visual methodologies comprise a small but growing field in sociological research (as I outlined above), in recent years there has been a surge of interest in visual research methods in education. Many of these studies share an interest in the analysis of cultural and social dimensions of the visual within education and many, like visual sociology more broadly, have an interdisciplinary methodological and theoretical orientation. Some recent examples of studies using visual methodologies in education include: the innovative uses of photo-elicitation in research with children and young people (Epstein et al. 2006; Margolis 1999; Prosser and Warburton 1999); the use of drawings, images and photographs in investigations of the visible but hidden curricula of school culture (Prosser 2007); teachers' use of video for reflective practice (Jaworski 1990; Walker 2002); and trainees' use of video for skills development during initial teacher education (Clarke 2009). While these studies explore the visual in compulsory and professional education sectors, higher education has seen parallel developments. For example, mobile phone images, cheap digital video and 'flip cameras' are increasingly being used in undergraduate education as a means to enhance teaching and learning through the promotion of student engagement (Hargis and Marotta 2011; Haw and Hadfield 2011); and at doctoral level, there is a growing interest in using video both as a narrative document of the doctoral journey and as a means to record skills development (Taylor 2011; Wisker 2008). The two higher education projects discussed in this chapter focus on research using video with undergraduates and doctoral students and, taken together, provide an empirical springboard for putting Deleuzian concepts on visuality to work in a practical sense.

Deleuze and Cinema: A Materialist Encounter

(A) Matter in Movement: Deleuze, Peirce and Bergson

Deleuze's writings on cinema, like the rest of his oeuvre, can be placed within an 'alternative' strand of philosophy, one which, with its emphasis on vitalism, materialism, change and difference, enables him to mount some important anti-essentialist challenges to the Western philosophical tradition (Parr 2005). For example, in Deleuze's view, the individual does not possess a 'self' which exists as a separable entity with a stable ego, people are not divisible into interior and exterior components, and neither do they possess internal will or agency to motivate external action. To think so is an illusion derived from Enlightenment rationality. Instead, Deleuze proposes, subjectivities are multiplicities, subjects are characterised by flows of forces, intensities and desires, and individuals are continually being formed through a process of 'dynamic individuation' (Deleuze and Parnet 1987: 93) from which the changing 'self' as an assemblage, a connective multiplicity, emerges. Deleuze uses the term 'becoming' to refer to this process of dynamic individuation. For him, becoming is first and foremost a material, sensible, intensive and embodied process, enabling us to experience life as a radically immanent fleshed existence motivated by desires and flows (Braidotti 2002). Deleuze sees becoming as immanent to all of life, human and nonhuman, and becoming, difference, change and variation as the hallmarks of life. I will pick up the concepts of becoming and multiplicity later. The main point to grasp now is that for Deleuze matter and mind are not separate but productively inextricable. In the *Cinema* books, this anti-essentialist, anti-dualistic philosophy is used to 'think with cinema', specifically to think how cinema has enabled new ways of conceptualising our connection to the world, how cinema has generated new modes of perception and experience, and how cinema has changed how we feel about time. In this, Bergson and Peirce are both crucial in helping Deleuze elaborate an approach to the visual which contributes to the development of a sociology which has the potential to reduce our 'over relian[ce] on words and their precious indexicality to establish relationships between visuals and meanings and to communicate ideas' (Prosser 2001: 3). In what follows, I focus first on what Deleuze took from Peirce and Bergson in order to develop his philosophical notion of the materiality of the image, then I deal with how he creatively appropriated Peirce's categories of non-linguistic signs to develop his concepts of the movement-image and the time-image. After that, I explore Deleuze's concepts in action through examples from empirical data.

A sign is something material, perceivable by the senses, which refers to something other than itself, and which is recognised by those who use it as a sign. Semiology, or semiotics, is the 'science of signs'. There are two main schools of thought about signs. Saussure thought signs functioned like a language, and that signs were ultimately an expression of (and signified) an underlying structure, whether social, cultural or unconscious. Peirce developed a radically different view. In Peirce's semiology, there is a triangular relation between the sign (an image, word, gesture, sound, etc., which refers to something other than itself), the object (that which the sign refers to) and its interpretant (the mental concept the sign evokes in the mind of a person as she experiences that object). Unlike Saussure, who was interested in how signs *reflected* 'deep' innate or social structures, Peirce's philosophy drew him to foreground *relations*, that is, the relations between people, their experience of signs, and objects. For Peirce, the sign's relationality, it's meaning, is expressed in the interpretant. It is important to realise that 'the interpretant is not the user of the sign . . . [the interpretant] is a mental concept produced both by the sign and by the user's experience of the object' (Fiske 1990: 42). In Peirce's view, this means that the sign is a form of thought which is 'given' (by the relation between the object and interpretant), interpreted, and open to further interpretation. Furthermore, 'what we know is based only on what we get', and what we 'get' and 'know' is 'a material intensity', which means the interpretant constitutes an articulation of 'what is real, present and observable, but abstract' (Dawkins 2003: 160). It is precisely this line of thinking which attracted Deleuze. Like Peirce, Deleuze held the philosophical view that matter exists prior to all formal expression, that matter is prior to 'potential actualization by the brain – a matter/brain coupling' (Dawkins 2003: 161). Deleuze used these ideas to think through how cinema becomes an expression of the immanent relation between real world and thought, whereby thought is 'the action of material intensity in the senses' (Dawkins, 2003: 161). This leads Deleuze to his innovative claim for the materiality of the image and his argument that 'the material element of the image is meaningful in its own right' (Dawkins 2003: 155). It also enables him to make interesting connections between image, movement and matter as I now show.

In *Cinema 1*, Deleuze (2005a: 2) contends that cinema 'does not give us an image to which movement is added, instead it immediately gives us a movement-image', because the movement-image extracts 'from movements the mobility which is their common substance' (Deleuze 2005a: 24). This 'extraction' of 'mobility' results from three things: the editing of shots into sequences (montage); shots taken from different angles and distances (the mobile camera); and the freeing of the viewer's gaze to rove over the image as she desires. Deleuze thinks that these three characteristics free cinema from space and produce it as a temporal experience, so that for him movement-images are 'mobile sections of a duration' (Deleuze 2005a: 23). Bringing in Bergson's idea of duration enables Deleuze to explain that the unceasing variation of cinema images works as a figuration of our consciousness. It was Bergson's view that we change without ceasing, that consciousness is continuous, unceasing variation (Bergson 1946, 2004). By connecting the concept of duration to the 'material elements . . . immanent to movement' cinema gives us an image of 'change which does not stop changing' (Deleuze 2005a: 4–8). Deleuze makes the specific point that cinema 'invented' this new way for us to be conscious of and experience temporal change; cinema gives us a new sense of time, a perception of time as a 'differing series of becomings beyond our organising point of view' (Colebrook 2002: 45). However, 'mobile sections' are not just temporal, they are also material. Drawing together Bergson's view that 'matter . . . is an aggregate of images' (Bergson 1946: viii) and Peirce's views, outlined earlier, Deleuze proposes that the movement-image includes the viewer's perception, sight and knowledge, as well as the 'force' of the object: the movement-image is 'the object; the thing itself caught in movement as continuous function', it is the 'modulation of the object itself' (Deleuze 2005b: 26). The viewer is intrinsic to this 'flowing matter', she is not separate or separable from the image or 'outside' the image in any sense, nor is the image a mere representation of an 'object' at a distance. In Deleuze's radical ontology, the viewer is related to the image, connected to it through brain and consciousness, combined materially and psychically: 'the thing and the perception of the thing are one and the same thing, one and the same image'; 'the set of images . . . is consciousness, immanent to matter' (Deleuze 2005a: 65, 63). Such an ontological shift brings with it profound implications, some of which I explore in the consideration of the empirical data below. Before that, I briefly outline Deleuze's categorisation of images.

(B) The Movement-Image and the Time-Image

Deleuze makes a basic distinction between the movement-image and the time-image (each image is respectively the subtitle of *Cinema 1* and *Cinema 2*). Drawing on what he called Peirce's 'great classification' of non-linguistic signs, he classifies images into nine signs with ten combinations (see the table, Deleuze 2005b: 277). The complexities of the total sign system don't need to concern us here, as my intention is to focus on the three main categories of the movement-image – the perception-image, the action-image, and the affection image – and the time-image.

The first category of the movement-image is the perception-image (equivalent to Peirce's 'sign') and designates 'the first material moment of subjectivity' (Deleuze 2005a: 66–8). The sign indicates the moment in which the individual emerges. From the universal variation of the 'whole', the viewer 'frames', that is organises and selects, a set of images which provide the information for thought, action and affection. The 'framing' of these images prompts perception. The second category of the movement-image is the action-image (which derives from Peirce's 'referent'). In Deleuze's analysis, the action-image is exemplary of American 'realist', 'classical', narrative cinema, with its internally motivated characters whose responses to challenges within the social milieu provoke changes and new situations. He uses the action-image to designate 'the second material moment of subjectivity', which explains the visual enactment of inner volition through materially embodied social acts (Deleuze 2005a: 67). The third category of the movement-image is

the affection-image. This occupies the gap or interval between perception and action; it is the moment in which subject and object 'coincide'
and, as the 'third material aspect of subjectivity', it captures the way
in which the subject 'experiences' and 'feels' itself 'from the inside'
(Deleuze 2005a: 67). In visual terms, the affection-image finds expression in the close-up and below I explore the affection-image through
Deleuze's concept of 'faciality'.

In *Cinema 1*, Deleuze explores the movement-image through its connection to the sensory-motor schema of 'classical', narrative cinema, a
system which begins to break down in postwar cinema with the advent
of successive 'waves' of new cinema, such as Italian neo-realism, the
French nouvelle vague and American new cinema. In Deleuze's theorisation, these new waves brought a crisis of the movement-image in which
the action-image tends to 'disappear in favour of pure optical situations'
(Deleuze 2005b: 17). This crisis brings a loosening of the sensory-motor
focus of the movement-image, and its replacement by the time-image.
The cinema of the time-image is characterised by absence of plot, an
emphasis on journeys and wanderings, and anonymised spaces rather
than 'real' and recognisable spaces. In Deleuze's view, the time-image
emancipates the senses from movement, from the sensory-motor dimension of the movement-image, and so discloses 'time, a little time in its
pure state'. The time-image brings the senses 'into direct relation with
time and thought' (Deleuze 2005b: 16–17).

In this brief overview I have discussed some key philosophical ideas
Deleuze creatively appropriates from Bergson (duration, change and
the materiality of the flow of images) and Peirce (the relationally and
materiality of signs as mental concepts). The task in the remainder of
the chapter is to put Deleuze's concepts to work in relation to empirical
instances from two recent research projects. My purpose in doing so is
to explore the analytical usefulness of the concepts as tools for thinking.
I am not aiming for systematisation and generalisation and I proceed on
the basis of Massumi's cautionary note that Deleuze's concepts are both
'slippery' and 'supple', with some pointing towards 'local encounters'
and others opening onto 'far-reaching speculation' (Massumi 1992: 15).
With this in mind, I now turn to the research data.

The data is drawn from two recent projects, one with doctoral students (the videonarratives project) and a second with undergraduate
students (the Student Transitions and Experiences Project). The projects
had some similarities in their use of a participatory, collaborative, emergent research design. Both projects had an open brief, low technical skill
requirement, invited participants to use video for creative, expressive

and reflexive purposes, and participants owned the videos they produced. Both projects aimed to use visual methods to garner insights into participants' experiences which may not have been so directly obtained though other methods (Packard 2008). It is worth highlighting that, in each project, participants filmed and edited video images of themselves, whereas Deleuze's *Cinema* books focus on documentary or fiction films produced by cinema professionals. However, this difference in the formal style and artistic/creative origin of the images obtained does not prevent the use of Deleuze's concepts as analytical tools for illuminating subjectivity, social relations and educational contexts, as I now go on to discuss.

The Perception-Image: Video as Machinic Assemblage

I think [video] is a process . . . an infinitely flexible product so . . . don't script it. Because you can feel it and if it isn't right on the first take you can do it again . . . plus you can edit it. So it's not like when you're handing in a thesis which is a very solid thing. (Yolande, videonarratives project)

Yolande here makes the obvious point that video is a form of technical assemblage. Matter, for Deleuze, as I indicated above, precedes all formalised expression. What video does is assemble the 'plastic mass' of the infinite relations of matter by, first, selecting images from the whole, then, through editing as a second selection, combining them as mobile sections. This makes video (like cinema) the 'machine assemblage of matter-images' (Deleuze 2005a: 87). One clear advantage of participant-generated video for Yolande is that it has such formal flexibility, a 'lightness' and potential for mutability which contrasts to the 'weight' and solidity of a written doctoral thesis.

More importantly, the technical assemblage entailed in video production has an ontological dimension, as Yolande's reflection on the assured, confident, academic demeanour she presented on her video and how this contrasted with an earlier self illustrates: 'It's not been massively difficult to shift into another class in some ways but being in that class you also have kind of residues of [things] that can't be erased.' Assembling images into mobile sections enabled Yolande to comment quite precisely on the emergence of subjectivity; her video image disclosed the emergence of an 'I', an 'I' which both 'frames' the self and an 'I' constituted in that momentary act of framing. This provides an effective illustration of what Deleuze means by the perception-image as a moment of emergence of an always indeterminate self which temporarily coheres in and through the flux of images. In Deleuze's terms,

Yolande's experience designates 'the first material moment of subjectivity' (2005a: 66–8). This is not to say that Yolande's emergence with the perception-image in her video establishes a centre, ground, essence or 'expression' of her subjectivity. For Deleuze, as I discussed earlier, no such stable ego exists. Rather, Yolande's emergence emphasises the different becomings possible from the 'whole' of the 'acentred universe of movement-images' (Deleuze 2005a: 64) and how this indeterminate, infinitely varied 'whole' is 'framed' in this one moment by this one individual.

Empirical instances from both projects provide insights into how video may disclose the micro-level working of social, familial and educational assemblages. Assemblage is a key term in Deleuze's writings and is used to describe the 'co-functioning' of entities which are non-linear, not successive, but related and relational in that alliances or 'alloys' are temporarily established between them (Deleuze and Guattari 1987). Deleuze's description of assemblages as 'machinic' refers to how the different components may be recombined in a temporary and contingent whole. Machinic assemblages work at macro, meso and micro levels and involve a combination of elements from all these levels. In the videonarratives project one participant, Rory, spoke of how the video he had made became an intensive component in a wider social assemblage which included him, his family, and his educational experiences:

> Friday evening when I got back the discussion enlarged . . . and it was as if [the video] acted as a stimulus for the conversation. So I got to learn something about my daughter and what my daughter knew . . . my family commented on the fact of 'Oh that's what you do at [name of city] on these weekends is it, you think about things like that?'

Rory's comment indicates how his video works as an 'expressive entity' (DeLanda 2006) as it affectively enters into a relational private-public-self-education-family assemblage. Rory's video 'inserts' his learning and education – things Rory had previously kept private to himself in a separate social and spatial sphere – into his family's relations. As they get to know something about him that he had not previously told them, and he finds something out about his daughter which he didn't know, the public act of viewing the video becomes an event at the micro-level reconstitution of family life, and of Rory's subjectivity within his family. We can say that his video becomes a heterogeneous component in the emergence of a new family assemblage: the transformations occasioned by the video work both at the 'molecular' level to reshape Rory's subjectivity within his education-family assemblage and, at the same time, the mobile sections of the video disclose the modulation of the 'object' (that is, Rory). Rory's video grants the viewer an indirect image of time in which the changing contingencies of the family social assemblage may be perceived.

The STEP project provides a more extensive example of how the visual matter of video materialises 'a machinic assemblage of bodies, actions and passions' and provides an empirical illustration of Deleuze's claim that 'each one of us [as] the contingent centre, is nothing but an assemblage of three images, a consolidate of perception-images, action-images and affection-images' (2005a: 68). Katrina uses her video to reflect on first coming to university:

> I remember Mum dropping me off and I walked to the car park and her driving away and I just broke down. I was running through the streets home to get out of the crowds and I was in tears and I just sat on my bed crying for ages. I remember that first night I just sat there so upset and I didn't know what to do with myself, I couldn't eat anything, and someone knocked on my door and said 'Do you want to come out?' and I said 'I'm too scared!' and they said 'Well come tomorrow' and I thought 'Okay, maybe'. The first few weeks were terrifying.

Katrina's comments exemplify three of the five modalities for using video in social research identified by Haw and Hadfield: extraction ('use of video to record a specific interaction'), reflection (using video for reflection on 'actions, understandings and constructions'), and articulation (video use which helps participants 'voice their opinions and communicate these to others') (2011: 2). The three modalities are useful in understanding Katrina's experience of coming to university and how it affects her physically and psychically. Katrina's emotional response and her view of herself arises in relation to the other students she feels she has to get away from, in relation to her bereft sense of distance from her mother, and in relation to new social contacts and invitations. The local, contextual and socially specific emergence of a new educational-family-friendship-spatial assemblage which Katrina reflects on in her video can be seen as an interesting, and complex, negotiation of the perception-image (framing the self), the action-image (location in social contexts which engender motivation to act) and the relation-image (reflexivity on one's own becoming). In this example, Deleuze's visual concepts enable us to gain insights into the expressive, material dimensions of subjectivity and, in particular, how our perceptual volition is materially embodied in social acts. Thinking of subjectivity as a 'contingent centre' composed of the entanglement of different forms of images connects well with an understanding of social interactions as hybrid, emerging and relational, as always co-constituted by the social assemblages we find ourselves within. Katrina's video provides an interesting empirical demonstration of the utility of some of Deleuze's cinema concepts and also discloses the affective dimension of plugging ourselves into new social assemblages.

The Affection-Image: Faciality and the Close-Up

One of the advantages of video is that it 'allows for the analysis of a social phenomenon at increasingly finer levels of granularity' (Haw and Hadfield 2011: 26). In both projects students used the camera to film themselves in big close-up often accompanied by talking directly into camera. In interviews in which the videos were used to prompt reflexive dialogue (Taylor 2011), participants commented on how they saw themselves.

> There are times when I know I'm on shaky ground academically, and that comes across . . . in the cicadic gazes around the room . . . my eyes are darting around the room hopefully looking for inspiration to try and get this thought out. (Rory, videonarratives project)

> No matter what you lot say I know what I look like now. You can't tell me anymore how I am because . . . that's me there. (Yolande, videonarratives project)

> This video's given me the chance to reflect back and think 'wow, what an experience'. I'm actually a lot different now. I was enthusiastic then, I wanted to learn, but I'm not really that interested in learning anymore. I feel the more I learn the more depressed I get. You realise how some views have got into your head and . . . there's no such thing as natural, things are constructed for you to think like that. I also became more aware of my position when I read bell hooks and I just realised that I didn't realise I was black, I didn't realise my skin was a barrier. And then to think, oh my god, when I go for a job interview I'm five times more likely not to get it because I'm black or because I wear a scarf and that was hard to take in, to think it's not about what you know, it's not about your personality, that this thing on my face can ultimately determine my life, that wasn't easy to take in. Imagine going your whole life, 24 years of never realising, even when people were racist to me, calling me a black bastard or a paki, I just thought they were stupid. (Mahveen, STEP project)

All three participants hone in on details of the face: in Rory's case the eyes, in Yolande's the image of her face, and in Mahveen's case her facial skin colour. Deleuze's concept of faciality is useful in helping think through the import of their comments. Faciality takes us in a different direction than traditional image-analysis might: while the latter would lead the reader to deduce 'inner' subjective states from 'external' visible images, a Deleuzian line refuses such a surface/depth interpretation. For Deleuze, the close-up does not offer a 'translation' of the face but, instead, shows its expressive becoming. The face, for Deleuze, may be 'intensive' or 'reflexive'. The 'intensive' face connects qualities or sensory materialities. Deleuze refers to the 'intensive expressive movement' of the face, of the face as an 'organ-carrying plate of nerves' which expresses 'micro-movements' or 'tiny local movements which the rest of the body usually keeps hidden' (2005a: 90). He elaborates his analysis of faciality by connecting the face first, to affect, that is to those perceivable forces, actions and processes which provoke change and initiate becoming (Colman 2005); second, to what Peirce calls 'firstness', that is to 'immediate and instantaneous consciousness . . . that which is as it is for itself and in itself what is new in experience, what is fresh, fleeting, but eternal' (Deleuze 2005a: 100); and third, to the affection-image ('the affection-image is the close-up and the close-up is the face' [Deleuze 2005a: 89]). It is quite easy to see how this concept of faciality, with its conjunction of affect, firstness and affection-image, provides a useful interpretive vehicle for Rory and Yolande's comments on their faces: as Yolande says 'that's me there' and the 'cicadic gazes' through which Rory divines and embodies his unstable identity as a becoming academic. However, it is the data from Mahveen which leads to an understanding of the more complex aspects of faciality.

Deleuze says 'there are two sorts of questions you can put to a face: what are you thinking about? Or what do you sense or feel?', and he contends that faciality enables an 'affective reading' of the film or video (2005a: 91). In prompting a 'microphysiognomy . . . that extends from the human face to the face of things' (Bruno 2010: 213), the affection-image tunes into the pre-personal, desubjectifying nature of affects as forces, intensities and events which resonate, interact and temporarily cohere in 'singularities'. These affects, as Kennedy explains, work as 'points that produce effects of transition', and which give way to 'an emergent self [which is] atmospheric, pathic, fusional and transitivist' (2002: 89). Mahveen's realisation that it is the visibility of her skin, its very colour, texture and materiality ('this thing on my face'), apparent in big close-up in her video, which she then connects to her transformative reading of bell hooks and her racist reception by others, indicates the 'singularity' of affective forces in/through which her becoming-self momentarily emerges. The affection-image, then, is not a gateway to uncovering

Mahveen's emotional 'depths' hidden behind the surface of her image, rather it points to how the 'surface' (of the image, of the skin) is already pleated or folded affectively with the forces of matter and memory, senses and spirit, culture and history. Mahveen's intensive face is the affection-image of her individual, sensory, material, embodied experience of the hate speech of racism. In *A Thousand Plateaus* Deleuze and Guattari refer to the 'white wall/black hole system' to describe an imperialist system in which the subject 'will be pinned to the white wall and stuffed in the black hole' by the force of a 'the faciality machine' (1987: 201). And we can see that, for Mahveen, the painful affects of racism find their molecular demonstration on her skin. Her video reflections are a powerful empirical example for understanding faciality as a deterritorialisation of the face, a production of the face as landscape, topography and zone of intensity, a flow of affects which abstract the face from the person in order to produce her socially as a black hole of subjectification.

These three empirical instances show how salient the concept of faciality may prove to be. In analysing Mahveen's face as an intensive component in an authoritarian, colonialist and 'othering' assemblage we can see how the affection-image may work as a conceptual vehicle to produce knowledge of the experiential, material, affective dimensions of racism, while the examples from Rory and Yolande lead to a radically alternative ontological understanding of subjectivity as an endless process of becoming.

The Time-Image: Becoming

As briefly outlined earlier, Deleuze thought the movement-image had been brought to a crisis in some forms of contemporary cinema and had been replaced by the time-image, a 'purely visual image' which is an instantiation of Bergson's notion of duration as change without ceasing. Philosophically, the time-image is a visual presentation of the 'living present' (Deleuze 1994: 71). As duration, the time-image is a 'contraction of instants', a combination of past and future in the present moment. It is time seen not as the linear succession of independent points but as dimensions of an event in which past and future coexist in the present. The significance of the time-image as a 'purely visual image' is that it 'contains' time, it does not represent or 'capture' time but instantiates it in the image, such that the visual presents 'a little time in its pure state'. How might the abstract and rather difficult concept of the time-image work as a thinking tool to help explain data from the two projects?

Halli from the STEP project reflected on her video:

I didn't want to edit any of it. What I really wanted to do is to put it to flow. I really wanted to put it all in. I wanted to see it back, you know [laughter], I want to see it as time goes by or when I've finished university I can watch it and say 'Right, yeah'. Well, the advantage is that you can see the changes, yeah?

And Yolande from the videonarratives project thought:

I thought I'd feel uncomfortable looking at myself but I don't, I find it reassuring, this sounds really weird, it's almost as if I'm not alone . . . it's like, you're always with yourself but it's which part of yourself are you with? Seeing your image there I think it makes it more embodied. That there is a body there and the words are coming from this body . . . because whenever you usually hear your words, the words are outside yourself. When I become conscious of the words is when they're already out there in the ether. Whereas looking at the image the words are coming from in here, they're coming from a place and that place is that body. It connects me even more . . . I feel like there's somebody with me. I feel that I'm not alone, this is who is with me, this person. We are together.

Haw and Hadfield point out that video is a multilayered 'indentation' of participants' meanings (2011: 28). Using Deleuze's time-image to think through Halli and Yolande's multilayered comments enables us to perceive that both their videos are about the 'direct presentation of becoming itself' (Colebrook 2002: 52). Halli says her video enables her to 'see the changes' in herself in the flow of images, a 'flow' which constitutes a time-image conjoining the past (the virtual duration past), the lived present (the actualisation of virtual objects) and the future (the virtual refraction of duration past). Deleuze refers to this synthesis of time in the time-image as the 'crystal-image'. Yolande, on the other hand, comments that the image shows her words actually coming from her body ('from in here'), and she apprehends this moment of embodiment as a spatialised, sensory materiality ('that place is that body') which 'connects' her even more to 'herself'. Yolande's immanent embodiment in her video image provides a momentary time-image. In this moment in Yolande's video the linear time and extended space which normally construct our everyday social lives have collapsed and Yolande experiences herself as a meeting point of multiplicities in the co-extensive present 'now'. Her image is experienced as a phenomenon passing through time. Thinking empirically with the concept of the time-image indicates, for Yolande, that time is not an external force but a means of experiencing her subjectivity as a becoming inside time.

Concluding Thoughts on Using a Deleuzian-inspired Framework for Visual Analysis

This chapter has explored some key concepts from Deleuze's cinema-philosophy and what they may offer visual sociology. The chapter has explained the concepts of the movement-image – with its divisions into the perception-image, the action-image and the affection-image – and the time-image, and has illustrated some ways of using these concepts in the analyses of empirical data from two higher education projects. In putting these key concepts to work the chapter has opened up some new ways for visual sociology to think about the emergence of the subject, the constitution of the subject through images, and the subjective processes of becoming through and in time. The most important feature we can take from Deleuze's cinema-philosophy is his insistence on the materiality of the image. It is his connection of consciousness with the materiality of the subject which forges a refreshing way of thinking about image and object; and it is this insistence on the materiality of the image which forms a radical challenge to representationalist modes of thinking and opens up new analytical avenues for visual sociology. While it needs to be acknowledged that some criticisms have been levelled at Deleuze's approach to cinema, for example the off-putting nature of his focus on male auteurs, his valorisation of European and other 'high brow' art cinema traditions, and his insistence that cinema is not principally a narrative form (Colebrook, 2002), in my view such criticisms do not diminish the power of the conceptual tools he has to offer, nor prevent us from appropriating and using them creatively ourselves in ways which are generative for empirical analysis. Such an endeavour itself is distinctly Deleuzian! As I stated at the beginning of the chapter, Deleuze is not interested in analysing cinematic form or style; his concern is with what the cinema image does for thinking (Trifonova 2004). If we start with the view that Deleuze's purpose in the *Cinema* books is to 'attempt to arouse the thinker in us' (Marks 1998: 158) then I would argue that that is good enough grounds for approaching Deleuze's concepts as materials to provoke fruitful discussions about methodology, research design and meaning-making. The *Cinema* books in themselves offer a set of flexible conceptual tools for analysing images and, when combined with other concepts from Deleuze's writings, provide a powerful conceptual framework for visual sociology more generally.

References

Altman, R. (1999), *Film/Genre*, London: British Film Institute.

Atkinson, R. and D. Beer (2010), 'The Ivorine Tower in the City: Engaging urban studies after *The Wire*', *City*, 14(2): 529–44.

Bergson, H. (1946), *The Creative Mind: An Introduction to Metaphysics*, New York: Kensington Publishing.

Bergson, H. (2004), *Matter and Memory*, New York: Dover Publications.

Block, M. (2010), *Situating the Feminist Gaze and Spectatorship in Postwar Cinema*, Newcastle-upon-Tyne: Cambridge Scholars Publishing.

Bordwell, D. and K. Thompson (2010), *Film Art: An Introduction*, 9th edn, London: McGraw-Hill.

Braidotti, R. (2002), *Metamorphosis: Towards and Materialist Theory of Becoming*, Cambridge: Polity.

Bruno, G. (2010), 'Pleats of Matter, Folds of the Soul' in D. N. Rodowick (ed.), *Afterimages of Gilles Deleuze's Film Philosophy*, Minneapolis: University of Minnesota Press, pp. 213–33.

Clarke, L. (2009), 'Video Reflections in Initial Teacher Education', *British Journal of Educational Technology*, 40(5): 959–61.

Colebrook, C. (2002), *Gilles Deleuze*, London: Routledge.

Colman, F. (2005), 'Affect' in A. Parr (ed.), *The Deleuze Dictionary*, New York: Columbia University Press, pp. 11–12.

Dawkins, R. (2003), 'The Problem of a Material Element in the Cinematic Sign: Deleuze, Metz and Peirce', *Angelaki: Journal of the Theoretical Humanities*, 7(3): 155–66.

DeLanda, M. (2006), *A New Philosophy of Society*, London: Continuum.

Deleuze, G. (1994), *Difference and Repetition*, trans. P. Patton, London: Athlone Press.

Deleuze, G. (2005a), *Cinema 1: The Movement-Image*, trans. H. Tomlinson and B. Habberjam, London: Continuum.

Deleuze, G. (2005b), *Cinema 2: The Time-Image*, trans. H. Tomlinson and R. Galeta, London: Continuum.

Deleuze, G. and C. Parnet (1987), *Dialogues*, trans. H. Tomlinson and B. Habberjam, London: Athlone Press.

Deleuze, G. and F. Guattari (1987), *A Thousand Plateaus: Capitalism and Schizophrenia*, trans. B. Massumi, London: Continuum.

Epstein, I., B. Stevens, P. McKeever and S. Baruchel (2006), 'Photo Elicitation Interview (PEI): Using photos to elicit children's perspectives', *International Journal of Qualitative Methods*, 5(3): 1–11.

Fiske, J. (1990), *Introduction to Communication Studies*, London: Routledge.

Girgus, S. B. (2007), 'Beyond Ontology: Levinas and the ethical frame in film', *Film-Philosophy*, 11(2): 88–107.

Grady, J. (2001), 'Becoming a Visual Sociologist', *Sociological Imagination*, 38(1–2): 83–119.

Hargis, J. and S. Marotta (2011), 'Using Flip Camcorders for Active Classroom Metacognitive Reflection', *Active Learning in Higher Education*, 12(1): 35–44.

Haw, K. and M. Hadfield (2011), *Video in Social Science Research: Functions and Forms*, London: Routledge.

Jay, M. (1993), *Downcast Eyes: The Denigration of Vision in Twentieth Century French Thought*, Berkeley: California University Press.

Jaworski, B. (1990), 'Video as a Tool for Teachers' Professional Development', *British Journal of In-Service Education*, 16(1): 60–5.

Jenks, C. (ed.) (1995), *Visual Culture*, London: Routledge.

Kennedy, B. (2002), *Deleuze and Cinema: The Aesthetics of Sensation*, Edinburgh: Edinburgh University Press.

Margolis, E. (1999), 'Class Pictures: Representations of race, gender and ability in a century of school photography', *Visual Sociology*, 14: 7–38.

Marks, J. (1998), *Gilles Deleuze: Vitalism and Multiplicity*, London: Pluto Press.

Massumi, B. (1992), *A User's Guide to Capitalism and Schizophrenia*, Cambridge, MA: MIT Press.

Nelmes, J. (ed.) (2011), *Introduction to Film Studies*, London: Routledge.

Packard, J. (2008), '"I'm Gonna Show You What it's Really Like Out Here": The power and limitation of participatory visual methods', *Visual Studies*, 23(1): 63–77.

Parr, A. (ed.) (2005), *The Deleuze Dictionary*, New York: Columbia University Press.

Pauwels, L. (2010), 'Visual Sociology Reframed: An analytical synthesis and discussion of visual methods in social and cultural research', *Sociological Methods and Research*, 38(4): 545–81.

Pink, S. (2007), *Doing Visual Ethnography*, 2nd edn, London: Sage.

Prosser, J. (2001), 'Editor's Introduction', *Visual Studies*, 16(1): 3–5.

Prosser, J. (2007), 'Visual Methods and the Visual Culture of Schools', *Visual Studies*, 22(1): 13–30.

Prosser, J. and T. Warburton (1999), *Visual Sociology and School Culture*, London: Paul Chapman.

Rose, G. (2007), *Visual Methodologies: An Introduction to the Interpretation of Visual Materials*, 2nd edn, London: Sage

Spencer, S. (2011), *Visual Research Methods in the Social Science: Awakening Visions*, London: Routledge.

Taylor, C. (2011), 'More Than Meets the Eye: The use of videonarratives to facilitate doctoral students' reflexivity on their doctoral journeys', *Studies in Higher Education*, 36(4): 441–58.

Taylor, C., Y. Downs, R. Baker and G. Chikwa (2011), 'I Did it My Way': Voice, visuality and identity in doctoral students' reflexive videonarratives on their doctoral research journeys', *International Journal of Research and Method in Education*, 34(2): 193–210.

Taylor, M. and E. Saarinen (1994), *Imagologies: Media Philosophy*, London: Routledge.

Tomlinson, H. and B. Habberjam (2005), 'Translators' Introduction' in G. Deleuze, *Cinema 1: The Movement-Image*, London: Continuum, pp. xv–xvii.

Trifonova, T. (2004), 'A Nonhuman Eye: Deleuze on Cinema', *SubStance*, 33(2): 134–52.

Walker, R. (2002), 'Case Study, Case Records and Multimedia', *Cambridge Journal of Education*, 32(1): 109–27.

Wisker, G. (2008), 'Doctoral Learning Journeys: Threshold concepts, conceptual threshold crossing and the role of supervisors and research development programmes', <http://www.vitae.ac.uk/CMS/files/vitaeconference2008-A4_B4%20Wisker,%20Gina.pdf> (accessed 16 October 2012).

Chapter 3

More-Than-Human Visual Analysis: Witnessing and Evoking Affect in Human-Nonhuman Interactions

Jamie Lorimer

There is a growing interest across the social and the natural sciences in the potential of moving image methodologies for researching the 'more-than-human' (Whatmore 2006) dimensions of life. The category 'more-than-human' describes the embodied, affective and skilful dimensions of our multispecies worlds that often elude research methodologies preoccupied with human representations. In this chapter I explore this potential by developing moving image methodologies for both witnessing and evoking human-nonhuman interactions. Drawing Deleuze into conversation with recent work in human geography, film theory, cultural anthropology and ethology,[1] I develop both a practical methodology and a critical, affirmative vocabulary for unpacking the work done by moving imagery. Engaging with work in political theory I develop techniques for attuning to the micropolitical power and promise of moving imagery. This analysis is illustrated through a focus on elephants and images of their behaviours, ecologies and interactions with diverse humans. Drawing on my own video material it outlines how moving imagery techniques can be used to witness and make sense of encounters between people and elephants. Focusing on Disney's famous animation *Dumbo*, I then map and compare two of the prevalent 'affective logics' according to which elephants are evoked in popular moving imagery. The chapter therefore aims to bring together two rather discrete sets of skills and debates relating to moving image methodologies. The first concerns the use of imagery in the field to witness interspecies encounters; the second interrogates existing evocations of such encounters. In conclusion I reflect on the relationships between these two and what they offer in conjunction towards new approaches for multispecies ethnographies (Kirksey and Helmreich 2010).

Moving Imagery

Much of the world now lives in an age of the screen, enmeshed in extensive media assemblages dedicated to the production, circulation and consumption of moving imagery (Shapiro 2008). New mediated ecologies constitute the spaces in which increasing numbers of people encounter distant peoples, organisms and landscapes. Such ecologies perform unprecedented geographies of international connection and are vitally important in shaping popular attitudes towards contemporary issues (Hansen 2004). In Doel and Clarke's (2007) terms, moving imagery frames our 'optical unconscious' organising the horizons of the visible and the sensible. There is a rich tradition of research in anthropology, media studies and film theory for engaging with such assemblages and the images they circulate (e.g., Rose 2007). This work draws primarily on a range of structuralist and psychoanalytic approaches where moving imagery is explored as a means for or mode of signification and representation. While such work is undoubtedly important, here I am interested in developing additional and commensurable means by which we might engage with the performative, haptic and affective dimensions to moving imagery and the importance of these registers for political ordering and intervention.

A 'more-than-human' research methodology encompasses at least three interwoven strands. First, it advocates a sustained inquisition of the modern divisions that establish which forms and processes have agency, challenging the ontologies of humanism to draw attention to the diverse objects, organisms, forces and materialities that populate the world and cross between porous bodies (see Hinchliffe 2007; Whatmore 2002). For example, a great deal of work has been done to unpack the category of 'the animal' to recognise the diverse modes of lively being it subsumes (Haraway 2008; Derrida 2008). Second, such ontological manoeuvrings have epistemological consequences. Rethinking humanism involves rethinking what forms of intelligence, truth and expertise count. Attention has turned from cognition and representation to issues of embodiment, performance, skill and affect, understood as relational and distributed forces and competencies that cut across any lay-scientist and human-nonhuman divides (Thrift 2007). Third, there are distinct politics and ethics to this approach. Appreciating nonhuman agencies and diverse intelligences foregrounds both our material connections to the earth and the varying ways these can be made to matter. The focus here is on modes of relational and/or affirmative ethics and politics that are open to difference (understood as a process) and the excessive and unpredictable nature of life. These are affective, micropolitical experiments, less certain about what bodies can become and how humans and animals can live together (Bennett 2010; Stengers 2010).

These more-than-human inclinations do not sit easily with the orthodox methodologies of the interpretative social sciences, including visual analysis. Many of these are geared towards the collection, interpretation and critique of texts. Such approaches can produce 'dead' accounts that struggle to appreciate the multi-sensory energies and intelligences of human and nonhuman bodies, gestures and events (as well as of images and texts themselves) (Massumi 2002). There is a widely shared sense amongst non-representational and more-than-human theorists that methods are lagging behind theoretical developments and that methodological invigoration and innovation are required. In response there has been a flurry of recent experiments which aim to stretch existing textual methods so that they might witness, analyse and evoke the affective and performative dimensions of imagery and writing.

For example, cultural geographers have experimented with creative writing, diagrams and montage as means to evoke affect and practice (e.g., Latham 2003), benefitting greatly from collaborations with artists and other creative practitioners (see Dwyer and Davies 2010). Such work can be connected to explorations in a new mode of cultural materialism that explores the relationships between matter, memory and place (e.g., Miller 2005; Tilley 2004). Similarly, a rich panoply of embodied and performative techniques has been developed to witness the practical, sensual and affective dimensions to human-nonhuman interactions. These involve autobiographical reflections on the processes of 'learning to be affected' and creative, mimetic techniques for sensing the world differently through the body of another. For example, Vinciane Despret (2004), combines methods from ethology and ethnography to encourage us to attune to the lived experiences and intelligence of nonhuman organisms and the skilled and awkward entanglements associated with interspecies interactions.

Advocates are at pains to point out that these approaches are supplementary to and do not aim to belittle or replace representational methodologies; they are best described as 'more-than-representational' (H. Lorimer 2005). They argue that any critical understanding of the power and provenance of representation is enhanced by attending to its material, practical and affective dimensions. I will return to the relationship between representational and non-representational methodologies in conclusion. Although they are central to moving imagery, affect and emotion have traditionally received little attention in work on film.

For many these are either trivial phenomena tangential to structuralist concerns with content, or the negative manifestation of psychoanalytic desire. There are some notable exceptions to this trend, which help inform the approach taken here. The first is the growing body of work in ecological psychology and film cognition that explores film as 'an emotion machine' mapping the techniques employed by film-makers to elicit emotional responses from their audiences (e.g., Carroll 2003; Smith 2003). This work draws attention to the role of narrative and characterisation, shot selection, editing, sound and lighting.

Anthropologists informed by phenomenology have theorised moving images as rich, mimetic, multi-sensory and affective media. For example, Totaro argues that we should understand cinema (and by extension most other modes of moving imagery) as: 'the ultimate synaesthetic art, incorporating sound, voice, music, colour, movement, narrative, mimesis and collage in a fashion so visceral and emotive that it can frequently move spectators to think and feel beyond the sensorial limits of sight and sound' (2002: n.p.). For writers like Laura Marks (2000; 2002) and Vivian Sobchack (2004) it is the 'haptic visuality' of moving images that give them their allure and evocative power. Here haptic refers to the sensory and affective register of touch – summing ambiguous associations with both bodily practice (I touch) and emotional energies (I am touched). In Eva Hayward (2005) and Donna Haraway's (2008) terms, moving images create 'fingery eyes', performing 'heterogeneous infoldings of the flesh' (after Merleau-Ponty) that trigger embodied senses of 'response-ability'.

These understandings of moving images chime with or are indebted to Deleuze's revolutionary rethinking of cinema through the philosophy of Henri Bergson and Charles Peirce (Deleuze 2005a; 2005b). In this two volume work Deleuze develops a vitalist philosophy of cinema that offers a number of useful concepts for more-than-human visual analysis, including a taxonomy of types of 'image'. For example, in his first volume on 'the movement-image' in classic cinema Deleuze (2005a) differentiates three types of cinematic images, which he terms 'perception', 'affection' and 'action' images. The first focuses on what actors see, the second on how they feel, and the third on the duration of their actions. Each image is associated, respectively, with long shots, close-ups and medium shots. Deleuze builds from this simple tripartite division to offer a complex eighteen-fold typology of images associated with the 'sensory-motor schema', this refers to prevalent perceptual sensibility that provides 'the commonsense temporal and spatial coordinates of our everyday world' (Bogue 2003: 5). In the second volume of his work

Deleuze (2005b) looks at how this sensory-motor scheme falls apart in modern cinema with the arrival of what he terms 'time-images'. These describe techniques like flashbacks, dream sequences and other disconcerting images that scramble linear notions of time.

Here Deleuze is especially interested in how moving imagery gives expression to the processes of life, time and movement, which are core concerns of much of his wider work. His understanding is grounded in a non-linear conception of time in which forms and events are understood as emergent and contingent. He argues that we should not understand film as a necessarily linear (and thus reversible) succession of still images, but as a process of montage with the ability to express the liveliness and dynamics of time and the nonhuman becomings of the world. Methodologically, Deleuze's taxonomy offers techniques for exploring how images can be strategically combined and juxtaposed to evoke form, affect and the processes of becoming. Politically, Deleuze provides radical new means of understanding and evaluating the work done by moving images. This approach dispenses with critiques relating to signification or desire to explore how films can provide a sensual shock to thought, catalysing or restricting lines of flight and affirming new ways of being. Critical analysis of moving images in this Deleuzian vein examines the techniques employed to relate images, sound and narrative in styles that evoke and mobilise particular 'logics of affect' towards various political ends (Carter and McCormack 2006; Shaviro 2010).

For political theorists like William Connolly (2002) and Brian Massumi (2002), moving images should be understood as important 'neuropolitical' mechanisms through which 'cultural life mixes into the composition of body-brain processes' (Connolly 2002: 75) to frame thought and action. Moving imagery and other media are vital components of affective 'resonance machines' that powerfully configure popular political landscapes. Jane Bennett and Michael Shapiro argue that this approach 'foregrounds the connections between affective registers of experience and collective identities and practices' (2002: 6). This radical rethinking of the relationship between moving imagery, affect and politics informs emerging styles of 'affirmative critique' that seek to reinvigorate left politics. For example in their work on 'affects and emotions for postcapitalist politics', Gibson-Graham contrast the resources offered to viewers of two British films that focus on 'the effects of deindustrialisation on communities and masculine identities' (2006: 9). They link the affective logics of the film Brassed Off to the moralistic 'structures of feeling that orient towards closure and brush with despair' that they understand to characterise much critical theory. In contrast, their work affirms a hopeful affective logic that is more open to a 'politics of becoming' that is expressed in the film *The Full Monty*. As I hope to demonstrate in the analysis that follows, the stance developed by these authors provides powerful critical and affirmative resources for engaging with moving imagery.

In the remainder of this paper I illustrate two of the different ways in which we might engage with moving images in a more-than-human fashion through a focus on elephant imagery. Here I am taking up the more general Deleuzian-inspired focus on affect and moving imagery as 'more-than-representational'. In the first, moving images are generated and analysed as a means of witnessing various forms of knowledge, skill and embodied practice. Here video provides a useful supplement for field observation and helps generate a rich data set for subsequent analysis. The second methodology develops existing visual methodologies to explore how moving images evoke affect and to what ends. It maps the techniques employed by image-makers to (dis)order their work and move their audiences. Developing Deleuze's identification of different types of images, it seeks to categorise elephant images according to the affective logics they evoke and to trace the micropolitical work done by different evocations.

More-Than-Human Moving Image Research Methodologies

Witnessing Elephants

There is a great diversity of methodologies and technologies for tuning into elephant behaviours and their encounters with humans. These can be found across the sciences (Sukumar 2003), social sciences (Bandara and Tisdell 2004) and humanities (Lorimer and Whatmore 2009). Moving images have long been used in this research. Ethologists have used film for researching animal behaviour for a long time. Early pioneers like Julian Huxley, Nico Tinbergen and Konrad Lorenz experimented with the medium from the 1930s onwards, developing innovative techniques and technologies for recording, analysing and narrating the natural world (see Bousé 2000). Successive further rounds of development have extended lay and scientific vision into previously inaccessible spaces, creating new mediated ecologies for comprehensive surveillance and analysis. The moving images generated by these new infrastructures generate rich new data sets and allow ethologists to manipulate time and space to subject new species and spaces to both detailed, slow-motion analysis and accelerated time-lapse monitoring and visualisations.

In my research on captive elephant behaviour I used video to record the activities of Rani, a female adult Asian elephant living at an elephant sanctuary in Sri Lanka. She previously belonged to a wealthy private individual who no longer has the time and money to look after her. Videoing Rani was straightforward. She remained stationary, spending her days rocking silently, chained to a post. However, the subsequent film does not speak for itself. Watching Rani I had initially assumed that her metronomic nodding was a sign of affection – like a dog wagging its tail – and it was only after conversations with elephant welfarists and cross-referencing her recorded behaviour to existing literatures and online video clip archives that I learnt otherwise and began to attune to her behaviour. Her mesmeric rocking motion is a stereotypic behaviour characteristic of elephants and other mammals which have been confined in environments lacking exercise, company and external stimuli. Veterinarians and elephant ethologists would argue that Rani has been lonely and bored for most of her adult life and that this evocative video material bears witness to a negligent history. This interpretation is contested by some captive-elephant owners who have learnt to be affected by elephants under different regimes of animal control (see Clubb and Mason 2003). Moving images of nonhumans are situated and contested, and learning to witness and evoke elephants requires identifying the multiple and contested 'professional visions' (Goodwin 1994) of those who claim to speak in their name. Here affective moving images make (different) sense when used in conjunction with talk and text-based techniques. They do not necessarily ensure a more accurate representation, but do help engage a broader range of senses. As I have argued elsewhere, this approach helps develop a more-than representational understanding of natural knowledge (see Lorimer 2012).

In parallel to ethology, there is an equally long tradition in anthropology of using film as a tool for witnessing field practices – including interactions with objects and animals. In the early days, the aim was to capture an objective representation of natural behaviour. Applications are now more reflexive, participatory and experimental and seek to represent the systems of signification of different cultural groups (Pink 2007; Banks 2001). Moving images have been employed differently within the sub-discipline of ethnomethodology, where the main concern is less to capture the symbolic content of practices and more to witness the liveliness, rhythms and contingency of their performance and the embodied dimensions of making sense (Knoblauch 2006). Ethnomethodological approaches have been developed by cultural geographers like Eric

Laurier who (with his co-authors) has used video recordings to explore subjects as diverse as travelling sales, eating, gestures, driving, fishing and dog walking. In this work Laurier et al. examine skilful negotiations with objects (like fishing rods), embodied and situated practices (such as seeing fish or communicating), reciprocal human-animal interactions (like walking and playing with dogs), and relational forms of canine mind and movement (see for example Laurier et al. 2006).

In my research using elephant imagery I filmed a range of embodied encounters between Western visitors to South Asia, Asian elephants and their mahouts. I also drew on archived collections of film material. Interpreting these materials I sought to juxtapose images of different provenance and from different periods to explore the character and persistence of power-laden forms of social and interspecies interaction. For example, in one short montage I choreographed archive footage of Queen Elizabeth II and Prince Philip hunting tigers from elephant-back in Nepal in 1961, video material I generated of a game of elephant polo, and a Western animal welfare volunteer washing an elephant in the company of a Sri Lankan mahout.[2] I used this montage to explore three of dimensions of the more-than-human geographies of human-elephant interactions.

First, these images help witness bodily practice – in particular what the ethologist Vinciane Despret (2004) terms 'isopraxis' – the time-deepened, skilful modes of relating that enable interspecies communication. The presence or absence of these within the multicultural and multispecies triangles formed between elephants, mahouts and visitors helps account for both the regimented order of the tiger hunt and the disarray of elephant polo. Video helps document the material specificities of this communicative performance and draws attention to the haptic interrelationships between the mahouts' calls, gestures and bodily actions and the elephants' responses. Watching Sally the volunteer, who is a skilled horsewoman, on top of the elephant, we can sense her uncertain attempts to translate an equine mode of engagement to a Proboscidean. For example, she orientates her scrubbing towards anatomical areas (the forehead) that give pleasure to horses but are perhaps sensed differently by elephants.

Second, these moving images illustrate the uncertain processes through which human and nonhuman protagonists learn to be affected by the unfolding of events. Attending to Sally's gestures and expressions we can begin to viscerally sense her experience. We feel her excitement and apprehension as the elephant descends into the water, the cold, wet shock as she is splashed and then the sensual, rhythmic (almost erotic) enfolding of her scrubbing. Watching the elephant in this encounter we note the scuttling fear induced by the ankus – the long pole wielded by the mahout. In contrast, in the footage of the tiger shoot we can detect the stern affectations of the (mem)sahib on the faces and in the gestures of the royals and their entourage. This is a dispassionate mode of comportment with a long colonial history.

Third, these moving images help deepen analyses of the power relations that run through the witnessed relationships. They foreground the complex micropolitics of domination, subservience, transgression and resistance played out in this unequal context. For instance we can note both the meek comportment of the elephants in the presence of the mahouts and their powerful potential for active or unwitting disobedience. Between the human protagonists we can also sense both the respect of the visitors towards the mahouts and their public deference – a complex sensibility with a long history that manifests itself in much postcolonial heritage tourism. These moving images thus help us to think through the materiality of history and draw attention to the persistence of particular modes of human-nonhuman engagement. This unsettles any simple colonial-postcolonial division and foregrounds the complex ways in which the past is materialised in the bodies, landscapes and technologies of the present.

Shooting video in the field, editing the generated and found footage, and interpreting the resulting imagery raises a series of practical and epistemological questions. Methodologically, one of the major contributions of video to ethnography is its role as both a recording and playback device. Having a video camera and screen in the field allows the researcher to relay sound and image almost immediately (albeit in raw form) to research participants in a familiar and accessible format for discussion and interpretation. In my work on elephants I was able to replay shot footage to research participants like Sally. By plugging the camera into a television in a local café I could slow down the actions and encounters I was interested in, highlighting embodied practices, and enabling us to discuss what she felt she was doing, thinking and feeling. Sally drew my attention to practices that I was not aware of – for example her equestrian riding skills. She sought to explain her own unfamiliarity with elephants and her search for interspecies communication as she saw it in the video material. Moving image technology thus offered an immediate and participatory mode of analysis that worked in addition to the written fieldwork diary I was keeping.

Using video in the field thus helps engage what Laura Marks (2002) terms the 'haptic visuality' of moving images. Even in its raw form, video footage has the ability to 'touch' an observer like Sally – especially as she had recently participated in the activity that was being relayed. Watching the images of her elephant-riding Sally began to become conscious of her actions. She tried to act out again what she was doing in an effort to explain to me her desire to communicate with the elephant. We found ourselves making similar gestures as we sought ways to act out modes of bodily performance that were proving difficult to put into words. In these acts of interpretation we achieved something of a shared feeling; a haptic sensibility that was significantly enhanced by the shared viewing of the video material. This is not to argue that video somehow provides a more real or authentic account, but that it helps witness other significant forms of meaning. The camera and the screen can create novel spaces for performance (Laurier and Philo 2006) and for participatory analysis.

Making moving images from this footage and other found materials requires a set of skills that are not that common or widely taught in the social sciences. In practice, film-making demands a familiarity with technologies and software, a sense of where best to direct attention to witness the phenomena of interest and an understanding of the grammatical conventions that determine what will be received as a coherent (let alone provocative) output. My own efforts to practise some of the concepts outlined above have been limited and amateur, but the exercise in composing this film helped sensitise me to some of the unseen skills and generally unacknowledged conventions that frame how we visualise human-animal encounters. A critical appraisal of these conventions is best (if perhaps unfairly) performed on the work of professionals, and that is what follows. The advent of cheap digital cameras, editing software, online archives and video-hosting websites offers significant potential for creative praxis. Video and animated material also offers great scope for research, presentation and intervention. In the next section of the chapter I present methods for examining how human-nonhuman relations are evoked in pre-existing moving imagery. In conclusion I reflect on how these methods might inform the types of image-making reported above.

Evoking Elephants

Jonathon Burt (2002) argues in his book *Animals in Film* that most existing analyses of animals in moving imagery are concerned with 'textual animals'. These are understood to be impoverished representations of 'real' animals that should be subjected to critical deconstruction to unpack their symbolic content and discursive power. This approach has produced a rich and important body of research that has revealed diverse ideological undercurrents in, and political economies of, animal representation. However, the lively and affective animal is absent from many of these accounts which pay little attention to either the agency of the moving animal itself or the ways in which moving animal imagery mobilises the complex affective logics associated with animals to cue strong emotional responses towards particular ideological political ends.

Elephants are charismatic and telegenic and provide an excellent example of the virtual animals that flourish in contemporary distributed mediated ecologies. Virtual elephants proliferate even as their fleshy kin decline. They are mobilised for diverse purposes – some directly connected to the bodies, ecologies and fates of their threatened progenitors, others more closely linked to art, commerce and entertainment. In all of these cases, different elephants are strategically evoked through presentations that catalyse different logics of affect. Each of these presentations has material effects of varying nature and magnitude on the animals themselves.

My aim in the final section of the chapter is to present and compare two of the multiple registers of moving imagery in which elephants are evoked. These registers are loosely categorised according to the affective logics they employ, the model of the moving animal they present, and the ethics they perform. Here I will compare sentimentality and disconcertion as they are evoked in Disney's classic animated film *Dumbo*. Elsewhere I have also written about sympathy, shock and curiosity (Lorimer 2010). The aim here is to nurture the potential of moving images to open thinking and feeling spaces for the mobile, mutable and emotional dimensions of nonhuman difference (in this case elephants). The intention is to push towards more convivial political/ethical sensibilities towards (non)human others.

The methodology for this analysis owes a great deal to existing approaches that explore images as representations. It involves both autobiography and a reflexive awareness of the cultural and political landscape in which any encounter with moving imagery occurs. Learning to be affected by moving imagery on a personal or group level is both straightforward and incredibly complex. On the one hand it involves going with the film, turning down the academic's instinct to detach and critique, and being swept through the emotional landscape on offer. On the other hand, to understand how particular affects are achieved requires a constant deconstructive attention to the syntax of moving imagery – attending to types of shot, sequencing, sound, music, etc. Furthermore, to be able to speak for the wider evocative power of an image we must situate it with the cultural norms of the audience – paying attention both to the evocation of universals and the constant possibility of confusion, transgression or offence at an unfamiliar or unexpected response.

Moving images adhering to an affective logic of sentimentality trigger and develop basic and often clichéd feelings in the audience. Powerful emotions like love, pity, anger and comedy are evoked in styles that can often drift towards mawkish nostalgia. A famous example of sentimentality in animal imagery can be found in *Dumbo*. This award-winning film was produced by the Walt Disney Company in 1941. It is perhaps the simplest and most moving of Disney's feature-length animations. It tells the story of an unfortunate baby circus elephant whose large ears and clumsy demeanour initially lead to his rejection from the troop but ultimately result in his salvation when he learns to fly. The sentimental force of this film is perhaps most clearly conveyed in the famous *Baby mine* sequence in the film, where Dumbo is reunited with his mother. This clip illustrates interwoven sets of filmic techniques that are used to catalyse an affect of sentimentality. The first is the universality of the narrative story. We identify with the main character and his relationships, which are framed within ubiquitous themes – here we have a bullied outcast, separated from his mother, who finds acceptance and success through heroic endeavours. Our affections are clearly directed from the start and are conducted by sophisticated narration and shot sequencing. It is the quality, credibility and evocative power of the animation that makes the film work.

The Disney animators did not aim to provide realistic representations but sought to caricature, reducing the complexity of an animal and accentuating the features and behaviours that they expected to be most affecting to their audience. This is perhaps best conveyed in their evocation of the cuddly charisma of infant mammals, of which Dumbo is an archetype. Indeed, *Dumbo* is the only Disney feature film in which the lead character doesn't talk. All of his characterisation is mimetic and the powerful associations we form with him are created and sustained through the careful use of close-up 'affection-images'. In the *Baby mine* sequence, Dumbo's weeping and gazing eyes (with uncommonly expressive eyebrows) and his prehensile touching trunk foreground basic human anatomical features.

Dumbo is a particularly stylised cartoon that works to a logic of sensation. The animators used broad brush strokes and broad washes of colour to suggest mood. At times this is riotous and uplifting – with imagery steeped in the gaudy visual vernacular of the circus (all primary colours) – at other moments the gloomy light and inclement weather combine pathetically to mirror Dumbo's dejection. These visual effects are accentuated by the pastiche musical score which ranges wildly from weeping strings to triumphant horns, punctuated by elephant trumpets and the full syntax of cartoon sonic punctuation – crash, bang, wallop and the rest. This brash and familiar sonic landscape provides the glue that holds the narrative together and propels us through its emotional peaks and troughs.

Disney's animations are incredibly successful at evoking an affective logic of sentimentality. They work off a lucrative formula that guarantees tear-jerking, heart-warming and teeth-grinding moments to sympathetic audiences. Childhoods steeped in such viewings no doubt influence citizens' sensibilities towards charismatic animals in later life. Indeed, it could be argued that efforts to conserve species such as elephants, pandas and tigers would not have got anywhere without the moving images of Disney and his colleagues in the middle of the twentieth century: sentimental appeals exert a powerful influence on the wallets and politics of the urban middle-classes. However, sentimentality has its critics, who can be found at different points on the political spectrum. For example, Deleuze and Guattari argue that 'anyone who loves dogs and cats is a fool'. They berate those concerned with 'individuated animals, family pets, sentimental Oedipal animals with their own petty history', which 'invite us to regress, draw us into narcissistic contemplation' (1987: 240). Writing about the problems with Freudian psychoanalysis they assert that safe and lucrative renditions of individual animals perform a conservative micropolitics that involves repetition and the continued reterritorialisation of affect according to an order of the same. Such evocations do not provide a shock to thought, nor (I would argue) do they do justice to the living difference of animals and their ecologies.

Many of these criticisms can certainly be applied to *Dumbo*. Disney's animators domesticate the elephant with their caricatured anatomy. By extending ears, curling tails, fattening bodies and shortening jaws they give Dumbo and his fellow elephants many of the features that archaeologists associate with organisms subject to generations of selective breeding. This cartoon 'petishism' succeeds where thousands of mahouts have failed. In Deleuze's terms, much of the film is classic 'movement-image' cinema in which the syntax and narrative of the imagery propel the viewer smoothly through a familiar if dramatic affective landscape towards an expected conclusion. There is little that surprises in this film, which was produced in 1941 against a backdrop of global rearmament and political upheaval for an American public seeking comfort in the sentimental nostalgia of animated elephants.

The notable exception to the slick striations of the film is the famous 'pink elephants on parade' scene, in which an inadvertently drunk Dumbo hallucinates surreal, shape-shifting and transgressive kinfolk who drink, dance and make merry. These trippy images resonate with scenes from both *Fantasia*, Disney's avant-garde experiment, which was produced in the previous year to little commercial success and *Destino* – a (then recently completed) collaboration with Salvador Dali. Although this sequence runs counter to the conservative logic of the main narrative, the psychedelic elephants it features have become yet more human, standing upright like Orwell's pigs to skate, jive and play musical instruments. In short, even in its most surreal moments, *Dumbo* as allegory reduces the alterity of emotional, living elephants to an anthropo-identity.

The affective, deterritorialising force of moving imagery is more explicitly and radically channelled in experimental image-making (Reekie 2007). This encompasses a diversity of fields, including surrealist wild-life documentary and postmodern animal art and experimental video, all of which share a desire to disconcert the viewer, using the affective force of moving imagery to provide shocks to thought, challenging the syntax of orthodox imagery and its associated animal evocations and inventing new techniques for imagining animal life and human-animal interactions differently. In his comprehensive review of the 'postmodern animal', the art historian Steve Baker (2000) identifies the use of similar techniques in the moving animal imagery of a number of contemporary multi-media artists – including Mark Dion, Damian Hirst and Joseph Bueys. In some of their experimental, non-representational work these artists – alongside others like Bill Viola – embrace the potential of what Deleuze (2005b) terms 'time-image cinema', where standard linear narratives are confused and left open and the affective force of the imagery is emergent and underdetermined. Chaotic and discontinuous images of animals and humans, together and apart, are layered over each other, repeated and reversed to catalyse comic, confusing and disturbing affects. With differing degrees of normativity, these works play with and challenge the clichéd affective logics of the popular vernacular reviewed above. They seek to provide disconcerting resources for rethinking and appreciating nonhuman difference.

Elephants are poorly represented in this genre, perhaps for the very reasons that make them so popular in images informed by affective logics of sentimentality and sympathy. Experimental, avant-garde artists and film-makers have tended to shy away from anthropomorphic animals and have instead focused either on the wild, the alien, the abject and the out of place – on disconcerting animals performing various challenging modes of radical alterity – or on unlikely and enchanting cross-species encounters with mundane nonhumans in unromantic, quotidian spaces. For example there is a rich minor tradition of experimental film-making in French wildlife documentary, which can be traced back to pioneers like the surrealist Jean Painlevé. Painlevé's films (largely produced between 1929–65) set the balletic movement of marine organisms to experimental electronic music. For example, in *The Love Life of the Octopus* the narrative is sparse, discontinuous and irreverent. The settings are wonderful and alien and the score is jaunty and jarring; avant-garde in its obvious presence (Hayward 2005). Painlevé's approach influenced Jacques Cousteau and it is clearly echoed in more recent work by the directors Claude Nuridsany and Marie Pérennou – including their film *Microcosmos*. This type of experimental wildlife film explores interspecies commonality and difference, employing a mode of anthropomorphism that aims to unsettle, educate and provoke curiosity by revealing unsentimental, absurd, violent and erotic universals that cut across species and spaces.

The micropolitics of disconcertion expressed in experimental image-making operates in different registers to sentimentality. At its most deconstructive and critical this work is steeped in postmodern irony and cynicism, concerned with either challenging modern divides or ridiculing obsessions with the cute and cuddly. In its more affirmative incarnations (that avoid the Romantic preoccupation with the wild and the sublime) it attends to mundane nonhumans and forms of practical, cosmopolitan companionship. Moving images forged in this model open a space for the emergence of unexpected affections and connections. Invoking Spinoza, they suggest that we do not know what a moving image can do and set out to explore this potential in a playful and open-ended style. Given the absence of surreal moving elephants it is difficult to judge and compare the political potential of this logic of disconcertion, though the colourful political history of experimental image-making hints at some interesting and fertile possibilities.

Conclusions

Through a focus on elephants this chapter has outlined visual research methodologies that help witness and evoke the more-than-human agencies, knowledges and politics that circulate in moving imagery. The methods presented here have great potential to supplement existing repertoires of representational methodologies. They help generate a rich panoply of primary audio-visual data that bear witness to phenomena that often escape talk- and text-based methods. They also provide lively materials for subsequent presentation and evocation. By attending to the affective logics mobilised in moving imagery and identifying a subset of the techniques employed by moving-image makers to evoke these logics, the chapter has also helped develop new means for categorising and critically interpreting existing imagery. There is much more work to be done here to unpack the relationships between moving imagery and affect to explore how images amplify or undermine the power of dominant discourses and ideologies.

This has been a chapter in two rather discrete parts. The challenge for academics interested in developing more-than-human (and other) visual methods for both witnessing and evoking their subject matter lies in reconciling these two discrete fields. There is no necessary obligation towards such a synthesis but it is rare at present to find researchers able to make high-quality films and to think and write critically about the work that these films do when they circulate. The culture, skills and methods required for each field are rather different. Film-makers prefer to let films speak for themselves, ethnographers are often more concerned with the film-making process, while Deleuzian film theorists and others in film studies stay firmly in the realms of critique. My own very modest efforts to date to craft effective and affective moving images from primary and secondary material testify to the difficulty of reconciling these different domains.

In choosing to focus this chapter on elephants I have deliberately picked an accessible and telegenic target. As living, sentient, terrestrial mammals, the ecology, behaviour, subjectivity and plight of elephants are more easily grasped. Nonetheless, many of the concepts and techniques that I have detailed could be applied to appraise and create moving images of social topics as well as more obscure forms, processes and interactions in the more-than-human world. The Deleuzian appeal that I have made in this chapter is to employ moving imagery to open thinking spaces for an affective micropolitics of curiosity in which we remain unsure as to what bodies and images might yet become.

Notes

1. Ethology is the science of animal behaviour, involving both laboratory and field-work. Deleuze and Guattari became interested in ethology through their engagement with the work of Jakob von Uexkull (see Buchanan 2008).
2. This film can be viewed at www.youtube.com/watch?v=wVAyj-wos0w

References

Baker, S. (2000), *The Postmodern Animal*, London: Reaktion Books.
Bandara, R. and C. Tisdell (2004), 'The Net Benefit of Saving the Asian Elephant: A policy and contingent valuation study', *Ecological Economics*, 48(1): 93–107.
Banks, M. (2001), *Visual Methods in Social Research*, London: SAGE.
Bennett, J. (2010), *Vibrant Matter: A Political Ecology of Things*, Durham, NC: Duke University Press.
Bennett, J. and M. Shapiro (2002), *The Politics of Moralizing*, New York: Routledge.
Bogue, R. (2003), *Deleuze on Cinema*, New York: Routledge.
Bousé, D. (2000), *Wildlife Films*, Philadelphia: University of Pennsylvania Press.
Buchanan, B. (2008), *Onto-ethologies: The Animal Environments of Uexküll, Heidegger, Merleau-Ponty, and Deleuze*, Albany: SUNY Press
Burt, J. (2002), *Animals in Film*, London: Reaktion Books.
Carroll, N. (2003), *Engaging the Moving Image*, New Haven: Yale University Press.
Carter, S. and D. McCormack (2006), 'Film, Geopolitics and the Affective Logics of Intervention', *Political Geography*, 25: 228–45.
Clubb, R. and G. Mason (2003), *A Review of the Welfare of Zoo Elephants in Europe*, Horsham: RSPCA.
Connolly, W. (2002), *Neuropolitics: Thinking, Culture, Speed*, Minneapolis: University of Minnesota Press.
Deleuze, G. (2005a), *Cinema 1: The Movement-Image*, trans. H. Tomlinson and B. Habberjam, London: Continuum.
Deleuze, G. (2005b), *Cinema 2: The Time-Image*, trans. H. Tomlinson and R. Galeta, London: Continuum.
Deleuze, G. and F. Guattari (1987), *A Thousand Plateaus: Capitalism and Schizophrenia*, trans. B. Massumi, Minneapolis: University of Minnesota Press.
Derrida, J. (2008), *The Animal That Therefore I Am*, New York: Fordham University Press.
Despret, V. (2004), 'The Body We Care For: Figures of anthropo-zoo-genesis', *Body and Society*, 10: 111–34.
Doel, M. and D. Clarke (2007), 'Afterimages', *Environment and Planning D: Society and Space*, 25: 890–910.
Dwyer, C. and G. Davies (2010), 'Qualitative Methods III: Animating archives, artful interventions and online environments', *Progress in Human Geography*, 34: 88–97.
Gibson-Graham, J. K. (2006), *A Postcapitalist Politics*, Minneapolis: University of Minnesota Press.
Goodwin, C. (1994), 'Professional Vision', *American Anthropologist*, 96: 606–33.
Hansen, M. (2004), *New Philosophy for New Media*, Cambridge, MA: MIT Press.
Haraway, D. (2008), *When Species Meet*, Minneapolis: University of Minnesota Press.
Hayward, E. (2005), 'Enfolded Vision: Refracting the love life of the octopus', *Octopus: A Visual Studies Journal*, 1: 29–44.

Hinchliffe, S. (2007), *Geographies of Nature: Societies, Environments, Ecologies*, London: Sage.

Kirksey, S. and S. Helmreich (2010), 'The Emergence of Multispecies Ethnography', *Cultural Anthropology*, 25: 545–76.

Knoblauch, H. (2006), *Video Analysis Methodology and Methods: Qualitative Audiovisual Data Analysis in Sociology*, Frankfurt: P. Lang.

Latham, A. (2003), 'Research, Performance, and Doing Human Geography: Some reflections on the diary-photograph, diary-interview method', *Environment and Planning A*, 35: 1993–2017.

Laurier, E, and C. Philo (2006), 'Natural Problems of Naturalistic Video Data' in H. Knoblauch, J. Rabb and H. Soeffner et al. (eds), *Video-Analysis Methodology and Methods: Qualitative Audiovisual Data in Sociology*, Frankfurt: Peter Lang, 181–90.

Laurier, E., R. Maze and J. Lundin (2006), 'Putting the Dog Back in the Park: Animal and human mind-in-action', *Mind, Culture, and Activity*, 13: 2–24.

Lorimer, H. (2005), 'Cultural Geography: The busyness of being "more-than-representational"'. *Progress in Human Geography*, 29: 83–94.

Lorimer, J. (2010), 'Moving Image Methodologies for More-Than-Human Geographies', *Cultural Geographies*, 17: 237–58.

Lorimer, J. (2012), 'Touching Environmentalisms: The place of touch in the fraught biogeographies of elephant care' in M. Dodge and M. Patterson (eds), *Touching Place/Placing Touch*, Farnham: Ashgate.

Lorimer, J. and S. Whatmore (2009), 'After "the King of Beasts": Samuel Baker and the embodied historical geographies of his elephant hunting in mid-19th century Ceylon', *Journal of Historical Geography*, 35: 668–89.

Marks, L. (2000), *The Skin of the Film: Intercultural Cinema, Embodiment, and the Senses*, Durham, NC: Duke University Press.

Marks, L. (2002), *Touch: Sensuous Theory and Multisensory Media*, Minneapolis: University of Minnesota Press.

Massumi, B. (2002), *Parables for the Virtual: Movement, Affect, Sensation*, Durham, NC: Duke University Press.

Miller, D. (2005), *Materiality*, Durham, NC: Duke University Press.

Pink, S. (2007), *Doing Visual Ethnography: Images, Media, and Representation in Research*, London: Sage.

Reekie, D. (2007), *Subversion: The Definitive History of Underground Cinema*, London: Wallflower Press.

Rose, G. (2007), *Visual Methodologies*, London: Sage.

Shapiro, M. (2008), *Cinematic Geopolitics*, New York: Routledge.

Shaviro, S. (2010), *Post Cinematic Affect*, London: Zero Books.

Smith, G. (2003), *Film Structure and the Emotion System*, Cambridge: Cambridge University Press.

Sobchack, V. (2004), *Carnal Thoughts: Embodiment and Moving Image Culture*, Berkeley: University of California Press.

Stengers, I. (2010), *Cosmopolitics*, Minneapolis: University of Minnesota Press.

Sukumar, R. (2003), *The Living Elephants: Evolutionary Ecology, Behavior, and Conservation*, New York: Oxford University Press.

Thrift, N. (2007), *Non-Representational Theory: Space, Politics, Affect*, London: Routledge.

Tilley, C. Y. (2004), *The Materiality of Stone*, Oxford: Berg.

Totaro, D. (2002), 'Deleuzian Film Analysis: The skin of film', *Offscreen*, 30 June.

Whatmore, S. (2002), *Hybrid Geographies: Natures, Cultures, Spaces*, London: Sage.

Whatmore, S. (2006), 'Materialist Returns: Practising cultural geography in and for a more-than-human world', *Cultural Geographies*, 13: 600–9.

Chapter 4

Affect as Method: Feelings, Aesthetics and Affective Pedagogy

Anna Hickey-Moody

> That bodies speak has been known for a long time. (Deleuze 1990: 285)
>
> Affects are precisely these nonhuman becomings of man [sic]. (Deleuze and Guattari 1994: 169)

In this chapter I suggest Deleuze's Spinozist notion of affectus can be read as an aesthetically based research methodology. Affectus measures the material equation of an interaction, the gain and loss recorded in a body, or your embodied subjectivity, as the result of an encounter. It is a margin of change. This is distinct from the affection, which is the *feeling* experienced by the embodied human subject. In between feelings and changes to what you can do are affects. An affect 'is a confused idea by which the mind affirms of its body, or any part of it, a greater or less power of existence than before; and this increase of power being given, the mind itself is determined to one particular thought' (Spinoza 2001: 158). As a confused idea, affect is what moves us. It's a hunch. A visceral prompt. Affect is a starting place from which we can develop methods that have an awareness of the politics of aesthetics: methods that respond with sensitivity to aesthetic influences on human emotions and understand how they change bodily capacities. I suggest affections, feelings, as a means for researching affectus, for understanding how the aesthetics of popular and high art make embodied shifts in capacity. This offers a methodological framework that is responsive to the aesthetics of research and the ways research design can be influenced by art. Taking affect as a method also shows the impact that everyday aesthetics have on our subjectivities. I explain my idea of 'affective pedagogy' (Hickey-Moody 2009), the concept that aesthetics teach us by changing how we feel, as one way this awareness can be brought into research. In so doing, I consider some of Deleuze's (1990, 2003) and Deleuze and Guattari's (1987, 1994) writings on the politics of aesthetics.

Research that maps affective pedagogy will teach us about the politics of aesthetics in new ways. It will demonstrate how embodied capacities are increased or decreased by sounds, lights, smells, the atmospheres of places and people. It allows us to understand the ways popular art such as films, games, pop music, wikis, popular dance and high art (visual art, theatre, dance), change people's attachments to subjects.

Confused Ideas, Feelings, Changes: Deleuze's Spinoza

Spinoza says: 'By affect I understand affections of the body by which the body's power of acting is increased or diminished, aided or restrained, and at the same time, the ideas of these affections' (2001: 98). For Deleuze, and Deleuze and Guattari, 'affect' refers to changes in bodily capacity. The body to which Deleuze refers is not necessarily human. It is a degree of power held within any given assemblage[1] or 'mixture'. Affects extend or decrease the limits of what a 'body' – or *a given assemblage or mixture* – can do. An affect, then, is the margin of modulation[2] effected by change in capacity: a material section in its own right that articulates an increase or decrease in a body's capacity to act.

For example: a car screeches to a halt, narrowly missing a woman pushing a pram. The busy intersection stops. The woman screams and her hands shake. The composition of her body has changed – as she responds to stress, her body reacts. The mental image of the near accident impacts not only her physical form, but her imagining of the intersection at which the near miss occurred. The place is changed in her embodied mind. She approaches it differently. A similar 'alteration of mixtures', in which experience changes mental images and/or images change physical responses, can be mapped through research and can be effected *by* research. The art of such cartography is also the science of affectus: mapping the ways mixtures or assemblages change, effecting alterations of subjectivities. Deleuze employs the term 'affect' like Spinoza, to refer to changing bodies, but he also uses the word to talk about art and the ways assemblages in art impact on embodied subjectivities. I begin with the notion of *affectus*, the increase or decrease in subjective capacity made by an affect. In *Spinoza: Practical Philosophy* Deleuze articulates *affectus* as: 'An increase or decrease of the power of acting, for the body and the mind alike' (1988: 49). He then expands this definition through arguing that *affectus* is different from emotion. While emotion is the psychological striation of affect, the way in which our experiences of change are captured by subjectivity, *affectus* is the virtuality[3] and materiality of the increase or decrease effected in a body's power of acting. Deleuze explains:

The *affection* refers to a state of the affected body and implies the presence of the affecting body, whereas the *affectus* refers to the passage [or movement] from one state to another, taking into account the correlative variation of the affecting bodies. Hence there is a difference in nature between the *image affections* or *ideas* and the *feeling affect*. (1988: 49)

Thus, *affectus* is the materiality of change: it is 'the passage from one state to another' which occurs in relation to 'affecting bodies'. The image affections, or ideas, to which Deleuze refers are generated by a specific kind of movement. Increasing or decreasing one's capacity to act is the modulation of *affectus*: the virtual and material change that prompts affection or the 'feeling of affect' in consciousness. Deleuze's work on this process of change begins with his reading of Spinoza.

In *Spinoza: Practical Philosophy*, Deleuze tells us:

the affections (*affectio*) are the modes [forms of life] themselves. The modes are the affections of substance [matter, the universal] or of its attributes . . . These affections are not necessarily active, since they are explained by the nature of God as adequate cause, and God cannot be acted upon . . . At a second level, the affections designate that which happens to the mode, the modifications of the mode [affectus], the effects of other modes on it. These affections are therefore images or corporeal traces first of all . . . and their *ideas* involve both the nature of the affected body and that of the affecting external body . . . [then, quoting Spinoza's *Ethics*] 'The affections of the human body whose ideas present external bodies as present in us we shall call images of things . . . And when the mind regards bodies in this way we shall say that it imagines.' (1988: 48)

This passage explains affection as a signifier of affectus; Deleuze is arguing that feelings mark embodied modulations. This is his Spinozist framework for thinking about the ways in which ideas and interactions create changes. For Spinoza, substance is the stuff of which life is made. It is expressed in modes, which are changed (affected or 'modulated') by affections (*affectio*). Affectio are *traces of interaction*: residues of experience that live on in thought and in the body. They make affects. Aspects of human bodies – molecules, muscles, blood, bones – communicate with each other, exist in relation to each other, and in relating, form an assemblage, mixture or body. Moving beyond the body, contexts and relations between human bodies are equally as constitutive of corporeal capacity.

Like Spinoza then, Deleuze (2003) and Deleuze and Guattari (1987, 1994) explore ways of thinking the body as a changeable assemblage that is highly responsive to context. For Deleuze and Guattari, each body's embodied mind is a performance of difference, the mind is the 'idea' of the body; human consciousness is a product of corporeality. Our subjectivity is the embodied accumulation of our actions. Every human mind is as different as its body. It is impossible to compare the individuality of each body: every person has 'the individuality of a day, a season, a year, a life (regardless of its duration) – a climate, a wind, a fog, a swarm, a pack' (Deleuze and Guattari 1987: 262). The relationship between Spinoza's philosophy and Deleuze and Guattari's idea of the body is evident in their often cited contention that every body is 'a longitude and latitude, a set of speeds and slownesses between formed particles, a set of nonsubjectified affects' (1987: 262). Here, as in the passage from Spinoza's *Ethics* quoted by Deleuze earlier, we are reminded that the body is an extension of substance, a variation of the two universal attributes of thought and extension. Human bodies are consistently re-making themselves through their actions: relations, interests, the contexts in which they live. In terms of my focus in this chapter, this re-making can be understood as the forms of art that bodies produce and consume, as these are technologies of subjectivation and ways of learning about the world. Aesthetic sensibilities are a means through which we become who we are and they are how we learn.

After Spinoza, Deleuze believes the materiality of sensation is the part of our imagination grounded in our body. To feel or sense is to imagine. The materiality of imagination, feeling, is relations between ideas and the bodies that are their objects: different attributes of substance. In his discussion of God (2001: 16) and his account of the origin and nature of affects (2001: 98), Spinoza argues that affect enables him to consider the constitution and power of emotions in terms of ontology. Emotions are a barometer of affectus and are one of the ways in which bodies speak. He says: 'affects . . . have therefore certain causes through which they are to be understood and certain properties which are just as worthy of being known as the properties of any other thing in the contemplation of which we delight' (2001: 98). In Spinoza's work, lines, planes, simple and complex bodies are methods for thinking about corporeality, feelings, actions and desires. He also employs this method to investigate the human mind. Embedded in this process of inquiry is the conviction that feelings and desires are powerful, affective aspects of bodies. Corporeality and emotion are the same attribute. They are shaped by the aesthetics of their encounters. By considering embodied affect and imagination as 'lines, planes and bodies' (Spinoza 2001: 98), reason is able to negotiate (make a road map of) the imagination, to understand the ways we make feelings. Processes of making feelings are mixtures, or 'assemblages' of bodies, places, times, events.

Spinoza sustains his focus on context by arguing that the affections of the human body lay down a range of paths in thought (Gatens and Lloyd 1999: 25). These paths arise from our patterns of experience. A variety of individual patterns exist in correlation with different people's lived experiences. All paths are the product of an individual's engagement with the community. Experiences form geographies of meaning that bind communities. Such a process of engagement occurs by virtue of a body's existence. Bodies' articulations of their surroundings are unique because they offer a distinctive extension of their context. How we feel about things impacts on how we can think about them. Emotions are confused ideas. They are a registration of affectus and they make coordinates for thought: our capacities to affect and be affected are set up by experience. For example, Spinoza suggests:

> All ways in which any body is affected follow at the same time from the nature of the affected body, and from the nature of the affecting body ... therefore the idea of these affections necessarily involves the nature of each body, and therefore the idea of each way in which the human body is affected by an external body involves the nature of the human body and of the external body. (2001: 63)

This illustrates Spinoza's belief that bodies are largely made *through* relations with others (Gatens and Lloyd 1999: 77). In arguing that 'the idea of each way in which the human body is affected by an external body involves the nature of the human body', Spinoza (2001: 63) reminds us that constructing bodies and actions in thought is an ethical enterprise. What a body might become, how a body is received, already 'involves the nature of the human body'. In other words, our understanding of the constitution of the body impacts on how we relate to, and 'deal with', the body. Consciousness shapes the possibilities we afford the body.

Spinoza sees human passion as operating in conjunction with, and being organised around, images (Gatens and Lloyd 1999). In constructing a relationship between human passions and sensory images, he acknowledges the aesthetic responsiveness of human subjects and opens up a space for thinking about how art and the aesthetics of daily life change what it is we are able to do. Art – film, games, dance, music, images – teaches us to feel in certain ways and these feelings have politics. The aesthetics of everyday life choreograph connections and resistances to people, situations and events. Sensory images cluster around points of emotional intensity (Gatens and Lloyd 1999: 40). Organised patterns of affect and image can be reworked through thought that is driven by emotion (Gatens and Lloyd 1999: 65). Research in the humanities and social sciences imagines bodies, societies and interactions in particular ways. Changing our imaginings through research, and researching to map such changes, are political acts grounded in the aesthetics of the practical. One route such research might take is to map the politics of feeling; unpack how aesthetics teach through making assemblages we learn through feelings.

Feeling Knowing, Changing Thinking

Following on from an understanding of the imagination as an awareness of bodies (one's own body in relation to others), Spinoza's theory of affect suggests that to comprehend something in thought, a person must have a previous emotional relationship to the subject (Gatens and Lloyd 1999: 22, 79, 82) – a prejudice against it, or fondness for it, based on an initial imagining, or first feeling. It is a relationship to this essence that generates affection, such as a sense of hostility or anxiety that the woman with the pram might retain towards the intersection at which she was narrowly missed by a car. The emotion experienced by the woman when thinking of the intersection might be anxiety. The affect of this would be the woman avoiding the intersection in the future and remembering or feeling something should she arrive at the intersection again – her heart rate might increase. Her breath becomes shallow.

Thinking more broadly about research in the humanities and social sciences, the first book that changed your mind on an issue might be a good example of the affective potential of research. For me, ethnography was opened up to be more than local interactions – to be cultural processes and global cultural flows – through reading Buroway et al. (2000), Gille and Ó Riain (2002), with Appadurai (1996, 2000) and Clifford (1997). I'm sure you can find similar moments in your research where your thinking and relating to the field has been affected.

Research, then, can change established patterns of thinking. One way it can do this is through affect and image. Methods that work with affect need to challenge the appropriateness of the images that lie at the core of organised structures of feeling. For example, my recent work on *The Margate Exodus* public art project (Hickey-Moody 2012) discusses how the project challenged racist community sentiments in Margate (Kent, UK). Through representing figures of black refugee youth in new ways, the project cited racist attitudes towards new arrivals and suggested ways of reimagining young people. Thus, the project challenged negative community imaginings of refugee youth and offered new images through which these young people might be known. Affect as method needs to make new mixtures of thought, to change research landscapes through shifting the registers on which particular issues or questions tend to be worked in the humanities and social sciences. It is a form of anti-fashion that makes us feel differently about things, calls us to think about how feelings are made. As a methodology, it performs the belief that patterns of human passion are grounded in the personal structuring of image and affect. Research that works affect as method recognises that processes of making meaning, crafting emotional responses and producing images in thought are practical and political acts. These acts inform *the possible* in social imaginings. Through this conceptual lens, embodied relations mapped by research and aesthetic responsiveness can be seen as a way of constructing new imaginings of the social.

In the next section, I suggest some ideas that can be put to work to build new landscapes of feeling through research. Taking up Deleuze's (2003) work on art and Deleuze and Guattari's (1987, 1994) *Capitalism and Schizophrenia* books to extend my reading of Deleuze's Spinoza, I suggest that processes of making meaning and producing affective images through art and mapping these mixtures with research, is one way we can change established patterns of affect. Working with aesthetic sensibilities can become core to how research in the humanities and social sciences is able to effect changes in research landscapes.

Affect and Art: Possibilities for Research

Deleuze and Guattari make a distinction between corporeal affects (which they also call becomings), that occur on a plane of sensation, and affecting change in thought (or making becomings of thought). Corporeal affect is 'the action by which something or someone continues to become other (while still continuing to be what it is)' (1994: 177).

Deleuze and Guattari's argument that works of art consist of collections of percepts and affects offers tools for unpacking the material thinking art undertakes. It also introduces a different concept of affect: the affects made in and through art. This idea contends that through crafting physical fragments of imagined worlds, artworks make new realities possible, the impacts and effects of which research in the humanities and social sciences is particularly well disposed to map. 'Percept' is the name Deleuze and Guattari give to physical fragments of worlds imagined through art. New realities imagined in art are communicated through kinaesthetic economies of affect, relays of sensation between an artwork and consumer. In this context, affect is meta-subjective; it is the sense or feeling that is enmeshed with the materiality of the artwork. Combined together in art, percepts and affects constitute what Deleuze and Guattari term a 'bloc of sensations'. They explain:

> Art is the language of sensations. Art does not have opinions. Art undoes the triple organisation of perceptions, affections and opinions [*doxa: the 'essence' of a body*] in order to substitute a monument composed of percepts, affects and blocs of sensations that take the place of language ... A monument does not commemorate or celebrate something that happened but confides to the ear of the future the persistent sensations that embody the event. (Deleuze and Guattari 1994: 176–7)

As compounds of percepts and affects, blocs of sensation are monuments, entities that propel the worldviews and knowledges of those for whom (and sometimes through whom) they speak. In doing so, they create a new sensory landscape for their beholder that can inspire different connections to bodies or make different feelings about subjects. These simultaneous acts of presenting a worldview and creating a sensory landscape occur through an artwork's affect. The materiality of the artwork, the blocs of sensation of which it is composed, embody the affect specific to the work. Each bloc of sensation has its own affective force or quality.

Deleuze and Guattari suggest that the person who experiences the force produced by an affect can retain this force and be changed as a result of their experience (1994: 166). Sensation is augmented by the body: 'sensation, when it acquires a body through the organism, is immediately conveyed in the flesh through the nervous wave or vital emotion' (Deleuze 2003: 40). However, the way a sensory affect is experienced, and the way(s) an affect works, will always be specific to a body. Whether or not a kind of art is perceived as having affect at all is specific to the body in its individuality: a work of art 'is no less independent of the viewer or hearer, who only experience it after, if they have the strength for it' (1994: 164). While they are material monuments and compounds of labour, skill, time and matter, the power of percepts and affects must be seen as context-specific and subjective. The forces produced by works of art exist in relation to those who experience them, those who 'have the strength for it'.

Artistic method serves to extract material, blocs of sensation, percepts and affects, from a 'territory' (Deleuze and Guattari 1994: 167). The nature of such a method is specific to the work, indeed, to the artist. It is a process that occurs on a plane of composition; in other words, it is a process of making material mixtures or assemblages that affect thought through modulating the body and its emotions.[4] Any artist's methodology is always contingent on process, the style of material with which they work, the context in which work is shown, and so on. These are just a few of the elements that are dismantled, reassembled, in order to create a block of sensations, an assemblage, with affective capacity.

This is not to say that a work will necessarily change its viewers in prescribed ways; rather, that art *can* create new associations and habits of clustering emotion around new images. Elsewhere, I have suggested that dance theatre can present a person with intellectual disability in very different ways from those in which people with intellectual disability are popularly characterised in public arenas, by working with the body's power to move, feel and sense (Hickey-Moody 2009). I argue that through placing bodies with intellectual disability on stage, embodied histories, cultural modes of imagining and responding to intellectual disability are taken up as raw material of art that is then redesigned through performance. This creates a material, aesthetic reconfiguration of bodies with intellectual disability and emergent cultural geographies of human feelings assembled in relation to bodies with intellectual disability.[5] It is but one example of how aesthetic affect can change bodily responses and of the capacity of research to map these modulations as indicators of social change.

The ideas of percept, affect and blocs of sensation offer critical conceptual resources for theorising the politics of aesthetics. These ideas need to be taken as an imperative for research in the humanities to map the politics of artworks and the affects they create. As concepts, they catalogue the time, labour and skill that are compressed in the materiality of sensation. By working with the body's capacity to feel, respond and imagine, aesthetics can re-map affective routes. These pathways of feeling activate or limit the capacities of bodies. Percept, affect and blocs of sensation thus offer us means of understanding the material labour that folds in to constitute aesthetic activism and offer us an applied way of thinking through the force, or power (*puissance*) of art. Research that explores and documents these changes will also map the construction of new social and emotional geographies. Such work is occurring (e.g., Henriques 2010), but the take up of Deleuze's work on aesthetics into practical research in the humanities and social sciences will offer a new level of critical engagement with, and understanding of, the politics of art.

Affective Pedagogy: How We Learn From Art

Art is a mode of producing subjectivity.[6] It is also a mode of augmenting community. Through constructing new milieus of sense, art changes collective knowledge bases that communities share as points of access. It does this through creating a language of sensations. As the citation above (Deleuze and Guattari 1994: 176–7) suggests, artworks are monuments. They are entities that propel the political agendas of those for whom they speak, create new sensory landscapes and systems of affective relay and responsive capacity for their beholders.

These simultaneous acts of propelling a political agenda and creating a sensory landscape occur *through* the way a work of art can make its observer feel; the connection(s) a work prompts its observer to make. The materiality of the work, the blocs of sensation of which it is composed, embody the affect specific to the work.

In suggesting that a bloc of sensations has an affective capacity, I am arguing that art has the aptitude to change a body's limits. Art can readjust what a person is or is not able to feel, understand, produce and connect. If an affect is a bodily change, it is registered as a sensible experience that, in the instance of affective pedagogy, is produced through art. This is, then, primarily a corporeal reconfiguration and secondly an emergent cultural geography of human feelings.

Deleuze and Guattari argue that percepts and affects exist within an artwork because they have been embedded in the assemblage that is a work of art, on the terms established by the work, terms specific to the *way* the work of art has been constructed. These terms are not established through the artist's intentions; they are pre-subjective, they are a performance of a wider assemblage of material and technique. The quotation below offers an example of an art-based assemblage in which Deleuze and Guattari consider relationships between the canvas, the brush's hair, and the paint texture folding together to create new imaginaries. Here, an affect is a new milieu of sense, or series of personal associations, created in relation to percepts: '*precisely these nonhuman becomings of man* [sic]' (Deleuze and Guattari 1994: 169). Such nonhuman becomings extend subjectivity and connect subjects to society in new ways. They are 'nonhuman' because, although an affect is an embodied change, a readjustment of personal 'limit' or capacity, it is not produced in relation to another person but rather in relation to the material product, the work, an artist has been involved in creating. For example, a dancer performing a choreographed ensemble piece is a de facto condition of the production of affect. The piece would not work without the dancer, yet the piece is more than the variable of a single body. A work of art is pedagogical to the extent it crafts new elements of difference and is able to imbue them on its spectator.

The term percept is a way of describing aspects of the physicality of the artwork in its completed form. Describing the way a percept works, Deleuze and Guattari explain: 'a percept is material crafted into a sensation ... it is difficult to say where in fact the material ends and sensation begins; preparation of the canvas, the track of the brush's hair, and many other things besides are obviously part of the sensation' (1994: 166). The affects produced by percepts are more than affinities of lived experience. They can only be developed 'internally' to a work of art, on terms that are specific to the work in question. However, new lived sensibilities, or personal vocabularies, are the *products* of artistic affects. On a work of art, blocs of sensation are offered up to the world. In describing this potential for the creation of newness and transformation, Deleuze and Guattari argue: '"blocs" of percepts and affects are innovative by *nature*; they are not about preserving previous events or works of art, but are the creation of a new solidarity ... Even if the material only lasts for a few seconds it will give sensation the power to exist and be preserved in itself in the eternity that exists for that short duration' (1994: 166).

Translating this sentiment into human terms, the implications of what Deleuze and Guattari suggest are that the person who experiences the force of an affect can retain this, and can be changed as a result of their experience. The forces produced by works of art exist in relation to those who experience them, those who 'have the strength for it' (1994: 164). In order to think about the ways everyday aesthetics fold in to make us who we are, and create space for research that is responsive to the importance of such everyday aesthetics, I want show some differences between a bloc of sensations (a work of art) and a cultural terrain (everyday habitat).

Compounds, Assemblages, Art and Ordinary Lives

The production of art requires opening up to chaos, a line of deterritorialisation that cracks open what they call a territorial refrain and connects it to other spaces (rhizome), other melodies. This connection, facilitated by opening up to chaos, forms a chorus. To employ Deleuze and Guattari's terms:

> Every territory, every habitat, joins up not only its spatiotemporal but its qualitative planes or sections: a posture and a song for example, a song and a colour, percepts and affects. And every territory encompasses or cuts across the territories of other species, or intercepts the trajectory of animals without territories, forming interspecies junction points. (1994: 185)

These 'interspecies junction points' are created through artistic methods, technical material workings, practices that craft compounds of sensations. A compound of sensations is distinct from a general collection of bodies, an unstructured dance, or the singular bodies and choreographies that are worked together until they pass into sensation. It must be artistic method that serves to extract blocs of sensation, percepts and affects, from a territory. Explicating the role of artistic method in constructing the force of a work of art, Deleuze and Guattari argue:

> By means of the material, the aim of art is to wrest the percept from perceptions of objects and the states of a perceiving subject, to wrest the affect from affections as the transition of one state to another: *to extract a bloc of sensations, a pure being of sensations. A method is needed, and this varies with every artist and forms part of the work.* (1994: 167, emphasis added)

Art encounters difference through creating and presenting differences yet unknown. The act of constructing new ways of feeling is at once a contextualised, local event and an enduring augmentation of existing aesthetic tropes. This is because an artwork occurs within, and writes over, a specific cultural territory and thus possesses a political significance relative to the cultural geography it re-inscribes. For example, every re-staging of *Swan Lake* reterritorialises Julius Reisinger's choreography and Tchaikovsky's score, creating senses that are experienced differently by each body in the audience. The texture of the dance work is an assemblage of the venue, the costumes, lighting and music, as well as the bodies on stage and the movements of the dancers. When assembled, these elements can be read analytically as an individual performance of a choreographic score, but read through affect, we see that the contextual specificity of every performance is absolutely what allows it to make sense. This sensory creation of meaning through feeling can be mapped onto thought. It is the product of the specific assemblage of the artwork, which is larger than the sum of its parts.

In 1995, English choreographer Matthew Bourne restaged *Swan Lake* in a fashion that was considered controversial by mainstream popular theatre audiences at the time. I dislike the 'musical theatre' aesthetic of Bourne's work, but it offers an example of how assemblages produce artistic affect that is likely to be accessible to many readers. Rather than casting ballerinas as swans – dancers who are chosen for their litheness and trained to possess a movement vocabulary that is often associated with stereotypical ideas of 'femininity' – Bourne cast men as swans. It was a decision that expressed a conscious choice to re-create lived affect produced by swans as animals. Bourne's swans were bare-chested, strongly built, athletic men. They articulated a reading of the character of the swan based on the sense, or affect, which swans as animals produce. They did so through combining power and anger, fighting each other, parading their bare chests. Bourne's production creates an assemblage of male bodies, costumes designed to invoke swans, music and choreography which 'accordion' together and connect with lighting, scenery and the performance space in ways designed to produce a particular affect. However, the individual nature of the affect as sense – the change registered in a body – is determined by the mixture of subjectivity and art created when the performance is witnessed and felt. Bodies need to 'mix with': to experience and respond to aesthetic affect as a nonhuman becoming of the human in order for affectio to occur, for bodily composition to change.

Because of bodily agency, the sensations produced in any assemblage that constitutes a work of art are not necessarily bound to the cultural terrain on which they are written. They abide in cultural memory, embodied memory and artistic vocabularies. Deleuze and Guattari explicate this through suggesting: 'If art preserves it does not do so like industry, by adding substance to make the thing last. The thing became independent of its 'model' from the start . . .' (1994: 163). As this quotation suggests, Deleuze and Guattari theorise works of art as affective entities that must be considered culturally active agents. In other words, in Deleuze and Guattari's philosophy, art (objects, events, or a relation between people, spaces and places) has the capacity to change people, cultures, politics. *Art is pedagogical.*

At times, Deleuze and Guattari presuppose the fact that a piece of art is evidence of the technical work of an artist(s) (1994: 163–4). For example, the following passage assumes, rather than explicates, the fact that a work of art is a substantiation of the methodological labour of the artist:

> The artist's greatest difficulty is to make it [an artwork] *stand up on its own.* Sometimes this requires what is, from the viewpoint of an implicit model, from the viewpoint of lived perceptions and affections, great geometrical improbability, physical imperfection and organic abnormality. (1994: 163–4, original emphasis)

While there is no discrete formula that will produce an artwork – indeed, peculiarity is always a defining and constitutive feature of art – the labour of the artist remains implicit in Deleuze and Guattari's idea of blocs of sensations. The artist is obviously a central determining factor in selecting the ways in which artworks are assembled. This labour is part of the mixture Deleuze and Guattari describe. It is useful to have this appreciation of creative labour written into their philosophical framework. However, the 'is-ness', or haecceity, of a work of art is of little use without a body to activate it. In *A Thousand Plateaus* we are reminded that while the particularities of kinds of affect needs to be specified in order to appreciate the political potential of art and the mechanics of subjective change, Deleuze and Guattari 'are not at all arguing for an aesthetics of qualities, as if the pure quality . . . held the secret of becoming' (1987: 306). The quality needs to be connected to a body: felt and given form in flesh, in order for its politics to be activated.

The analytic tools of blocs,[7] beings of sensation and aesthetic figures thus serve to theorise the ways in which artworks, as entities, hold power, or force. Building on, or consolidating blocs of sensation, a *being* of sensation is the sensibility of a work of art. A being of sensation can also be thought as the inhabitant of an artwork, as living upon the work and consisting of its affective potential. Operating in a similar way, yet in relation to the cultural context of an artwork, aesthetic figures offer us a way of thinking through the cultural politics of art. Deleuze and Guattari describe aesthetic figures by suggesting that 'Aesthetic figures, and the style that creates them, have nothing to do with rhetoric. They are sensations, percepts and affects, landscapes and faces, visions and becomings' (1994: 177).

Aesthetic figures are inhabitants of artworks. By inviting us to think outside the boundaries of 'majoritarian' thought, aesthetic figures push sensory becomings into the realm of the conceptual by creating experiences in which one is challenged to partake in 'the action by which the common event itself eludes what it is' (Deleuze and Guattari 1994: 177). Beings of sensation are created within artworks and these beings 'think for' (1994: 63–8) the observer, in the respect that they translate a particular sensation into materiality.

Affective pedagogy mobilises the idea of a being of sensation to interrogate the nature of affective forces produced by art. Every artwork has the potential to imbue a new sensory vocabulary and catalogue of images upon its viewer. Art modulates subjectivity. Working with affect as method, research in the humanities and social sciences can map the ways in which the affect of art is a whole greater than the sum of its parts, a sensory milieu that encompasses, but extends beyond, the products of human labour. The 'affective pedagogy' of aesthetics is a spatial, temporal assemblage in which historicised practices of art production, ways of seeing, spaces and places of viewing are plugged into one another and augmented. Critically, people give them political power. Subjective change is part of a broader assemblage of social change that is activated by the production of new aesthetic milieus. Research needs to better understand and illustrate how *affectus*, the rhythmic trace of the world incorporated into a body-becoming, makes new geographies of meaning. Examples of work that does so performatively and powerfully include Kathleen Stewart's *Ordinary Affects* (2007), Eve Kosofky Sedgwick's *Touching, Feeling* (2003) and Elizabeth Ellsworth's *Places of Learning* (2005). The aesthetics of the research design in these books make just such geographies.

Researchers can develop an awareness of the affective register of their research through thinking about the design of their projects in terms of the kinds of 'voices' being heard (for example, dance can be read as an expression of minoritarian voice), or the kinds of literacies being acknowledged (style can be read as a cultural literacy). More than this, focusing on the affective assemblages of research contexts: the smells, sounds, aesthetic economies of research sites, the indirect discourses through which research subjects speak, constitute simple ways in which affects of our everyday lives can inform research method. For those in a position to be more specific about the role of affect in their work, understanding the ways in which art (music, visual art, dance, theatre) facilitates bodily changes by increasing or decreasing a body's capacity to act will allow for a greater understanding of political economies of how feelings and responses are made.

While the examples I have used in this chapter are either from my research in dance theatre or reflect my interests in what is often understood as 'high' art, popular cultural texts also need to be considered as kinds of affective pedagogy. Texts such as films, games, zines and online practices of creativity (wikis, blogs, YouTube, etc.) need to be read as the most accessible and therefore culturally powerful means of changing subjectivity through aesthetics. For example, the 2010 Hollywood feature film *Black Swan* (directed by Darren Aronofsky) is likely to have made an affect of dancing swan available to far more contemporary viewing audiences than the musical theatre example discussed above. *Black Swan* is not Bourne's *Swan Lake*, which has a critical politics to the extent it points out that swans are not, necessarily, light beings of grace, and in so doing, draws viewers' attentions to the biopolitical control required to produce popular ballet aesthetics. The affect of dancing swan in *Black Swan* is not inspired by swan birds, rather it is an expression of female sexuality. Specifically, the figure of the dancing swan is a case study of repressed female sexuality and the ways many young women negotiate what Judith Butler (1990) calls the heterosexual matrix through channelling libido into physical activity.

Working with affect as method is a political agenda which acknowledges that the critical agency of human feeling is choreographed by the aesthetics of existence. This can include thinking about how it is that popular culture and high art teaches people to feel and respond, but it might be as general as designing research that pays attention to embodied responses and the ways in which contexts make feelings. The former research agenda can be assisted through Deleuze's work on art. The latter, a comprehensive engagement with how assemblages make bodies feel, is a 'humanities and social sciences' version of Spinoza's ethics. It is important to the extent that it can be used to understand and change the politics of academic thought, which unfortunately remains a predominantly hegemonic, white masculine discourse. It can also be employed to think about how our actions in the world make people feel. Perhaps this is what matters the most.

Notes

1. An assemblage is a contextual arrangement in which heterogeneous times, spaces, bodies and modes of operation are connected.
2. I choose the term modulation because it avoids teleological overheads that accompany the idea of 'transformation'.
3. See Deleuze's book on Bergson (1991) for an explanation of 'the virtual'.
4. In theorising the process of making artworks, Deleuze and Guattari suggest that such an endeavour 'entails a plane of composition that is not abstractly preconceived but constructed as the work progresses, opening, mixing, dismantling, and reassembling increasingly unlimited compounds' (1994: 188). Art is an assemblage.
5. See Hickey-Moody (2009) for an elaboration of this idea.
6. After Deleuze, I read subjectivity as 'a specific or collective individuation relating to an event' (Deleuze 1995: 99). Human subjectivity is a collection of individuations, which are activated differently in various machinic arrangements.
7. A *bloc* of sensation is a compound of percepts and affects, a combination of shards of an imagined reality and the sensible forces that the materiality of this micro-cosmos produces.

References

Appadurai, A. (1996), *Modernity at Large: Cultural Dimensions of Globalization*, Minneapolis: University of Minnesota Press.

Appadurai, A. (2000), 'Disjuncture and Difference in the Global Cultural Economy' in F. J. Lechner and J. Boli (eds), *The Globalization Reader*, Oxford: Blackwell, pp. 322–30.

Burawoy, M., J.A. Blum, S. George, Z. Gille, T. Gowan, L. Haney, M. Klawiter, S. T. Lopez, S. Ó Riain and M. Thayer (2000), *Global Ethnography: Forces,*

Connections, and Imaginations in a Postmodern World, Berkeley: University of California Press.

Butler, J. (1990), *Gender Trouble*, New York: Routledge.

Clifford, J. (1997), *Routes: Travel and Translation in the Late Twentieth Century*, Cambridge, MA: Harvard University Press.

Ellsworth, E. (2005), *Places of Learning: Media Architecture Pedagogy*, New York: Routledge.

Deleuze, G. (1988), *Spinoza: Practical Philosophy*, trans. R. Hurley, San Francisco: City Lights Books.

Deleuze, G. (1990), *The Logic of Sense*, trans. M. Lester with C. Stivale, New York: Columbia University Press.

Deleuze, G. (1995), *Negotiations*, trans. M. Joughin, New York: Columbia University Press.

Deleuze, G. (1991), *Bergsonism*, trans. H. Tomlinson and B. Habberjam, New York: Zone Books.

Deleuze, G. (2003), *Francis Bacon: The Logic of Sensation*, trans. D. W. Smith, Minneapolis: University of Minnesota Press.

Deleuze, G. and F. Guattari (1987), *A Thousand Plateaus: Capitalism and Schizophrenia*, trans. B. Massumi, Minneapolis: University of Minnesota Press.

Deleuze, G. and F. Guattari (1994), *What is Philosophy?* trans. G. Burchell and H. Tomlinson, London: Verso.

Gatens, M. and G. Lloyd (1999), *Collective Imaginings: Spinoza, Past and Present*, London: Routledge.

Geertz, C. (1973), *The Interpretation of Cultures*, New York: Basic Books.

Gille, Z. and S. Ó Riain (2002), 'Global Ethnography', *Annual Review of Sociology*, 28: 271–95

Henriques, J. (2010), 'The Vibrations of Affect and their Propagation on a Night Out on Kingston's Dancehall Scene', *Body and Society*, 16(1): 57–89.

Hickey-Moody, A. C. (2009a), *Unimaginable Bodies: Intellectual Disability, Performance and Becomings*, Netherlands: Sense Publishers.

Hickey-Moody, A. C. (2009b), 'Little War Machines: Posthuman pedagogy and its media', *Journal of Literary and Cultural Disability Studies*, 3(3): 273–80.

Hickey-Moody, A. C. (2012) *Youth, Arts, Education*, London: Routledge.

Sedgwick, E. K. (2003), *Touching Feeling: Affect, Pedagogy, Performativity*, Durham, NC: Duke University Press.

Spinoza, B. (2001), *Ethics*, Wadsworth.

Stewart, L. (2007), *Ordinary Affects*, Durham, NC: Duke University Press.

Chapter 5

Desire Undone: Productions of Privilege, Power and Voice

Lisa A. Mazzei

In the preparation of contributions for this edited collection, authors were encouraged to think carefully about the methodological implications of Deleuze's work and how thinking with Deleuze informs our research processes. What I aim to do in this chapter is discuss the ways in which strained meanings and representations 'may emerge through a rigorous engagement with the work of Deleuze and Guattari toward transformations of research practices and knowledge' (Mazzei and McCoy 2010: 503). I specifically draw on this stretching and straining of language to present examples of how this happens in my own thinking about research, data and voice *with* Deleuzian concepts, specifically that of desire. I present a genealogy of sorts that traces my movement to Deleuze and how, as a result of my strained/strange encounters with Deleuzian desire, I am as researcher undone as a result.

Strained/Strange Language

In the mid 1990s I began a qualitative research project whose purpose was to consider how a group of white teachers in an urban school district in the United States understood their racial position and to examine how that understanding impacted their curricular decisions and work as teachers. The two most notable learnings emerging from that initial research were the realisation that the white teachers who participated in the study, including myself, had little or no experience of themselves as having a 'racial position', and that their experience of having lived in a world of white privilege severely limited their ability to see or express themselves as 'Other'. This lack of awareness led to noticeable silences in the conversations related to race, racial position and racial identity, subsequently reflected in the pedagogical and curricular decisions made by these teachers. In the course of the research these silences were shown to be both purposeful and meaningful in reaffirming the espoused perspective of the participants. For example, on more than one occasion when I asked the group of white teachers from my initial research to describe their own racial identity, individuals would couch their responses in how they saw themselves in relation to a non-white Other. Another instance of a 'non-response' or purposeful silence resulted when discussing the issue of white privilege. Instead of a critical examination of how whiteness is privileged as presented in an article that we read by Peggy McIntosh (1990), and how this privilege affects one's perception of white in relation to the Other, the conversation shifted to a discussion of what whites enjoy by virtue of their privileged position as white. Even the very idea of white as privileged was resisted (and thereby silently articulated) by some of the participants (Mazzei 2004: 29). As a means of acknowledging the importance of these silences and addressing their relevance in circumscribing identity, a methodological strategy was developed to identify and examine the significance and myriad meanings inhabiting the silences.

Out of this initial project and subsequent research with pre-service teachers, much of my methodological writings have been concerned with accounting for the silences that occur in conversations with participants, both literal and metaphorical. In doing such work I have leaned heavily on Derrida to theorise silence as data and to develop strategies to account for such in the records of research that we name and collect in discourse based research (see for example Mazzei 2004, 2007, 2009). While thinking with Derrida was very productive in that he had much to say about the absent present, I began to brush up against the limits of methodological thinking about voice with Derrida. Derrida helped me consider the trace, the always already absent present. In considering the absent presence, I began to account for previously unthought voices, silently spoken but full of meaning. While these previously unthought voices in the form of silence had much to add to what I might now consider as data worthy of a hearing, such an accounting failed to help me interrogate why the absent present in the form of these previously unthought silent voices might be inhabiting the narratives. Why were there persistent silences in the data and what did they produce? How might the straining of language possible with Deleuze produce a different way of thinking?

One of the hallmarks of the writing of Deleuze and Guattari is their creation of a new language. They stretch language and its possibilities by intentionally using words to connote something other than what we ordinarily take them to mean as a way to interrupt and rupture our ways of thinking. Deleuze does this through a creation of concepts that 'reach beneath the identities our world presents to us in order to touch upon the world of difference that both constitutes and disrupts those identities' (May 2005: 19). Concepts expressed with words like *becoming* or *rhizome* or *desire* can be easily appropriated without sufficient attention to the radical shift in thinking and the nature of ideas that each portends. As described by Philip Goodchild, 'Deleuze and Guattari's writing ... instead of directly throwing aside theoretical norms ... offers a whole range of digressions and alternatives that carry thought elsewhere, shattering the coherence of hegemonic discourses' (Goodchild 1996: 2) that in a post-positivist tradition of research concerns itself with meaning, truth and interpretation. Such an emergence of thought that shatters previous ways of thinking and knowing can only occur, according to Deleuze, with signs and images that have never before appeared in the same way in a process of becoming. By providing these differently designated signs and images, Deleuze and Guattari give us a new language and new concepts with which to interrogate data, voice and ethics in qualitative research.

In further theorising and accounting for the silences, I went first to Deleuze's writings in *Cinema 1* and *Cinema 2* and his philosophical concept of the 'image' of the speech-act in cinema. Such thought produced a consideration of how voice in qualitative research is conveyed in a cinematic sense, particularly if one is to consider silent films as Deleuze does in *Cinema 1*, as being conveyed through actions, intertitles, out-of-field cues, and other means. Thinking with Deleuze's philosophical concept of the 'image' of the speech-act in cinema (see Deleuze 2005, 1989) allowed a re-imaging of voice (Mazzei 2010). Such a re-imaging encouraged/permitted a thinking of the 'speech-act' as an 'image' in keeping with the visual because, as Deleuze states, 'The heard speech-act, as component of the visual image, makes something visible in that image' (Deleuze 1989: 223). To think with the 'image' of speech-acts and how voice is conveyed in a cinematic sense, particularly if one is to consider silent films, was to think not just about the ways in which we listen to participant voices or read the transcripts, but also about a shift to 'viewing' voice in qualitative research, and how such viewing might make it possible to 'read' the image of voice from a multi-dimensional perspective. Deleuze compares the components of the silent image with the talking image and in so doing makes it possible to question what is made 'visible' in the image of voice, or the speech-act broadly defined. It was the discussion of how voice was constituted in silent films and a reimagining of the image that allowed me to make this methodological move from merely listening to viewing.

As previously noted, while Derrida helped me account for the silence, Deleuze's work on cinema produced different strategies for 'reading' the silences; but the question still remained, why did they persist, what were they producing, and who was benefiting? Because Deleuze's philosophy is one of immanence, he helped me focus not on the question of what is there (e.g., silence), but on what is being produced as a result. And so, I went to Deleuze to move beyond a mere theorising and accounting of the silences to consider how silences work and what they produce. To ask the Deleuzian question: how does it work, and who does it work for?

Why Desire?

I went to Deleuzian desire (or it came to me) to consider how the forces of desire are acting through and with our research participants to produce silences, what those silences often produce (e.g., privilege, power and voice), and to make sense of what results from such interaction. Desire, according to Deleuze and Guattari, is not a 'thing' or a characteristic, but rather a force. It is a coming together of forces/drives/intensities that produce something. Taking up Deleuze and Guattari's notion of desire in my work is also concomitant with a necessary rethinking of the intentional, rational humanist subject. It is a thinking of a 'subject group' rather than *a* subject. Commenting on Deleuze and Guattari's schizoanalysis, in which desiring production produces a transformation of human relations, Mark Seem writes that once we loose ourselves from *an* ego, 'where singularity and collectivity are no longer at odds with each other', there is the possibility to 'de-normalize and de-individualize through a multiplicity of new, collective arrangements against power' (1983: xxi).

It is important to emphasise that my treatment of desire in the context of this chapter and in previous work is not in keeping with desire as lack in a Lacanian sense, but as Deleuzian desire that is generative and seeking, resulting in the production of privilege, power and voice. Both Deleuze and Guattari discuss the debt they owe to Lacan. While the debt is properly acknowledged, it is also properly disclaimed by them as they 'want to free it [desire] from the normative cage within which psychoanalysis has enclosed it' (Deleuze 2002: 13–14). If desire does not begin from lack (i.e., desiring what we do not have), then where does it begin, or, put differently, what spawns desire?

In a conversation about *Anti-Oedipus*, Guattari discussed the fact that while psychoanalysis has been compromised, it discovered 'desire, machineries of desire':

> They're constantly whirring grinding away, churning stuff out, in any analysis. And analysts are always starting up machines, or restarting them, on a schizophrenic basis. But they may be doing or setting in motion things they're not fully aware of ... There's no question that psychoanalysis has ... been like a bomb smuggled inside ... it's forced people to organize things differently, it's uncovered desire. (Deleuze 2002: 16)

As it is Deleuzian desire that I mobilise to understand the silences, I have to ask, how does desire function to produce silence? What are the machineries of desire that are constantly 'churning stuff out' to produce connections? What are the silences producing? The charge then becomes not to define desire, but to understand the interests that produce desire and the interests that desire seeks to produce and/or protect: to ask the Deleuzian question, how does it work? In the context of both previous and ongoing research, the purpose of a Deleuzian reading of desire is to understand why silence is produced in our conversations with research participants, what is producing this silence, and what this silence produces.

In thinking with Deleuzian desire, both in my research with white teachers (Mazzei 2011) and in a study that I conducted with Alecia Jackson with first-generation academic women (Jackson and Mazzei 2012), I look for how desire circulates in ways that produce the unexpected. As such, I go to desire to examine the unexpected silences in the narrative accounts by research participants to ask how desire is functioning to maintain sameness and privilege through the production of a silence. For example, in the research project with first-generation women in the academy, what emerged were places in the transcripts where our research participants were articulating purposeful silences that were maintained, sometimes for years, because they were produced by a desire – a desire to maintain smooth and uncomplicated (or less complicated) family relationships, family dinners, long-term friendships, acceptance both inside and outside the academy, spousal conversations, and possibilities of intimate relationships. Thinking with Deleuze and Guattari requires me not merely to think with desire, but to turn desire on its head in order to open up a consideration of how silences work, and why they persist, because those *speaking* with silence act and are acted upon in a transformative process. Thinking with this notion of desire as productive calls us to ask, what are the competing forces, intensities, and interests (e.g., privilege, status, the ability to maintain sameness) with which we approach our conversations with research participants through the lens of desire? What are the desiring machines they are plugging into, and that are plugging into them, to produce this desiring silence? To think with Deleuze is to consider the forces of desire that are acting through and with our research participants and to make sense of what results from such interaction.

For Deleuze, desire is about production. We desire, not because we lack something that we do not have (as Lacan would insist), but because of the forces and actions that are actively becoming. To turn desire on its head in my methodological project is to open up a consideration of how silences work, and why they persist, because those 'speaking' with silence act and are acted upon in a transformative process. Rationality and intentionality are not part of Deleuzian desire; nor is fear of 'loss, failure, . . . and the ontological lack' (Braidotti 2002: 57).

Deleuze and Guattari further explain and provide a sense in which their conception of desire differs from a psychoanalytic perspective:

> To a certain degree, the traditional logic of desire is all wrong from the very outset: from the very first step that the Platonic logic of desire forces us to take, making us choose between production and acquisition. From the moment that we place desire on the side of acquisition, we make desire an idealistic (dialectical, nihilistic) conception, which causes us to look upon it as primarily a lack: a lack of an object, a lack of the real object. (Deleuze and Guattari 1984: 25)

What matters for Deleuze and Guattari is not what desire means; instead, they want to know 'whether it works, and how it works, and who it works for' (Deleuze 2002: 22). How is desire working to produce a silence that maintains privilege, the status quo and smooth social relations? How does such thinking with desire demand of us to unthink our received notions of data and voice?

Unthinking Data and Voice

Alecia Jackson (2009) first coined the term 'desiring silence' in her chapter '"What am I Doing when I Speak of this Present?": Voice, Power and Desire in Truth-Telling'. Jackson's chapter mobilises Deleuzian desire to posit an explanation of what is happening in the context of her research as she describes how desire functions to produce certain truths (or certain silences). In the article, 'Desiring Silence: Gender, Race and Pedagogy in Education' (Mazzei 2011), I extend her thought to consider how desire is functioning in the form of a silence that serves to produce and protect white privilege – in other words, the ways in which desire, power and voice coalesce (Jackson 2007, 2009). It is this not said, this silent and desirous voice, that is produced by a longing for maintaining a normative and unchallenged (even unrecognised) white-ness (i.e., privilege).

In both of the aforementioned projects, the impetus was not to return to the safe space of knowing, in other words, to attach or fix meaning to the silences, but instead to explore what was producing the silence. Prompted by Deleuze, the question was to consider how desire was coalescing with these forces of power and voice – in my research with both white teachers and first-generation women academics – to produce silence, and what was being produced as a result. As I read through the transcripts *with* Deleuze, I began to see/hear what might be examples of a desiring silence.

There seemed to be instances in the data that fit with what both Alecia Jackson and I had written about previously as a 'desiring silence' (Jackson 2009; Mazzei 2011; Jackson and Mazzei 2012) – a productive relationship between desire and silence – and so the task was to see if sense could be made of the silences that I was seeing/hearing/missing, engaging a Deleuzian mapping of desire. Embracing a Deleuzian notion of mapping is so important methodologically for qualitative inquiry as it pushes us to flee from the safe space of knowing that might cause us, as researchers, to 'emulate practices and analyses that are known and predictable' (Mazzei and McCoy 2010: 506), resorting to what Deleuze and Guattari would call tracing. Tracing relies on the 'basis of an over-coding structure or supporting axis, something that comes ready-made' (Deleuze and Guattari 1987: 12). Deleuze and Guattari distinguish tracing from mapping, not to present the intrusion of the trace as an error, but as a way to identify the places of blockage and repetition (1987: 13). The trick then is to fashion a map that 'is detachable, revers-ible, susceptible to constant modification', one with 'multiple entryways' that produces encounters that come up against and move through these blockages, inhibiting a return to 'the same' (1987: 13–24).

Resisting the urge to return to the same, I did not wish to overlay the transcripts and trace the silences in order to fix meaning or explanations, but rather to produce a mapping of the silences as understood through the counter-intuitive framing of desire. Setting out with the Deleuzian map, I began to notice examples of silences, understood through a desiring silence. As I read this and other data, what emerged was how research participants described episodes where they or someone else kept quiet. I began to hear these silences as desire functioning to produce an effect/affect.

My encounters with Deleuze promoted a return to earlier data from my research with white teachers. In my work with white teachers, predominantly female, I assert that 'desire' was functioning to produce silent discourses that seek to maintain a status quo. Such a return produced the question, not of why the silences were present, but of what they might be producing: a desire to voice whiteness in ways that function to maintain privilege. The desire with these white teachers then does not spring from what they/we lack, but from a desire to preserve and re-produce more of what they have, in other words, white privilege. Many of the pre-service teachers with whom I worked either came from rural communities, or lived in the white suburban enclaves that form a perimeter around the cities in which they work and/or go to school. They have lived most of their lives in a white world where race has not been part of their own identification of self, and where, if it was spoken of in reference to others, race was an uncomfortable topic to be avoided.

In response to an assignment discussing her experiences growing up as the daughter of a career military father, Jan wrote:

> I would never think to identify myself as white. In the military, race is not an issue; rank is. I didn't even know what race was until we moved back to the United States [from Germany] . . . I rode on a bus for one and a half hours a day to attend an all-black school [in Florida]. My introduction to racism was as a minority white person in a black school.
>
> I think the fact that I never think of myself as white and Felice defines herself as African American [a woman that she interviewed for this assignment] speaks volumes about the differences that exist between our cultures even though I don't readily see those differences. The only time my being white was ever an issue is when I was in an environment where I was the minority and those in the majority treated me poorly because of it. The rest of my life being white has put me in the majority and has probably given me advantages of which I wasn't even aware.[1]

That Jan recognises her place in this racialised discourse and what is potentially at stake is reflected in the comments above. That she and other students in the class fail to articulate the inconsistencies, omissions and silences that pay returns for their reinvestment in whiteness is an example of how desiring silence works. Desire and a production of power through silence are certainly at work in the above example. Jan notices her whiteness when put in a situation of being the minority, where her white body is obvious when she becomes the Other. She also doesn't 'see' why Felice defines herself according to race (African American) but she does not. While she states that being white has probably given her advantages of which she was unaware, she fails to see her whiteness as an issue unless she was in the minority – in other words, her white body becomes visible *against* other non-white bodies when the silence of sameness is interrupted. She discounts the differences that Felice articulates, for to do so is to voice white privilege.

Furthering my illustration of what this mapping might produce, I return to the research project with first-generation academic women that I undertook with Alecia Jackson. In this project, we interviewed ten first-generation women faculty and administrators in order to understand their educational, socio-cultural and professional experiences. In response to the question: What relationships in your life have changed as a result of becoming an academic? Sera, one of the women in the study, describes her changed relationships with family and talks about what she can't say, or won't say to her mother:

> She's a massively born again Christian. She's evangelical, right wing, loves president Bush, she's always been poor, single parent. And I was reading about this, they're called hidden messages. A rhetoric of morality, in this case, and it was talking about this one evangelical preacher whose name is Joel Osteen or something like that. And I haven't heard of him, but it took apart like these are really issues of class that are housed in issues of morality, and this is how it works. And so I said to my mom have you heard of this Joel Osteen or whatever? And she's like I love him. I love him.
>
> I was like okay, but what about the part where – how do you feel about prosperity theology? And she was like I just think it's right on. And I'm looking at her life thinking how can she think this? What she's saying is that God doesn't bless her. She's not living good enough because God hasn't given her material resources. And yet she believes in it. It's like poor people that believe in individualism or whatever. It's like this *so* doesn't serve you. And what I realise is that I can't then have the conversation. I can't turn around and say blah, blah, blah, academics, blah, blah, blah because she'll just dismiss it as ridiculous, and she's never going to see it.

Turning desire on its head results in an opening up of how silences work, and why they persist, because those 'speaking' with silence act and are acted upon in a transformative process. Sera is silent with her mother in the above example and she is produced by the effect of a desiring silence as being a good daughter, rather than being criticised for being too uppity, too book smart, but not street smart, as described by Sera: 'So I know that my mom and my dad brag on the fact that I have a PhD, but they also are very quick to say oh, you're just a PhD, you don't know about stuff.' This is not to suggest that Sera is always consciously making decisions about how to speak and act, but that she plugs into a desiring machine that is continually whirring away and that 'churns stuff out'. The desiring machine of family plugs into Sera's becoming in the academy in ways that seek to reterritorialise and freeze her becoming. Such arresting is not *finally* possible because desires still circulate and plug into one another, resulting in a becoming that produces a new desiring silence.

A movement *away* from tracing and fixity of meaning does not lead to a shunning of attempts to know or understand what is being communicated by Sera in this and other examples. It is a movement away from an 'easy sense' (Mazzei 2007) that, through an engagement with Deleuzian desire, focuses on what is producing the silence (i.e., desire) and/or what the silence produces (i.e., power, privilege, status). A movement away from an easy sense is an ethical response that attempts to disturb thought so as not to reproduce what we already think, know and experience. As researchers in this process of thinking with a Deleuzian theory of desire, the question is not what is lacking, but, what desires are producing the silences and what do these silences in turn produce?

Becoming Undone

> Thinking is not something 'we' do; thinking happens to us, from without. There is a necessity to thinking, for the event of thought lies beyond the autonomy of choice. Thinking happens. (Colebrook 2002: 38)

As stated at the beginning of this chapter, Deleuze and Guattari's major contribution to social theory and research is how they stretch language and its possibilities by intentionally using words to connote something other than what we ordinarily take them to mean as a way to interrupt and rupture our ways of thinking. Such a use of language produces a stuttering and way of thinking that if taken seriously produces an emergence of thought that shatters our previous ways of doing qualitative research. It requires that we become undone with signs and images that have never before appeared in the same way in a process of becoming. By following Deleuze and Guattari's lead, these differently designated signs and images give us a new language and new concepts with which to interrogate data, voice and ethics in qualitative research.

Elizabeth St. Pierre makes a distinction between what she calls 'conventional' qualitative inquiry, 'a methodology turning toward interpretivisim but still very dependent on positivism' (2009: 221), and what Patti Lather calls a 'post-methodology' (2007: 70). Whether we will call this work 'qualitative' inquiry, according to St. Pierre, 'remains to be seen' (2009: 232). The point she is making, and that is consistent with a willingness to give up on our compulsion as researchers to fix our current practices, is to become undone in ways that produce new practices and ways of thinking/doing/being researchers.

As Deleuze's practice of straining language carries thought elsewhere, it serves to shatter the coherence of the hegemonic discourse of interpretation that continues to limit 'thinking' qualitative research differently. A conventional, dominant, or traditional reading of data would have me seek an analysis that reduces data to themes, 'writing up transparent narratives that do little to critique the complexities of social life' (Mazzei and Jackson 2012: vii). In returning to the data excerpt from Sera in the previous section, it would have me compare her response to the question of changed relationships to that given by other participants in the study in order to see if her 'experience' can be discussed thematically in accordance with the other responses. It would have me produce an 'easy sense' that is understood, articulable and knowable.

In *The Logic of Sense* (1990), Deleuze maintains that it is only out of nonsense that thinking can occur. Following an incoherence or seeming non-sense sometimes encountered with Deleuzian thought, a decentring of the subject, of myself as researcher, and an interpretation of experience must occur. What is to become of us as researchers if we give ourselves up to nonsense and don't interpret? Can we still call ourselves qualitative researchers, or does this, as St. Pierre intimates, remain to be seen? What if we let ourselves be carried away or be undone by Deleuze? What if we face up to how our old vocabulary has failed us, causing us to not appropriate Deleuzian concepts – rhizome, becoming, desire – but to allow the rupture to occur – to enter the desiring machine and to be undone by the flows and intensities that persist.

John Rachjman has written, 'Language becomes the limits of our being' (1985: 24). If we allow the rupture to occur, and recognise the limits of our being, then we can no longer use the old vocabulary of our received methodologies. While the process of deconstruction is important, as St. Pierre notes, in order to identify the trace or vestiges that limit our methodology, deconstruction can only take us so far. Merely deconstructing and naming the always already absent presence can help us locate and decentre the binaries of meaning, presence and truth, however, it fails to undo us. If language becomes the limits of our being, then the language of research, if strained, becomes the possibility of our undoing. By this I refer to a process of becoming undone that demands a giving of ourselves up to a straining of language.

In my most recent project with Alecia Jackson (2012), we wrote in the last chapter about how we were undone in the place of the threshold where we brought theory and data together to produce a new analytic in the context of post-humanist qualitative inquiry.[2] Such a process meant that we could no longer merely rely on a straining of language (in other words, to continue to use words like meaning and interpretation), we had to take up new language as prompted by Deleuze and Guattari. We would have to consider 'thought' rather than 'meaning' or 'thinking' rather than 'interpretation'. Such a taking up of new language required us to rethink methodology in the hope that it would get us out of the representational trap of trying to figure out what the participants in our study 'mean' and that would help us to avoid being seduced by the desire to create a coherent and interesting narrative bound by themes and patterns. For example, instead of focusing on themes that emerged through a sameness present in the data with our participants who were all first-generation women in the academy (e.g., imposter syndrome; continuing male privilege; double standards for men and women; the importance of mentoring), we used theoretical concepts to ask questions that might serve to open up (undo) rather than foreclose meaning. In such a way, thinking with Deleuzian desire prompted the question: How does a desiring silence function to keep/maintain/produce smooth social, familial and professional relations? While our project involved thinking with different theorists and concepts, we were aware of how we began to think and enact data analysis differently in this process of becoming undone. The analytical question in the above example was informed by the key concepts of Deleuzian desire, that might serve to help us 'think' about what was happening rather than to try to construct 'meaning'.

Becoming undone forced us and forces me into a place of trying to articulate how I think with Deleuze in ways that I cannot do with anyone else. In writing about plugging data, myself and thinking into a Deleuzian concept of desire, I wrote the following in my research log:

> I'm not sure as I attempt to explain how desire is functioning, if I am indeed, using a new language to talk about an old practice. Maybe it is the process of a plugging/unplugging/replugging that produces something different. I am thinking of an electrical circuit that cannot transmit without the connection being complete. And there are many ways to complete the circuit – some that are safe and sanctioned and others that are dangerous, often resulting in death. Is death what I fear? Death of research, of meaning, of easily publishable manuscripts?

So what does such becoming produce? How is this research that is not safe and sanctioned articulated and practiced? As previously stated, such becoming (or un-becoming) attempts to re-name the hegemony of presence and interpretation that limits our ability to become undone in the context of interpretive or traditional qualitative research. This hegemony of traditional qualitative research would have us stay close to the stories presented by the white teachers or the women academics as 'evidence' of sexism, racism, classism. Instead of staying close to the stories in order to develop the places where they overlap with one another as traditional approaches would have us do, becoming undone would have us stay close to the stories in order to be tripped up by what they may not be telling us overtly. This is not done in an attempt to get the real story, or the most nuanced story as 'experienced' and re-told by Sera and Jan in the data excerpts presented above, but involves examining what is produced in their process of becoming and the becoming produced through my production of a research text and of plugging into this data.

When Deleuze and Guattari wrote about the 'body without organs', they did so in an attempt to enact thinking without a subject and to confront our reliance on essential objects or material representations to understand and explain. To take the metaphor seriously, in other words, to try to conceive of a literal body without organs, is to return to our interpretive roots and to miss the point entirely – it is to resist becoming undone. Thinking with Deleuze and Guattari then calls us not to seek evidence, or to make easy sense, or to fashion an interpretation, but to give a direction. Like Braidotti, who also thinks with Deleuze, 'I do not support the assumption of the critical thinker [or qualitative researcher] as judge, moral arbiter or high-priest(ess)' (2002: 9).

Returning to the concept of desire, it is not a 'thing' or a characteristic, but rather a force. It is a coming together of forces/drives/intensities that produce something. As qualitative researchers, if we let ourselves become undone and swept up in this coalescing of forces and drives and intensities, we look at the data, not to ask what our research participants are doing, but what is happening. I want to know how they are becoming and how I as a researcher am undone in the process. I want to look for the drives that emanate from the intersecting desires of myself as researcher, of my participants, and of those with whom they/we interact.

Continuing with Rosi Braidotti, she maintains that 'As readers [and I would add researchers] in an intensive mode, we are transformers of intellectual energy, processors of the "insights" that we are exchanging' (2002: 9). Becoming undone then requires that we approach our role not as conduits of meaning, but as transformers of thought and processors of insights as we provide direction in our thinking with Deleuze.

Notes

1. Quotes from students' assignments and response journals are used with their permission.
2. See Chapters 1 and 8 in Jackson and Mazzei 2012 for a more nuanced and detailed discussion of this process.

References

Braidotti, R. (2002), *Metamorphoses: Towards a Materialist Theory of Becoming*, Malden: Polity Press.

Colebrook, C. (2002), *Gilles Deleuze*, London: Routledge.

Deleuze, G. (1989), *Cinema 2: The Time-Image*, trans. H. Tomlinson and R. Galeta, Minneapolis: University of Minnesota Press.

Deleuze, G. (1990), *The Logic of Sense*, trans. M. Lester with C. Stivale, London: Althone.

Deleuze, G. (2002), *Negotiations: Interventions and Interviews 1971–2001*, trans. E. Rottenberg, Stanford: Stanford University Press.

Deleuze, G. (2005), *Cinema 1: The Movement-Image*, trans. H. Tomlinson and B. Habberjam, London: Continuum.

Deleuze G. and F. Guattari (1984), *Anti-Oedipus: Capitalism and Schizophrenia*, trans. R. Hurley, M. Seem and H. R. Lane, London: Athlone.

Deleuze, G. and F. Guattari (1987), *A Thousand Plateaus: Capitalism and Schizophrenia*, trans. B. Massumi, Minneapolis: University of Minnesota Press.

Goodchild, P. (1996), *Deleuze and Guattari: An Introduction to the Politics of Desire*, London: Sage.

Jackson, A. Y. (2007), 'Desiring Silence', paper presented at the 3rd annual International Congress for Qualitative Inquiry, Champaign-Urbana, IL, May 4.

Jackson, A. Y. (2009), '"What am I Doing when I Speak of this Present?" Voice, Power, and Desire in Truth-Telling' in A.Y. Jackson and L. A. Mazzei (eds), *Voice in Qualitative Inquiry: Challenging Conventional, Interpretive, and Critical Conceptions in Qualitative Research*, London: Routledge, pp. 165–74.

Jackson, A. Y. and L. A. Mazzei (2012), *Thinking with Theory in Qualitative Research: Viewing Data Across Multiple Perspectives*, London: Routledge.

McIntosh, P. (1990), 'White Privilege: Unpacking the invisible knapsack', *Independent School*, 49(2): 31–6.

May, T. (2005), *Gilles Deleuze: An Introduction*, Cambridge: Cambridge University Press.

Mazzei, L. A. (2004), 'Silent Listenings: Deconstructive practices in discourse-based research', *Educational Researcher*, 33(2): 26–34.

Mazzei, L. A. (2007), *Inhabited Silence in Qualitative Research: Putting Poststructural Theory to Work*, New York: Peter Lang.

Mazzei, L. A. (2009), 'An Impossibly Full Voice' in A. Y. Jackson and L. A. Mazzei (eds), *Voice in Qualitative Inquiry: Challenging Conventional, Interpretive, and Critical Conceptions in Qualitative Research*, London: Routledge, pp. 45–62.

Mazzei, L. A. (2011), 'Desiring Silence: Gender, race, and pedagogy in education', *British Educational Research Journal*, 37(4).

Mazzei, L. A. and K. McCoy (2010), 'Thinking with Deleuze in Qualitative Research', *International Journal of Qualitative Studies in Education*, 23(5): 503–9.

Rachjman, J. (1985), *Michel Foucault: The Freedom of Philosophy*, New York: Columbia University Press.

Seem, M. (1983), 'Translator's Preface' in G. Deleuze and F. Guattari, *Anti-Oedipus: Capitalism and Schizophrenia*, Minneapolis: University of Minnesota Press, pp. xi–xxiv.

St. Pierre, E. A. (2009) 'Afterword: Decentering Voice in Qualitative Inquiry' in A. Y. Jackson and L. A. Mazzei (eds), *Voice in Qualitative Inquiry: Challenging Conventional, Interpretive, and Critical Conceptions in Qualitative Research*, London: Routledge, pp. 221–36.

Chapter 6

Data-as-Machine: A Deleuzian Becoming

Alecia Youngblood Jackson

What I was told at the time was that they needed someone here to teach and enhance diversity, and so they had gotten a very large grant that allowed them to bring in minority, primarily African-American students, to get their master's degree in [my field] and they wanted someone to serve as their mentor and also to develop a course and some programs that would promote diversity within the profession, and so that's what I came here to do. I absolutely loved working, actually, the first year or two. I absolutely loved what I was doing. I thought it was something I would be doing for the rest of my life and I would love going to work every single day. But within the first year of being here at [Regional State University] I had a huge disappointment.

I had been brought here to be a mentor to the African-American students and to create courses and programs and so forth to talk about diversity, and so some of the white students felt that I was paying too much attention to the black students and so they wrote these long, very critical letters of me that accused me of reverse discrimination and that I was showing favoritism to the black students because they would come in to my office. My office is small now, but it was even smaller then and they [the black students] would be sitting all on the floor and everything and we just hung out together. I was a mother figure. That was pretty much the same thing that I did at [Southern State University], so I knew how to work with those students and I knew that they needed a lot of personal attention. Now there was never a time when I didn't give the same amount of attention to any white student who wanted it. But it became so huge that it went all the way up through the provost's office, and I found myself spending a lot of time writing letters of rebuttal and that kind of thing. The university came up with some funding and sent several of us to a conference in Atlanta on racial issues to find solutions to the problem. I still quote some of the stuff to this day that came out of that. It was very supportive of what I had been doing [mentoring minority students] and it made me feel good, but that was a rude awakening for me because up until that point I really did think that the university wanted me here to do what I was doing. But slowly over the course of the next two years I realised that that was not necessarily why I was here. They needed someone to fill that position in that grant and they wanted it to look like they were making an effort.

And I've had students to actually challenge me. It was so obvious that they thought that I didn't even know what was in the book, in the text-book, because they would ask me a question that was right there, some-times within the first few pages of the chapter that we were studying. It was if they felt that I hadn't even read the book, that I wouldn't know the answer to that question that they were asking, which I thought was rather stupid, but I would answer the question. There would be those little things that they would put out there especially earlier in the semester to see if I really knew what I was talking about.

Some of the students from time to time have actually gone to my col-leagues and told them what I said and asked them what they thought about it. Then sometimes my colleagues come back and tell me that it had hap-pened and then other times the students themselves would come back and tell me, 'Well, yes I was talking to Dr. So-and-so and they said . . .' what-ever. Most of the time [my colleagues] would support me, but there would actually be sometimes that my colleagues would disagree with what I said. Even though it was on a topic where I was considered the expert, and they were not, and I would never challenge their expertise in their area, but they would say, 'I don't agree with that.' And the students would then feel that I obviously didn't know what I was talking about because Dr. So-and-so didn't agree with me.

This is my 39th year in university teaching and I really feel like I am such a misfit for academic culture. I don't know how I lasted in the culture because I don't fit in neatly with what you would generally think of as being academic, the academic culture. In terms of when I'm sitting around with people and the kinds of things that they love to talk about and they get excited about certain topics. Even though I'm located in [this unit of the university], I was never trying to be an educator. I was trying to be a [prac-titioner in my field]. I fell into being an educator. So, a lot of the theories, or the philosophies, and so forth that would be of interest to people who are true educators would probably not be of that much interest to me. My focus and my research and my writing and my practice have been delivery of services to people who are from culturally diverse backgrounds and I don't know of anybody else here on campus who does that. One of the good things that came out of my coming here to [Regional State University] is that I was very content at [Southern State University] with just being a teacher, playing the teacher/ mentor role, but there wasn't really much of an emphasis on research. I was told that that would not be the case when I came here, but I found out after I got here that there was, in fact, an unwritten expectation that you would do certain kinds of things. I wrote a textbook, which I would never do if I had stayed [at Southern State University], which has been very well received.

The book is ten years old and, but I still keep getting these checks and so that has opened up all kinds of doors for me in terms of name recognition and in terms of offers to do conferences and things and I've become, in some circles, the go-to person for an answer to that kind of thing. So when people ask certain kinds of questions they either email me or they will call me to do conferences. I had an opportunity to do one videotape on that kind of a topic and so it has just really made me feel good about carving out my little niche and doing well in that professional endeavour. So even if someone challenges me, I'm not at all affected the way that I would've been prior to having done these kinds of things . . . I'm not afraid to say, 'I don't know the answer to that.' And then I will either say, 'I will try to find out for you' or 'Perhaps you could go to this particular source.' . . . I've come to the point that I can say, 'I don't know' and not feel bad about not knowing because I always felt, for many, many years, for most of my life, actually, that I just couldn't say that. I've gotta, I've gotta know. I'm supposed to know, but now I can say 'I don't know' and I don't feel bad about it.

As an assemblage, [data] has only itself, in connection with other assemblages and in relation to other bodies without organs. We will never ask what [data] means, as signified or signifier; we will not look for anything to understand in it. We will ask what it functions with, in connection with what other things it does or does not transmit intensities, in which other multiplicities its own are inserted and metamorphosed, and with what bodies without organs it makes its own converge. [Data] exists only through the outside and on the outside. [Data] itself is a little machine. (Deleuze and Guattari 1987: 4)

The insertion and bracketing of [data] for Deleuze and Guattari's word 'book' is the first of several acts of contagion in this chapter. They refer to a book (or representation) as 'an assemblage . . . a little machine'. How they use 'little machine' and 'book' is easily interchanged with how I position/use/work with data. So already here I emphasise the fluidity and productive force of Deleuzian concepts; for this chapter it is *becoming*.

I began this chapter with a conventional, descriptive/inscriptive piece of data taken from a larger transcript, a strategy that is not uncommon or unfamiliar in qualitative research representations. At first read, you-as-reader may wonder, Who is this person (subject)? Where did these words come from? What is the backstory? Who is the researcher? Is this journal data or interview data? From one interview or multiple? Is this 'raw' data? Why is this chapter starting off with such a conventional data representation? And so on. Yet I do not begin this chapter simply with data but with a *machine*: a productive force that functions immanently in its becoming. In its becoming, the data is already multiplicitous – it is not dependent on being stabilised or known in an onto-epistemic project of qualitative research 'interpretation' and 'analysis'. As a machine, data 'works' when it enters and interrupts a flow, or is 'plugged in' to produce different ontologies. Data-as-machine exchanges a traditional qualitative research question, 'How do we accurately represent being?' for 'How does being *become* in the act of representation?'

Deleuze and Guattari write, 'When one writes, the only question is which other machine the literary machine can be plugged into, *must* be plugged into in order to work' (1987: 4). Colebrook (2002) offers an example of machines 'plugging in' in order to work differently. The bicycle is a machine that does not work or have a particular meaning or use until it connects up with another machine. When it connects up with a cyclist, it becomes a vehicle; when it is placed in a gallery, it becomes an artwork. Similarly, my task in this chapter is to see how two machines 'work' when they are plugged into one another:[1] Cassandra's data as represented above and Deleuze and Guattari's concept of becoming. What does the data (or Cassandra's being-as-representation) *become* when connected to Deleuze's theory?

Because I do not seek the pure meaning of the data, I do not offer traditional 'categories', 'themes', or 'patterns' that emerged from within the inherent truth of the words purely retrieved by me, the researcher, during a two-hour interview. I do not treat the data as speaking for itself by stabilising the essential 'being-ness' of the subject, Cassandra, who is a late-career, first-generation academic black woman who lives and teaches in the southern US. (Though the categories have been named, they flow in and out of the connectives to come – interrupting and transforming.) In the analysis for this chapter, I allow the data to contaminate Deleuze's theory in its own act of *becoming*. The plugging in is an activity to provoke, explain and elaborate the assemblage. Data-as-machine positions 'data' as fluid, multiple, and this analysis shows what the connectives open up and what they close down (e.g., how might it be possible to make a shift in thinking about and representing ontology?). Also flowing out of this plugging in, this method-machine, is my attempt to push Deleuze's theory to its limits and make it 'groan and protest' (Foucault 1988: 23) as it connects with an onto-epistemological project in the impossibility of representing Cassandra's alive-ness and her power to live in the ways that her becoming incites her to live.

In the next section, 'Deleuzian Ontology', I first consider Deleuzian difference as a theoretical construct. After detailing Deleuze's ontology of difference – or *becoming* – I then work with the data-as-machine as I 'plug in' Deleuze's concept.

Deleuzian Ontology

Becoming and difference are key themes of Deleuze and Guattari's work; they are their response to Western philosophy's reliance on becoming as a transcendent, linear process being diluted to difference-from-the-same, which relies on a stable identity (or sameness) for external comparisons and relations, as in grouping. Traditionally, philosophy applies universal characteristics to groups; for example, the social category of *woman* possesses consistent traits and remains stable because of its distinction from *man*. Another relevant example would be the social category of *academic woman* as possessing coherent essences that might be easily and readily recognisable and predictable.

However, with Deleuze and Guattari, difference does not exist in opposition to sameness; rather, difference is immanent to sameness. In other words, while becoming is directional (away from sameness), the movement creates something unique and particular *within* that would render the entire category imperceptible. Becoming, then, is immanent to (not outside of) the social field to which it applies. Furthermore, becoming is not a linear process between two points. There is no origin, no destination, no end point or goal. Though becoming can be described as an escape, it always 'takes place *in* the World As We Know It . . . Bodies in flight do not leave the world behind . . . they take the world with them – into the future' (Massumi 1992: 105). I elaborate this idea further, but for now, think: Cassandra plays the academic game, and in the middle of the game lines of flight are immanently created, forming passageways for (temporary) escapes, transformations, becomings. And, repeat.

But for now, let's stay with becoming and what it *does*. Deleuze and Guattari illustrate becoming this way:

> A line of becoming is not defined by points it connects . . . on the contrary, it passes *between* points, it comes up through the middle . . . The line of becoming that unites the wasp and the orchid produces a shared deterritorialization: of the wasp, in that it becomes a liberated piece of the orchid's reproductive system, but also of the orchid, in that it becomes the object of an orgasm in the wasp, also liberated from its own reproduction. (1987: 293)

The *becoming* is in the relationship between the wasp and the orchid. The *becoming* is the something else, the newness that is created.

Becoming is the movement through a unique event that produces experimentation and change: a state of being in-between.

Let's consider the threshold, as it is an important in-between space in a Deleuzian becoming. In architecture, a threshold is in the middle of things. It exists as a passageway. A threshold has no function, purpose, or meaning until it is connected to other spaces. That is, a threshold does not become a passageway until it is attached to other things different from itself. Thresholds contain both entries and exits; they are both/and. A single threshold can be not only an entryway, but also an exit; therefore, the structure itself is not quite as linear and definitive as one might think. In other terms, thresholds can denote excess, such as in having a low threshold for pain. The excess of a threshold is the space in which something else occurs: a response, an effect. Once the threshold is exceeded, something new happens.

I offer the figuration of the threshold as a way to situate the relationship between Cassandra and her academic life. The threshold can also be conceived as a 'plugging in' space in which data and theory are put to work to create new analytical questions. In the space of the threshold, qualitative researchers can became aware of how theory and data constitute or make one another – and how, in the threshold, the divisions among and definitions of theory and data collapse. Just as the wasp and orchid are transformed into something else through their *becoming* – just as they break from their essential categories – Cassandra, via the thresholds described in the interview excerpt, is transformed into something else. To think with Deleuze is to show the possibilities of both Cassandra *and* her academic life transforming into something else as an effect of their becomings. Cassandra and her academic life meet, collide and contaminate one another in thresholds, and the effect of the 'crossing and impregnating' is becoming (Deleuze and Guattari 1987: 276).

In the threshold, Cassandra and academia as an institutional structure meet (enter), flow (or pass) into one another, and break open (exit) into something else. Each re-makes the other. Each depends on the other for transformation. For example, in the data excerpt from Cassandra's interview, there are multiple thresholds, or sites (physical places and social spaces) in which things collide and create: her office and black and white students; her classroom and white students; her attending a professional conference on racism; her relationships with colleagues. In thresholds, multiple micro-particulars exist as in-between points of activities to encourage lines of flight from the middle of things. For example, lines of flight such as writing letters of rebuttal and writing a textbook are immanent to her becoming. Each act of writing/responding is a specificity, or a single, concrete instance of how she responded to her others. We can return to the wasp and orchid again, and remember that becoming happened in the event of connection. In a threshold. We can think of Cassandra's becomings as that which connects micro-events to a threshold in order to unleash desire, to evoke experimentation.

Movements. Connections. New possibilities. These descriptors convey action and productivity, and they capture transformation; we move from 'Cassandra is . . .' to an expression such as 'to make Cassandra' which is a product – or an actualisation – of a particular confluence of forces (Stagoll 2005). Cassandra's becoming is no longer merely a quest for meaning (what she 'is' to be); that is, I follow Foucault in an attempt to suspend the serious yet unavoidable imperative to locate meaning. 'We are condemned to meaning', Foucault wrote (cited in Dreyfus and Rabinow 1982: 88), yet rather than stabilising meaning once and for all, I want to play at the edges of what is going on as Cassandra is made – or becomes – as an effect of the production and interaction among immanent dynamics. Cassandra's life involved seeking and expressing her difference, or her *becoming*. She struggled against the overcoded expectations of teaching in a dominantly white academic institution of higher education in the southern US. To return to Massumi, the guiding question for the remainder of this chapter is, 'How does living more fully [i.e., becoming] work?'

Contours of Becoming

Becoming is a constant, fluid process of changes, interactions and transformations that work to destabilise *molar* forms and relations. Molar – and its companion concept, molecular – are important to a Deleuzian becoming. Molar is something that is well-defined, massive and governing – such as large structures, or identity categories. Cassandra occupied a molar territory of academia; in particular, a predominantly white institution of higher education in the southern US: a molar territory with a dominant form that attempted to stabilise her identity. Let's turn to the molar territory of US southern white academia to explore the immanent dynamics (or, the 'wasp' and 'the orchid') that get contaminated in the threshold. I attempt to elaborate these dynamics as those 'happenings' that meet in the threshold without regard to time; things that 'happen' in a threshold include all that has occurred before as well as that-which-is-yet-to-occur (or the unimaginable and undetermined line of flight). So rather than looking on the surface to 'see' how Cassandra 'fits into' a particular category of, for example, a black woman academic, the challenge in a Deleuzian *becoming* analysis is to notice how Cassandra unfolds through micro-particular movements with her others. Her specificities were single, concrete instances of how she responded to student and faculty criticisms, how she attempted to redefine the practices of teaching and mentoring minority students in a predominantly white institution, how she expressed her desires. These 'singular and concrete forms' make up the activity of *becoming* (Badiou 2007: 40). So in a methodological sense, thinking with a Deleuzian *becoming* is a double move: noticing Cassandra's movements and lines of flight in the data, and positioning the data-machine as not something stable with inherent meaning but as that which needs a plugging-in in order to work. The contours of considering the data-machine as becoming as well as theorising Cassandra's tellings as lines of flight are illustrated in the remainder of this section.

Cassandra was aggressively recruited to her current institution, Regional State University, in 1992. She said that the university needed someone to 'teach and enhance diversity, and they had gotten a very large grant that allowed them to bring in minority, primarily African-American students, to get their master's degree in [my area of academic specialty] and they wanted someone to serve as their mentor and also to develop a course and some programs that would promote diversity within the profession, so that's what I came here to do.' So in 1992, Cassandra was hired into RSU as an African-American woman academic at the level of associate professor to recruit and mentor African-American students in her area of specialty – a role that she had filled for fifteen years at Southern State University, a smaller, historically black university. Cassandra, then, entered RSU, a university that was predominately white in terms of faculty and students, a mid-sized comprehensive university that, as of 1992, had never promoted to full professor an African-American woman. Cassandra herself had been educated, as an undergraduate student in the late 1960s, at Southern State University, and she had returned there to teach while completing her master's and doctoral degrees. Cassandra explained that she took seriously her role as a mentor and used similar practices with minority students (e.g., open-door policies that welcomed students into her office for 'hanging out time') that she had been using for many years before at Southern State, where she had begun her academic pursuits and firmly established herself as an effective teacher.

'Friction in the molar machine' (Massumi 1992: 106) happened within the threshold as a group of white (molar) students resisted her mentoring of minority students. Cassandra explained, 'White students wrote long, very critical letters that accused me of reverse discrimination and that I was showing favoritism to the black students.' The accusations travelled all the way up to the university's provost's office, and Cassandra wrote letter after letter of rebuttal. That particular case was resolved in Cassandra's favour, yet the molar machine cranked out continuous struggles in the threshold; what met there were molar definitions of good teaching, learning and mentoring at the predominately white university and molecular practices by Cassandra that were her expressions of more than twenty years of mentoring minority students at a molecular institution (Southern State University). More instances that attempted to block a flow occurred in the molar machine. Cassandra explained that a group of her white students accused her of incompetence. The students wrote long letters to her Dean, and again, she had to write a rebuttal and the case was dismissed. She re-counted many events during which students challenged her knowledge base during class by asking her 'simple', 'obvious' and 'factual' questions. These singularities of students challenging Cassandra (with her in turn having to justify her teaching) were further elaborated by students when they involved colleagues. She explained that some students had 'actually gone to my colleagues and told them what I said [in class] and asked them what they thought about it'. Cassandra, as a black woman professor, was caught up in the molar machine with white students and white colleagues who attempted to stop a flow, to contain her expression. They continually attempted to consume and produce Cassandra as incompetent and less knowledgeable when she did not conform to molar expectations. 'Molarity is an apparatus of capture', according to Massumi, seeking sameness and equilibrium. The Molar Gaze is not a static but a productive process: a making-the-same (Massumi 1992: 101, 106).

The contours of this particular flow – this meeting in the threshold – are shaped not only by present 'happenings' but also by the historical past. Molarity as apparatus-of-capture and making-the-same produces shared deterritorialisation: a deterritorialisation of molar expectations (i.e., lessening critiques of Cassandra's teaching and mentoring style) and a deterritorialisation of Cassandra's academic life (i.e., Cassandra questioning and revising her own teaching and scholarship practices). Though the academic molar machine (i.e., RSU) is made of molarised bodies and bundles of complex forces of rules, laws and traditions that make expectations of 'white' teaching and mentoring, Cassandra continually defended her disciplinary expertise: these zig-zags within the molar machine kept expression on the move. So each time students challenged Cassandra's mentoring style, or sought out a colleague to 'test' her teaching competence, Cassandra directed her molecular freedom towards working that tension between molar limitations of academia and her molecularity. And each time Cassandra expressed her molecularity, her academic life expanded (or in Massumi's terms, 'became more full and livable') in ways that engendered and sustained her own becoming. That is, in the interview data, we learn that while the molar machine is never fully dismantled, we see how both the molar and the molecular share a deterritorialisation in that they are both *becoming* – they collide and contaminate and liberate one another via continual unfoldings and lines of flight. These movements – these passings – exist as *racial* relations of force that seek to contain: white student expectations (i.e., confidence and expertise) seeking to contain black epistemologies of teaching and learning (i.e., relationships and mentoring). These flows work in other directions as well, given Cassandra's own practices of directing her molecular expressions towards minority students while being perceived as ignoring white students' needs.

Molecularity, or counter-actualisation, is a becoming that 'first must be understood as a function of something else' (Deleuze and Guattari 1987: 275). That something else is what produces the molecular; the molecular involves micro-entities, processes, creations – tiny things (singularities) that destabilise the perception of a whole. Becoming is 'directional (away from molarity), but not directed (no one body or will can pilot it)'; it is not intentional (Massumi 1992: 103). Becoming happens in the middle of molar structures that break apart dichotomies that organise bodies, experiences, institutions and histories (Sotirin 2005); the molecular is the *effect of this breaking apart*. The molecular is a deterritorialisation of the molar, obviously, but more-so the molecular relates to singularities, to individual responses, to becomings. Cassandra's rebuttals and writing of a book are the very substance of her molecular becomings. And the molecular processes of her becoming deterritorialised the molar space that attempted to define her academic life.

Cassandra gives an account of breaking apart/temporarily escaping the molar machine when she explains how molar others 'expected' her to 'be' an academic by pressuring her to achieve in the areas of teaching and scholarship when she would have rather focused her work on providing professional, therapeutic services in her discipline to the community; she sees herself more as a practitioner than a scholar. Molar rules in academia persist in Cassandra's language when she uses phrases such as 'true educators' and as she describes academic culture as equated with philosophy and theory. Cassandra's becomings make her into a particular type of professor who, in some ways, conforms to academic expectations, yet the conformity – that meeting in the threshold – also produces a deterritorialisation of expectations: 'My focus and my research and my writing and my practice have been delivery of services to people who are from culturally diverse backgrounds and I don't know of anybody else here on campus who does that.' Cassandra's molecularity – her line of flight from the middle of things – is that which is immanent. The molar conditions of the academy produced her molecular (or resistant) 'doing' of scholarship, teaching and service, a doing that Cassandra described as more practitioner-oriented than philosophically or theoretically oriented. Cassandra's becoming is immanent to (or within) the molar machine. It cannot exist without such threshold. Furthermore, Cassandra's becoming is directional – or away from molarity – and produces her transformation: she would not have emphasised *her* expression of scholarship without the infiltration of molar expectations. So we can return to the wasp and the orchid, as each of them liberates the other, or takes them elsewhere *within*. That is, Cassandra's becoming is a transformation of how she thinks about and enacts her own academic life. Not transformation in a transcendent sense, but one of immanence and folds: movement that is simultaneously asymmetrical, instantaneous, a zig-zag between the general and the singular. Becomings (or transformations) are more like tiny frictions, little moments of counter-actualisations that are unfinalised. Lines of flight never return to the same as they sweep and pass through thresholds that keep becoming immanent, and each passing through produces an approach to a limit that is never reached. Thus, becoming happens over and over and over again, yet in each moment everyone and everything become something else.

Interrupting, Only to Interrupt Again

Becoming implies 'two simultaneous movements, one by which a term (the subject) is withdrawn from the majority, and another by which a term (the agent) rises up from the minority' (Deleuze and Guattari 1987: 291). I attempted to show in this chapter the zig-zag movements of Cassandra passing through the molar and expanding her own molecularity – while also forcing the molar gaze into its own becoming: that of inclusion, even if it is superficial in the form of academic promotion. Furthermore, and as a caution, Cassandra's becoming is merely a capture. We have only one glimpse of the transformation of her academic life becoming more livable and full; it is never final, complete, or coherent. But the point is that the molar is never stabilised; neither is the molecular. That the molar machine continued to work on Cassandra throughout her career – continually making and re-making her academic life – points to Deleuze's idea that machines are processes, not products or things or concepts.

My goal in this chapter was to attempt to map Cassandra's immanent becomings in the threshold of academic teaching, mentoring and scholarship. I centred on a couple of specificities to play with a limit that is never reached. I highlighted the becoming-processes of Cassandra's intensities with others and the breaking apart, and breaking open, of her subjectivity. These intensities depended on a relationship, a connection – much like that of the wasp and orchid – to transform. A Deleuzian approach can re-think connection and transformation: Cassandra was becoming in that she was a site of struggle over the materiality and the transgression of what an academic *does* – not what she is. I mapped how Cassandra destabilised the perception of a whole: the perception of an academic woman who is contained and bound by molar (i.e., white male) definitions of academic practices. Becoming is never finalised and complete, yet the connections and micro-events create tiny explosions that keep new creations on the move. 'The goal is a limit approached, never reached; what is important is the process' (Massumi 1992: 106).

Where does such an analysis of *becoming* take us as qualitative researchers who work with Deleuze in our thinking with data? First, the data included in this chapter is, obviously, excerpted from a much longer interview segment with Cassandra. In the entire interview, Cassandra indeed described her movements with/in white academic culture as a zig-zag: a constant, continual negotiation of her expressions as a first-generation black academic woman. Yet Cassandra has remained at Regional State University; the molar apparatus has neither pushed her away nor absorbed her into the cumulative making-the-same. Rather, both Cassandra and RSU branch out in their becomings to destabilise the whole. While neither transformation is revolutionary, the tiny processes of destabilisation and deterritorialisation create something different for Cassandra; as she put it, 'I feel good about carving out my little niche and doing well in that professional endeavour. So even if someone challenges me, I'm not at all affected the way that I would've been prior to having done these kinds of things.' Here, Cassandra is referring to the scholarship that infuses her professional service and teaching – expressions of molecularity that offer what she gestures towards as a livable academic life. For a moment, in the threshold, everything and everyone become something else. The in-between-ness of a Deleuzian *becoming* analysis offers up new ways to think about difference, transformation and social structures. For qualitative researchers, such a mapping of difference allows multiple entries and exits to keep us 'present to the present' (Badiou 2007: 39). We avoid traps of tracing data that can lead us to generalities and a reliance on structural definitions of difference that depend on so-called group likeness. As Foucault explained, 'If we want to pose problems in a rigorous, exact way that's likely to allow serious investigations, shouldn't we look for these problems precisely in their most singular and concrete forms?' (2000: 285). Deleuzian difference – or becoming – accentuates the concrete, the specific, the singular, and teaches us that there is radical possibility in the unfinalised.

Data-as-machine flows along the same connectives and moves from molar forms to molecular forms. The data is becoming in that, as a machine, it was a productive force in its potential for difference. In a molar form, qualitative interview data has been treated as pure, foundational, truth-as-presence. Yet in its molecular form, machinic data stays on the move, seeking connectives and assemblages to interrupt (and to be interrupted). In this chapter, data's ontological journey depended on the joining of Deleuze's thought in order to *become*, yet the data-as-machine can be connected to another assemblage to *become* again. Furthermore, Massumi warns that becoming 'cannot be adequately described. If it could, it would already be what it is becoming, in which case it wouldn't be becoming at all' (1992: 103). What Massumi explains here is that the event of becoming cannot be predicted or prescribed *in advance*; that is, no one can write out rules for what becoming should be in a particular social field (e.g., in the case of qualitative methodology, fitting into pre-determined or even emergent grounded-theory type themes and patterns). This is a crucial methodological point for data 'analysis' and 'interpretation' in qualitative research that uses a Deleuzian frame: a data-machine has supple substance, but what matters most are its relations, affects and machinic potential to interrupt and transform other machines, other data, other knowledge projects, and so on. Data-machines never stand alone, isolated and elevated; rather, they keep things on the move, keep things *becoming*. As such, data-machines are always becoming molecular. So, to repeat, there is radical possibility in the unfinalised.

In this little analysis I have only merely interrupted a flow. For anything to become, there needs to be the potential for more movement, another break, another connectivity. More plugging in of data to other machines, and more becoming-molecular (Jackson and Mazzei 2012). As Massumi writes, 'Only one thing can rival the BOREDOM of this endless reproductions of representations of the unrepresentable: endless deconstructions of them' (1992: 193, n. 46).

Note

1. Lisa Mazzei and I elaborate on Deleuze and Guattari's concept of 'plugging in' and offer exemplars of the activity in our book *Thinking with Theory in Qualitative Research: Viewing Data across Multiple Perspectives* (Jackson and Mazzei 2012).

References

Badiou, A. (2007), 'The Event in Deleuze', *Parrhesia*, 2: 37–44.
Braidotti, R. (1994), *Nomadic Subjects*, New York: Columbia University Press.
Deleuze, G. (1990), *The Logic of Sense*, trans. M. Lester with C. Stivale, London: Althone.
Deleuze, G. and F. Guattari (1987), *A Thousand Plateaus: Capitalism and Schizophrenia*, trans. B. Massumi, Minneapolis: University of Minnesota Press.
Dreyfus, H. L. and P. Rabinow (1982), *Michel Foucault: Beyond Structuralism and Hermeneutics*, Chicago: Chicago University Press.
Foucault, M. (1988), *Power/Knowledge: Selected Interviews and Other Writings: 1972–1977*, New York: Pantheon Books.
Foucault, M. (2000), *Power: Essential Works of Foucault, 1954–1984*, New York: New Press.
Jackson, A. Y. and L. Mazzei (2012), *Thinking with Theory in Qualitative Research: Viewing Data across Multiple Perspectives*, London: Routledge.
Massumi, B. (1987), 'Translator's Foreword: Pleasures of Philosophy' in G. Deleuze and F. Guattari, *A Thousand Plateaus: Capitalism and Schizophrenia*, Minneapolis: University of Minnesota Press, pp. ix–xv.
Massumi, B. (1992), *A User's Guide to Capitalism and Schizophrenia: Deviations from Deleuze and Guattari*, Cambridge, MA: MIT Press.
Sotirin, P. (2005), 'Becoming-woman' in C. J. Stivale (ed.), *Gilles Deleuze: Key Concepts*, New York: McGill-Queen's University Press.
Stagoll, C. (2005), 'Becoming' in A. Parr (ed.), *The Deleuze Dictionary*, New York: Columbia University Press.

Chapter 7

Looking and Desiring Machines: A Feminist Deleuzian Mapping of Bodies and Affects

Jessica Ringrose and Rebecca Coleman

This chapter is an attempt to explore how Deleuze's geophilosophy might be put to work methodologically. Geophilosophy is for Deleuze and Guattari (1984, 1987) an attention to the connections between different things that come to constitute an assemblage. It is a kind of cartography that takes place on a plane of immanence, as connections are made and re-made horizontally, immanently, rather than (only) as a result of vertical hierarchies. As such, assemblages are diverse and multiple – 'the synthesis of heterogeneities as such' (Deleuze and Guattari 1987: 330) – and machinic – connections are made between human and nonhuman things. Deleuze and Guattari theorise the machine in terms of desire, in that desire is a productive force that forms relations between different aspects of an assemblage. We argue that geophilosophy can be understood and put to work as a methodology – a means of *mapping* the relations in desiring machines. We reflect on the methodological dilemma of how one might map machinic relations, and question the directionality, flow and ethico-political workings of the machines under question. Mapping connections is not only a task of investigating what there is, then, but is also concerned with unpacking what might be. It is a methodology of looking differently at connections, and, possibly, a methodology of tracing how these connections might be made differently.

In this chapter, we take up a methodology of mapping through different empirical research projects with young people. This includes research on the relations between teenage girls' bodies and images (Coleman 2009) and teens' uses of social networking sites (Ringrose 2011, 2012; Ringrose et al. 2012). These projects are clearly interested in different issues, and our aim here is not to flatten these differences but rather to flag up points of connection and to develop a methodological position on how we have interpreted data produced in them. In particular, our focus is on how our research has been interested in affect and the politics of looking, that is, in how looking comes to constitute affective relations between bodies. In this sense we work with the oft-cited phrase from Deleuze that 'a body affects other bodies, or is affected by other bodies; it is this capacity for affecting and being affected that . . . defines a body in its individuality' (Deleuze 1992: 625). We treat the capacity of affecting and being affected as a series of relations that we can map according to the ways in which the capacity of becoming is extended (the molecularity of lines of flight, for example) or captured (as molar categorisations).

As our research has been on how bodies come to be constituted via contemporary visual culture, this chapter examines how looking is an affective capacity that extends or fixes the ways in which bodies become. We pay specific attention to how these processes of movement or capture are gendered and/or sexualised. Key questions we therefore address include: How does looking work and how does the body become in particular ways through looking? What type of looking is at work? We will suggest there are affective dynamics of looking, what we call 'looking machines' that inscribe bodies, cultivated in 'post-feminist' media contexts that celebrate objectification. However, we outline how a feminist Deleuzian methodology of mapping can help demonstrate both how objectification and bodily relations work, and how coercive practices might be disrupted.

A Feminist Deleuzian Mapping Methodology

There has been a range of important theoretical writing about Deleuze and the body (Guillaume and Hughes 2011) and also on Deleuze and gender, feminism, sexuality and queer theory (e.g. Colebrook and Weinstein 2008; Beckman 2011). This work has elaborated how bodies are reconfigured in ways that disturb the subject/object binaries of Western metaphysics and explored how new thinking tools are available that disrupt the naturalisation of essential gender difference, drawing particularly on tools from Deleuze and Guattari's *Anti-Oedipus* and its epic critique of familial, conjugal and Oedipal organisation of sexuality and desire. Elizabeth Grosz has been especially important in underscoring feminist uses of Deleuzian thought for understanding the 'volatility' of the body, which

> in its active relation to other social practices, entities and events forms machinic connections . . . The body is thus not an organic totality which

is capable of the wholesale expression of subjectivity, a welling up of the subject's emotions, attitudes, beliefs or experiences, but is itself an assemblage of organs, processes, pleasures, passions, activities, behaviors, linked by fine lines and unpredictable networks to other elements, segments and assemblages. (Grosz 1994: 120)

What is specific about the *feminist* approach to this framework is that it seeks to make sense of how these machinic bodies and assemblages work to materialise the coercive norms of patriarchy and gender. Grosz is explicit that Deleuze helps us to understand how gender, sexuality, and other 'great divisions and global categories' function through the body because his work produces a conceptual framework with the potential of 'rendering more complex the nature and forms that these oppressions take' (1994: 173).

Our aim in this chapter is to illustrate the methodological value of this feminist Deleuzian thinking about bodies and gender and sexuality in the analysis of empirical research practice. Thus, our focus is not so much on processes of research collection – although this is important and worthy of more consideration – as on what a feminist Deleuzian approach opened up for how we came to understand and interpret the data that our research generated. We take seriously Deleuze's disruption of any clear demarcation between theory and practice, and suggest that how data is made sense of – theorised – is a methodological practice. Indeed, Guattari, speaking of his work with Deleuze, said 'Theoretical expressions should function as tools, as machines . . . and this is true in every field . . . The most desirable effect that can be anticipated in the conceptual field is not in the order of comprehension but in the form of a certain efficiency. "It works or it doesn't work"' (2009: 22).

According to Deleuze and Guattari, this logic of efficiency encompasses 'methodological' thinking and, moreover, as part of their project of 'transcendental empiricism', empirical research should find new ways to see and transform the social. In thinking through the implications of this approach for empirical research we need to ask: in what ways does it enable us to demonstrate in new and different ways how things work in research encounters? In what ways is noticing different things in research data a methodological project?

This chapter considers how a Deleuzian approach enables us to think differently about gender and bodies by insisting that we ask: How can we map how desiring machines work? What can bodies do and not do? Indeed, Mark Bonta and John Protevi have called the Deleuzian approach 'geophilosophical', because it offers what in our Introduction we call 'clusters' of ideas; conceptual mapping to help us understand time, space and movement differently. Bonta and Protevi provide an important outline of the political nature of Deleuze and Guattari's 'geophilosophy', arguing that

> A key dimension of Deleuze and Guattari's work is the investigation of 'bodies politic', material systems or 'assemblages' whose constitution in widely differing registers – the physical, chemical, biological, neural and social – can be analysed in political terms. Such an analysis proceeds along an ethical axis (the life-affirming or life destroying character of the assemblage) and a structural axis, the poles of which Deleuze and Guattari name 'strata' (the domination or putting to work of one body by another in a fixed hierarchy) and consistencies (what Deleuze and Guattari also call 'war machines' or 'rhizomes' which entail the formation of a network or assemblage of bodies with multiple, shifting and increasingly intense internal and external connections). (Bonta and Protevi 2004: 10)

Our aim is to put this geophilosophical understanding to work in a feminist Deleuzian methodological mapping exercise. Mapping as a methodology for research has been developed through concepts of rhizomatic movement (e.g., Alverman 2000) to highlight connectivity, the middles, becomings and difference in research processes, where mapping is distinguished from repetition and tracing patterns. Rhizomes are highlighted as tuberous structures that connect to other things, rather than the singular roots of one tree. In this chapter, we develop a cluster of concepts related to 'mapping' (Kaufman and Heller 1998) and apply these methodologically to demonstrate the machinic, connective aspects of bodies – what Deleuze and Guattari called desiring machines – which form relations between parts and bodies in assemblages. Our interest is in mapping affect and bodily capacities; we are interested in how bodies affect and are affected by things, and to therefore think of bodies' potentials for movement or fixity in space. One of the specific concerns of our research is the relationship between bodies and images, or visual culture, and we unpack the affective intensities and dynamics of how images work. We explore how young people relate to images in their everyday lives offline, but also in online spaces of social networking sites, drawing on a range of empirical data with teens from several studies, asking: How do the relations of looking work differently according to gender and sexual 'dualism machines', as Deleuze and Guattari might call them?

The chapter specifically contributes to thinking about visual methodology and how images work affectively in online space. For instance we show *how* extensive gender norms create fixity through gender and sexual dualisms when *looking* captures girls, reducing them to their body parts or the 'wrong' sexuality, as 'skets'. But we also examine how these are unfixed and disrupted to show when we find life-affirming potentialities in assemblages.

The Becoming of Bodies: Looking, Images, Affect

Rebecca Coleman's book *The Becoming of Bodies* develops a Deleuzian feminist approach to help move from problematic and much critiqued analyses of media *effects* upon bodies (expressed for instance in debates surrounding body image), to a discussion of media *affects* – an affective analysis to reconsider the relationship between bodies and images. Media effects arguments position images as a 'hypodermic needle' that penetrates the minds of young people in particular in ways that damage self-esteem and confidence (see Egan and Hawkes 2008 for a critique). Drawing on focus groups, individual interviews and image-making sessions with young white women, aged thirteen and fourteen, which explored the knowledges, understandings and experiences of bodies that different types of image make possible, and impossible, Coleman argues that images do not operate in such simplistic ways because 'bodies and images are not separate but experienced through each other. Images therefore do not reflect or represent bodies but produce the ways in which it is possible for bodies to become' (2009: 94). As part of this argument, Coleman considers the role of looking in constituting images of bodies; for example, the girls discussed how other people's views of them gave them a particular image of their body. As such, Coleman restages looking as not simply a one-way gaze, as feminist work on the 'male gaze' might imply, but rather as an affective relation between bodies. Looking is understood in terms of the capacities of bodies to affect and be affected. Moving away from a simple feminist pronouncement of objectification, she elaborates Deleuze's transcendental empiricism to map out how these capacities are extended or fixed via gendered relations. She draws attention to how the girls discuss views from boys and girls operating differently. Gender in this sense is an extensive molar category that comes to capture and fix the molecularity of becoming:

Fay: If someone said that to me, like I don't know said something horrible to me, like a boy, then I'd just think 'well you've got a load of spots on your face today' [Laughter].
Dionne: Yeah but girls don't say it, boys that are cocky and confident . . .
Fay: say it . . .
Dionne: and popular sort of like say 'oh you look really fat' and then like the other boys laugh and . . .
Dionne: but if we were like to say something like 'oh you're really

	spotty' then they would be like 'oh shut up you big ugly cow' or something and then you wouldn't know what to say back because like it hits you harder than it hits them.
Anna:	That's what happens though, like you say one thing and they can say as much to you and you can't say anything back.
Dionne:	Yeah.
Anna:	And the minute you say something back and they just flip and say . . .
Dionne:	Yeah even if you said the same amount of stuff it still wouldn't hurt their feelings as much as it would hurt you.

Mapping out the capacities of affecting and being affected makes clear that the knowledges through which the girls' bodies are fixed through relations with boys are not equal or reversible, since girls are 'hit harder' by the affect of the words from boys. The girls are not able to 'fight back' and fix and objectify boys' bodies in the same ways:

Beckie:	So boys make comments about girls' appearances, can girls do the same back to boys?
Tina:	No cos boys don't . . .
Casey:	boys don't really care.
Chloe:	No we can't.
Catherine:	They'll just hit ya.
Chloe:	We can't just go up to someone and say 'you've got a smaller willy than him ain't ya, ain't ya?'
Tina:	Cos then they'll be like 'ergh'.
Chloe:	'Why you looking at my dick for?' or they'll go 'c'mon let me show you it, what can you do with it'.

This mapping marks a shift away from a psychological reading of the individual girl's or boy's intentions or psyches to the social and affective relations through which their bodies become in particular ways. It is, then, an approach that maps the connections between different elements in encounters or assemblages. Coleman shows how bodies become through and are constituted by gender and sexual relations, which enable or delimit bodily movement and possibility in time and space.

In thinking through this data, however, Coleman also argues that Deleuze's transcendental empiricism insists that capacities cannot be known *prior to or in advance of* material bodily encounters, which means there are unknown spaces for movement. Indeed, she explores how girls resist and fight back against the fixing of the body through looking. Through analysis of the interview data, she identifies how the girls' position looks or appearances in opposition to self or personality.

For example, in the extracts discussed above, looks are an 'intense' organ of the body that reduce the girls' bodies to this specific aspect of the body; looks become the way in which that body is fixed. But girls also resist the force of looking by privileging 'personality' as an organ of the body to disrupt the power of looking:

Emily: When Tasha said, like when she was saying that whenever she fancies someone they won't go out with her cos she's really fat and ugly and stuff and I said it wasn't, that's not what it should have been but no offence to my sister or anything but she isn't really that pretty but she's got a boyfriend and everything and so I don't really think it is how Tasha said it is.

Beckie: Ok, so how do you think it is?

Emily: Well, I don't think you should go for looks, it's just like, if you're a nice person and you've got a really nice personality and stuff then, yeah, you should go out with them

Beckie: That's more important?

Emily: Yeah.

Beckie: Do you think Tasha was saying that or do you think she was saying you shouldn't go out with someone?

Emily: Well, I don't know cos, she was saying, cos I know she's got a really nice personality cos I know her, but she kept saying that no boy would want to go out with her cos she's really ugly and she's really fat and everything, but I don't think she is.

Here Emily suggests that personality not only should be but often is prioritised over looks, since she offers an alternative analysis of 'how it is' that affective relationships happen. Coleman argues that Emily knows Tasha through her personality, which does not reduce the body to looks, and explores how complex affective relationships of trust and honesty between girls can disrupt the fixing of girls' bodies in time and space.

Looking on Digital Social Networks: Desiring Machines, Affective Assemblages and Bodily Capture

In her solo writing and with co-authors, Jessica Ringrose (Renold and Ringrose 2008, 2011; Ringrose 2011, 2012; Koefed and Ringrose 2012) has used a similar Deleuzian framework to explore girls' relationships with popular media images to consider the affective dimensions of bodily capture through looking, organised through what has been termed a 'post-feminist' media context (Gill 2007). Media contexts have been discussed as *post*-feminist because in a reversal of feminist thinking about sexism and the male gaze, self-objectification of the girl's or woman's own body is now commonly viewed as a space of consumer-based freedom in what some have called 'commodity feminism' (Tasker and Negra 2009); *and* more intense objectification of the male body has been positioned as a democratisation of looking now available to girls and women.

As we saw with Coleman's work, however, some Deleuzian-inspired questions about the body turn the relationship away from subject/object dualisms and from understanding a one-way direction of images causing harmful media effects *upon the body* to an investigation of how looking works and how bodies are relationally and affectively experienced through images. Deleuzian thinking means we must change the question from simply asking 'who is objectified, and in what ways?' to: How does the (self-)objectification of girls' and boys' bodies *work* through relations of looking and through images? What are the affective and bodily relations through which images operate?

Ringrose's work has explored how these relations work in social networking sites among young people (14–16) at secondary school through interview and online ethnography based research.[1] Social networking sites require the construction of a visual cyber-subjectivity constructed through multiple modalities of signs, but largely photographic images. The body is signified through gendered and sexualised discourses through the photos and other mediums, but feminist Deleuzian thinking goes beyond semiotic, discursive and cultural analysis (Gilbert 2004). This approach can prioritise how young people experience images of the self and others, to *map* how bodily captures happen and when movement occurs, exploring the affective quality of these flows through their machinic interactions in assemblages.

As noted above, Deleuze and Guattari consider the body as complex, multifaceted and machinic, that is, plugging into and out of other machinic parts. The body is therefore what they call a 'desiring machine', not bound up as a singular entity but always coming into being through relations with other bodies and things in various assemblages. They argue that 'machinic assemblages' are complex social configurations through which *energy flows* and is directed (Malins 2004). The concept of 'assemblages' provides a useful way to think about social entities as 'wholes whose properties emerge from the interactions between the parts' (De Landa cited in Tamboukou 2010: 685). Assemblages are 'characterised by relations of exteriority ... [that] imply that a component part of the assemblage may be detached from it and plugged into a different assemblage in which its interactions are different' (De Landa cited in Tamboukou 2010: 685). There is never a neutral flow of power, however, and bodies are affected and affect through their relations in assemblages.

Using Deleuze and Guattari's concept of assemblages, Ringrose (2011) has theorised social networking sites as relational 'affective assemblages'. These concepts can help us to think of virtual space and relationality in new ways that disturb the online-offline binary and the human-nonhuman dimensions of distributed agency in much thinking about cyber space and real life (Clough in Kuntsman 2012: 9). Take for example the virtual spatial geography of online social networks like Facebook (Paparachissi 2009). These can be understood as assemblages, where desiring machines plug into each other via virtual Facebook profiles which then plug into other profiles. Crucial for this chapter are the findings in Ringrose's research that young people often feel they have to 'look good' to plug into the assemblage in ways that resonate with Coleman's findings of how girls related to photographic images of the self:

Daniela (14): Girls, I think, take more care over how it looks and like their pictures.

Marie (16): You don't really want to put, put a picture on there that makes you look like you just woken up in the morning!

Nicola (14): You only put a nice picture up. Not one of you looking awful.

Louisa (16): You can airbrush yourself ... you can make yourself look better then, well – what can I say? – I've been doing it all the time!

The 'geophilosophical' task for the social scientist is to map out how the internet 'works' (Buchanan 2007) and the networked assemblages become in specific time/space instances. In the young people's social networking sites under study, 'looking good' is an embodied assemblage of meaning and experience; it is constructed in relation to a flow of images and affects where the local and global come together in 'glocal' (Montgomery 2007) networked becomings in relation to idealised versions of girl and boy bodies as: 'sexy', 'buff' and 'well-fit'.

This returns us to Deleuze and Guattari's over-riding concern with the body and their repeated question: 'what can a body do' within a particular assemblage of relations? Using these geophilosophical concepts, we can think through how to map how gender *works through images* and how it enables or disables desiring machines in particular ways. Indeed, as with many feminists inspired by Deleuze (for example, Grosz and Braidotti), it is critical to underscore the *ethico-political* aspects of the geophilosophical mapping afforded by this approach. It enables us to gauge the relations through which the body or desiring machine is captured and territorialised, creating fixed gendered sexual(ised) differences, through dualism machines, in this case via injurious heterosexed norms (to also invoke Butler's [1993] important conceptual work on bodies and the heterosexual matrix, which confines normative gender identity to heterosexual masculine and feminine identities).

Drawing on these concepts, we can map what is repetitive of the molar (wide scale, extensive) norms and how these norms striate space, or (to blend a Foucauldian idea with Deleuze's thinking) carve out the 'conditions of possibility' for movement. If, as we will argue, the body is captured through these processes and denied movement (that is, flows of desire are constrained in specific ways), we also want to ask, how might these constraints be disrupted or de-territorialised (Renold and Ringrose 2008) and how do we account for this?

As one example of addressing this question, Ringrose explored sexual regulations where girls are disciplined as 'sluts' when they are viewed as giving off the wrong type of gendered 'looks' in their peer relations. She looked at the affective force of 'slut' to 'stick' onto girl bodies (Koefed and Ringrose 2012) to 'pin them' (Deleuze and Parnet 2002) into a difficult set of social relations since they must balance looking 'sexy' in the right ways:

> Daniela (14):   I think like if you've got like say a slutty girl, she'll take a picture of her body or whatever and have it as her image . . . If I came across a Bebo[2] that's someone's got a picture of their cleavage and their body, and nothing else. I'll think, 'Well, they obviously think too much of themselves.'

Daniela is describing how the image creates a look of conceit but also the look of 'slutty-ness' if girls display 'too much' rather than shielding their body from looking. Mapping the micro nuances of what girls do online through a Deleuzian analysis of immanent becomings (rather than mimesis or cultural reproduction) is critical, however, because girls can also disrupt this fixing and bodily capture by using the less-regulated space of social networking sites to experiment with 'digital' slut 'looks'. For example, Daniela actually adopted the online social network (Bebo) user profile name of 'slut' while her best friend, Nicola (14) used 'whore', after older girls called them 'sluts' at school, describing they would say about each other:

> Daniela: She's my whore and I'm her slut. Whatever. Get over it!

Daniela and Nicola's Bebo profile-assemblage partly disrupted the molar and extensive organisation of gender and sexuality used to regulate girls' overt sexual expression as 'sluts' by taking up, using and becoming sluts in a new way that was life-affirming rather than life-destroying. This was not a one-way-total line of flight from the molar, injurious norm of 'slut', however, as there was continual risk in inhabiting this space for teen girls, as we continue to explore below.

Ideal Looks and Body Parts: Boobs, Pecks and 'Back Off'

To further demonstrate the methodological work that Deleuze makes possible we will use a few examples from Jessica's most recent project on young people and 'sexting' (Ringrose et al. 2012). This project explored how young people (13–15) communicate sexually through digital technology including social networking sites such as Facebook and mobile phone networks like Blackberry messenger (BBM).[3] The project was explicitly undertaken with the methodological aim of mapping online space and exploring experiences of this with young people. We looked at Facebook activity online then discussed images with young people and were talked through their interactions on Blackberry messenger. The following analysis continues to explore how 'looks' orient digital spaces shaping bodily relations in particular ways, asking: What are the ideal looks for engendered bodies?

Tropes from advertising and popular media circulate within social networks and work to orient particular ideal girl and boy bodies on social networking sites as part of an 'affective assemblage' of meanings (Ringrose 2011). A Deleuzian frame helps to illustrate how this contains and striates the space around what constitutes an ideal gendered bodily pose. For instance, our sample included a teen girl who did some professional modelling, posting copious amounts of these images on Facebook, which introduced specific terms of photographic bodily reference into the peer group of a slim and mechanically mannequin-like posed feminine body. Other typical examples of 'sexy' girl body photos include a genre of self-produced images of the poser in the mirror taken with a camera from a high angle to emphasise cleavage and a diminishing size of body (thin-ness).

| Jodie (13): | Like when girls take pictures they like take it from above like this and you can see down their top and I think they do that on purpose and like some girls like they squeeze their boobs together to make them look bigger and everything. |

To map how these looks work relationally within a particular assemblage we have to find out what happens when this type of image is plugged into the peer networks under study. Jodie talked about how 'sexy' images generate more 'looks' and 'adds' of your profile and further requests for images of girls in bikini and bra:

> Jodie (13):   Some boy asked me, 'Can I have a picture of you', I was like, 'My display picture' and he was like 'No I mean a special photo' and I was like, 'What special photo' and he was like, 'Like you in your bra' and I was like 'No', and I was like, 'I have one of me in my bikini' And he was like, 'can you send it anyway' and I was like, 'Victoria's got it' because he knows my cousin. And then them two went to the same school, so I was like, 'you can ask her to send it' and then I was like, 'Victoria delete the photo and don't send it to him'. Like when you say no to people, like you fall out with them, so I just make excuses.

The attention to breasts illustrates a particular form of 'looks' around specific body parts in the peer social network, where breasts become an intensive or 'special' organ of high value for the female body.

Images of idealised masculinity included topless pictures taken in the mirror of boys' six-packs and back muscles. Evaluation of the 'looks' of the images happens through 'likes' and 'dislikes' from peers in the assemblage. For instance Kamal talked proudly about having forty-two people like the image of his back muscles on Facebook. There was, however, a danger that people might not like the six pack photo, or possibly that a boy could be seen to be effeminate or gay by being too vain about his appearance. And while we found multiple instances of boys posting and commenting on their six packs and aspiring to post photos even if they didn't feel they could, this was organised through ideal 'looks':

> Nathan: Nah nah nah! For me to do that [post a photo of his chest] I would have to be completely big. I'd wanna be proper big to do that. I wouldn't want to do some little half, got a little peck here, little peck there. I'd want to be fully big. And I wouldn't do it in the mirror. I'd get someone to take it of me. Outside or something, not in my house, in the gym I'd get someone to take it of me in the gym like this.

These relations of looking in the 'looking machines' of social networks can be highly pleasurable. Jodie is pleased to be asked for a photo in her bra and Kamal enjoys having forty-two people 'like' his back muscles on Facebook. But the Deleuzian framework for analysis we are showing encourages us to map out how the relations between the images the bodies and the young people capture and fix their bodies and capacities (for desire, as desiring machines) in particular ways. Jodie has described the high value of 'big boobs', and Nathan of 'completely big' muscles. Jodie has described carefully negotiating a refusal to post or send such a photo, and Nathan did not want to post up images of any 'little pecks'.

The way that a particular body part can come to contain the whole (i.e., how the body can be reduced to one organ) emerges more clearly through a further investigation of how the young people used another social network, Blackberry messenger (BBM). The relations of the looks of bodies organised the social relations of looking through BBM in textual and photographic ways. In order to get BBM contacts you do a broadcast in order to have others 'add' you to their contacts. These broadcasts also revolved in large part around particular looks, highlighting particular valued body parts. As Cherelle and Mercedes (both 13), explain:

Jessica:	Okay, so what did people say about you when they do a broadcast?
Cherelle:	They say, 'Stop what you are doing, add Mercedes, she's gifted' that means pretty and stuff like that. Yeah stuff like that and 'she has good conversations'.
Jessica:	Okay, is it mostly about your appearance?
Cherelle:	Yeah mostly about appearance when it comes to broadcasts.
Jessica:	Okay so tell me exactly what they would say?
Cherelle:	If it is a boy and a girl told a boy to BC their pin then they will say, 'Oh she has big tits and a big bum . . . and if you get to know her, she's nice.'
Mercedes:	Like 'add this chick she got a back off'.
Jessica:	What's the back word?
Mercedes:	Back off. That is a big bum.
Jessica:	So that's a good thing?
Mercedes:	Yeah, it is what they are like expecting in girls. It is like good features.
Mercedes:	Yeah, like their dream girl is probably like a big bum, nice breasts and long hair and like a nice skin tone . . .
Jessica:	A girl wrote this about you and who did she want to add you?
Mercedes:	I don't know she was helping me . . . I have this friend yeah, like she is really popular yeah, like loads of boys yeah. So she asked me because she wanted me to have more people, she broadcast it yeah about like forty boys added me.

Again, while there is affirmation and pleasure (Mercedes is pleased she got forty adds) the Deleuzian analysis of the bodily relations helps us to very simply understand how the broadcasts reduce the girl to her looks and her body parts 'tits and bum', which are highlighted to get 'adds'. Cherelle (13) explained that several boys moved from responding to broadcasts and seeing her display photo to asking her 'can I have a picture of your tits?' As we saw Jodie (13) similarly described receiving requests for photos in her bra. The girls also discussed how the politics of the broadcasts reduced their bodies to the ideal 'looks' around certain parts like their 'breast' size and 'skin tone':

Jessica: So do you think the size has like some bearing on whether girls are popular or not?
Mercedes: Eve is popular and she ain't got big.
Veronica: Yeah she ain't got big breasts.
Cherelle: But she is a lightie.
Veronica: I can't remember but one boy told me yeah, I asked him yeah, 'What's the first thing you see in a girl yeah?' and he is like, 'Oh her tits' . . .
Ashley: I hate it when guys yeah, like 'What do you see in me first yeah?' they will be like your eyes or something and what they think really is our breasts.

Deleuze helps us to think about how images work energetically, that is, to enable or contain flows of energy around sexuality and what is possible or impossible to imagine about a body as result of the look that is created in an image. From this conceptual starting point, we can then methodologically get to grips with trying to discover the value that can be derived from a photo through its relation in the affective network or assemblage of connections. How do the looking machines here constrain girl and boy bodies, materialising sexual difference?

To demonstrate the gender dualisms, the sexual difference created and that *becomes* through the looking machines online, consider another image on Facebook. Assad posted a photo of his six pack and tagged some girls in the photo so they would be sure to see it. One of the tagged girls then commented under the photo that she would look forward to seeing it (his body) for real when they 'hooked up' later in the week. In this instance, Assad confidently displays his body and receives a positive evaluation and response with the implication of real intimacy. Girls, however, had a more difficult time posting or sending body photos, which could be subject to the 'hard hitting' from girls and boys that we discussed above. To investigate further how the images of girls' bodies work in the networked assemblage we are mapping we return to the images of breasts that are requested in the assemblage. There were numerous examples discussed of boys using these photos on their social networking site or even as their profile photo on Blackberry messenger profiles. For instance, there was much discussion in interviews of photos of girls' body parts with the name of the boy written on it (with a marker), most commonly on part of the cleavage.

Love, Respect and 'Skets': Bodily Capture, Fixing and Disrupting

The feminist Deleuzian approach we are elaborating enables us to think about how the photos work or what they enable or stop the body from doing or becoming. In one way, the photos work by generating value for the boy who is signalled in the photo as owning the valued body parts (the breasts) – it operates as potential proof of a sexual relationship with the body in the photo (Ringrose and Harvey 2012).[4] The photos also work through the extensive categories of gender and sexuality which striate (that is carve up and limit movement in) both online and offline space. Most boys and girls described *girls* who took or sent such photos as 'stupid' girls who did not respect themselves. This was because the 'look' of these images would categorise the girl as a 'sket':

Irina: But most girls who do that and send the pictures they already
             have had sex or will do it or are ready to do it, yeah. It is like,
             you know 'skets', as in like they will give some random one to
             anyone and they show off their body.

Alexandra: I wouldn't want people to see – I just don't do it, I don't think
             it is the right kind of messages . . . I think I have like respect
             for myself. I wouldn't like other people – like I'm not really
             bothered to get attention from other people, like I wouldn't be
             like posting my naked pictures on my – I wouldn't even take
             naked pictures, because I think that is very stupid.

The images stick to and pin down and fix the body in the photo as 'sket' because they 'send the wrong message' through the look, that the body is to be sexually available instead of shielded, as mentioned earlier. The Deleuzian approach goes beyond reading representations or attitudes, however, to unpack how the 'look' of the images materialises gendered bodies which become in dualising and hierarchical ways through the relations with and to these images. Indeed, the look of this type of image also worked to de-value the girl as shameless and not worth a relationship:

Kaja: She is not the type of girl I would want to go out with . . .
           I wouldn't like want to be seen with her . . . girls like this
           I wouldn't love. I don't know why, I just wouldn't love. I
           wouldn't have respect for them . . . It might sound rude yeah
           but girls like that, I'm not being rude yeah, but I would just have
           sex with her and then leave her. I wouldn't want to – I would
           talk to her, but I wouldn't get in a relationship with her.

Again we see the relations of sexual difference, the dualism machine of
gender. Kaja can gain value from the photo at the same time that he
that devalues the girl. He wants to look (online) but not be 'seen with'
because he cannot 'love' or 'respect' the girl. This same gendered difference was evident in Monique (15) and Kylie's (15) discussion of how the
images worked:

Kylie: But the thing is the girl shouldn't be so stupid as to send it.
Monique: If the boyfriend really wants to see it he can see it in person and
           that's it.
Kylie: The girls want to impress their boyfriends but they don't want
           them to do nothing with the photo.
Monique: But that is what most of the younger lot think.
Kylie: Impressing them, that is losing respect.
Jessica: What do the younger lot think?
Kylie: They think, 'Oh if I wear this, and I do this for him then he is
           going to love me, and I am impressing him.'
Monique: Love, hum!
Kylie: The thing is yeah like if the girls are going to send them the
           picture that is also leading the boys on.
Monique: You are fuelling their disrespect.
Kylie: They think then maybe she will also do this. And then when the
           boy tries it –
Monique: And it doesn't work, they are confused. Because you are sending
           mixed messages.
Kylie: For me as a girl if I sent a picture to that boy and it has got
           passed on, it is my fault, because one I shouldn't have took the
           picture, however that boy is in the wrong also.
Jessica: What if they ask you for a picture for example, which I have
           seen the year eights saying they are like, 'Oh like they are asking
           for a picture of me in my bra like every day.'
Monique: Yeah, and it's like 'No'!

Here complex relationships between images, looks and the engender-
ing of bodies or how gender and difference *become* are apparent. The
images of girls' body parts seem saturated with the affects – affective

intensities – where sending or posting such images seems to be a doing or becoming that creates sexual 'wrongness' or 'stupid-ness' more so than for boys. As Kaja, Monique and Kylie suggest, this looking won't generate 'love' but rather 'disrespect' for girls, but they also tried to resist this gender dualism:

Kylie: We try to challenge it all the time. Like if we have sex, straight away, we are a slag. The second a boy has sex, you are real player you got in there. The minute the girl does it, it's bad, and we always say to the boys 'so if I do this with this person I'm a slag but if you do it with that person no one says anything to you?'

Monique: They have never said it to me but they did say about me that I was a slag and I made a point in front of all the girls of saying it is my body what I do with it is up to me. My mum knows I have spoken to her about it.

Kylie: And everyone respected you more for it.

Monique: Do you get what I'm saying? I use protection, I have done my research, I'm not stupid, I didn't just go and have sex freely and thought, 'Yeah let's just do it because he wants to do it.' I made the decision by myself and I said to all the girls, so all of you lot want to call me a 'sket' because you are not sexually active whatever, whatever, so be it. I don't care, and I carried on with my life and eventually they all respected me because they said, 'Do you know what she's not hiding it, she's confident about what she does', so they left me.

This passage foregrounds an explicit 'challenge' to the double standards of the sexual difference machine where girls are called 'sket' or 'slag' for sexual activity and boys called 'players'. Monique resists the injury of 'sket' by declaring her sexual activity, which disrupted the relations of looking and the fixity of 'sket' by the peer group, so that the intensity of slut eventually 'left'. The bodily relations that enabled this unfixing of her from 'slut' included her relationship with her mum, a teen mother who told Monique she could always come to her to discuss sex, and friends like Kylie, who were part of a peer group that undertook a joint visit to the local sexual health clinic to get condoms and familiarise their friends with birth control. The Deleuzian attention to when something injurious can unfix from a body, affording more space and movement, is crucial in helping us see how Monique can stage her gendered body somewhat differently (see also Renold and Ringrose 2008, 2011; Jackson 2010).

Conclusions

In this paper we have explored how a feminist Deleuzian approach creates useful cartographic tools that help us map out what bodies can do. This basic starting point enables us to re-think our understandings of how bodies relate to one another. This aids in moving away from a simplistic media-effects approach to one that considers the rich affective complexity of relations between bodies and images and how and when images engender and capture and fix bodies. In particular, we explored the idea of looking machines on social networks that inscribe sexual difference and the gendered and sexualised affects attached to images by young people. For instance, we showed how girls' bodies were captured as 'slut' or 'sket' or 'slag' but also how they challenged this, unfixing their bodies from these captures.

Bringing together our diverse data to demonstrate the methodological usefulness of Deleuze is part of contributing to the 'transcendental empiricism' Deleuze insisted could change the ways we understand and act in the world. Indeed plugging our research findings into one another, as we've done here, creates an assemblage to demonstrate how concepts can work to enable new types of seeing and thinking about our research. There is always an ethical dimension, which we have sought to make explicit – methodologically we isolated clusters of concepts that work to take forward our political projects, in this case a feminist consideration of the workings of gender and sexual dualisms and hierarchies.

When social scientists' create cartographies that demonstrate the machines and relations that striate (e.g., dualise) the social they are illustrating ethical and political dimensions of life (exploring power) through their research process. As Hickey-Moody and Malins argue, 'Deleuze's philosophy makes socio-political empiricism an imperative, because the assemblages that social researchers and practitioners form with the world necessarily have implications for bodies and their capacities' (2007: 18). When social scientists find and map the capture, fixing and unfixing of the body and its machinic connections they offer hope and possibility for something different in the social. With this chapter we have sought to make just this form of methodological intervention.

Notes

1. For a longer discussion of the research methods see Ringrose, 2012.
2. Bebo was a popular online social network for young people in 2008 at the time of this research project; usage is now largely supplanted by Facebook.

3. Blackberry messenger is a social network for Blackberry phone users. The user creates a profile and can 'add' other Blackberry messenger contacts through a pin number, which is broadcasted by other users.
4. See Ringrose and Harvey (2012) for a much fuller analysis of the exchange value of these images within the affective economy of 'sexting'.

References

Alverman, D. E. (2000), 'Researching Libraries, Literacies and Lives: A Rhizoanalysis' in E. St. Pierre and W. Pillow (eds), *Working the Ruins: Feminist Poststructural Theory and Methods in Education*, London: Routledge.

Beckman, F. (2011), *Deleuze and Sex*, Edinburgh: Edinburgh University Press.

Bonta, M. and J. Protevi (2004), *Deleuze and Geophilosophy: A Guide and Glossary*, Edinburgh: Edinburgh University Press.

Buchanan, I. (2007), 'Deleuze and the Internet', *Australian Humanities Review*, 43 <http://www.australianhumanitiesreview.org/archive/Issue-December-2007/Buchanan.html> (accessed 11 September 2012).

Butler, J. (1993), *Bodies That Matter*, London: Routledge.

Colebrook, C. and J. Weinstein (2008), *Deleuze and Gender*, Edinburgh: Edinburgh University Press.

Coleman, R. (2009), *The Becoming of Bodies: Girls, Images, Experience*, Manchester: Manchester University Press.

Deleuze, G. (1992), 'Ethology: Spinoza and Us' in J. Crary and S. Kwinter (eds), *Incorporations*, New York: Zone, pp. 625–33.

Deleuze, G. and C. Parnet (2002), *Dialogues II*, trans. H. Tomlinson and B. Habberjam, London: Continuum.

Deleuze, G. and F. Guattari (1984), *Anti-Oedipus: Capitalism and Schizophrenia*, trans. M. Seem, R. Hurley and H. R. Lane, London: Athlone.

Deleuze, G. and F. Guattari (1987), *A Thousand Plateaus: Capitalism and Schizophrenia*, trans. B. Massumi, London: Athlone.

Egan, D. and G. Hawkes (2008), 'Endangered Girls and Incendiary Objects: Unpacking the discourse on sexualization', *Sexuality and Culture*, 12: 291–311.

Guillaume, L. and J. Hughes (eds), *Deleuze and the Body*, Edinburgh: Edinburgh University Press.

Gilbert, J. (2004), 'Signifying Nothing: "Culture", "discourse" and the sociality of affect', *Culture Machine* <http://culturemachine.tees.ac.uk> (accessed 11 September 2012).

Gill, R. (2007), 'Post-feminist Media Culture: Elements of a sensibility', *European Journal of Cultural Studies*, 10(2): 147–66.

Grosz, E. (1994), *Volatile Bodies: Toward a Corporeal Feminism*, Bloomington: Indiana University Press.

Guattari, F. (2009), *Soft Subversions: Texts and Interviews 1977–1985*, Los Angeles: Semiotext(e).

Hickey-Moody, A. and P. Malins (2007), *Deleuzian Encounters: Studies in Contemporary Social Issues*, London: Palgrave.

Jackson, A. Y. (2010), 'Deleuze and the Girl', *International Journal of Qualitative Studies in Education*, 23(5): 579–87.

Kaufman, E. and K. J. Heller (1998), *Deleuze and Guattari: New Mappings in Politics, Philosophy, and Culture*, Minneapolis: University of Minnesota Press.

Kofoed, J. and J. Ringrose (2012), 'Travelling and Sticky Affects: Exploring teens and sexualized cyberbullying through a Butlerian-Deleuzian-Guattarian lens', *Discourse: Studies in the Cultural Politics of Education*, 33(1): 5–20.

Kuntsman, A. (2012), 'Introduction: Affect Fabrics of Digital Cultures' in E. Karatzogianni and A. Kuntsman (eds), *Digital Cultures and the Politics of Emotion*, Basingstoke: Palgrave.

Malins, P. (2004), 'Machinic Assemblages: Deleuze, Guattari and an Ethico-Aesthetics of Drug Use', *Janus Head*, 7(1): 84–104.

Montgomery, K. C. (2007), *Generation Digital: Politics, Commerce, and Childhood in the Age of the Internet*, Cambridge, MA: MIT Press.

Papacharissi, Z. (2009), 'The Virtual Geographies of Social Networks: A comparative analysis of Facebook, LinkedIn and ASmallWorld', *New Media and Society*, 11(1–2): 199–220.

Renold, E. and J. Ringrose (2008), 'Regulation and Rupture: Mapping tween and teenage girls' "resistance" to the heterosexual matrix', *Feminist Theory*, 9(3): 335–60.

Renold, E. and J. Ringrose (2011), 'Schizoid Subjectivities?: Re-theorising teengirls' sexual cultures in an era of "sexualisation"', *Journal of Sociology*, 47(4): 389–409.

Ringrose, J. (2011), 'Beyond Discourse? Using Deleuze and Guattari's schizoanalysis to explore affective assemblages, heterosexually striated space, and lines of flight online and at school', *Educational Philosophy and Theory*, 43(6): 598–618.

Ringrose, J. (2012), *Postfeminst Education? Girls and the Sexual Politics of Schooling*, London: Routledge.

Ringrose, J. and L. Harvey (2012), 'Ratings and Hating: Teen peer culture and the affective, digital economy of "sexting"', Sexual Cultures Conference, Brunel University, UK (20–22 April 2012).

Ringrose, J., R. Gill, S. Livingstone and L. Harvey (2012), *A Qualitative Study of Children, Young People and 'Sexting'*, London: NSPCC.

St. Pierre, E. A. (1997), 'Nomadic Inquiry in the Smooth Spaces of the Field: A preface', *International Journal of Qualitative Studies in Education*, 10(3): 365–83.

Tamboukou, M. (2010), 'Charting Cartographies of Resistance: Lines of flight in women artists' narratives', *Gender and Education*, 22(6): 679–96.

Tasker, Y. and D. Negra (2007), *Interrogating Postfeminism: Gender and the Politics of Popular Culture*, Durham, NC: Duke University Press.

Chapter 8

Disrupting 'Anorexia Nervosa': An Ethnography of the Deleuzian Event

Sarah Dyke

Paradox is initially that which destroys good sense as the only direction, but it is also that which destroys common sense as the assignation of fixed identities. (Deleuze 2004: 5)

There is some evidence to suggest that applying a psychiatric diagnosis and the theoretical models associated with them ... leads to a worse outcome for some. (CAPSAID 2011)

This chapter is based on a Deleuzian analysis, interpretation and writing of data gathered during eighteen months in the field of a mobile or connective ethnography (Hine 2000) on anorexia. By drawing on Deleuze's work in *The Logic of Sense* (2004), particularly his notion of the event, it became possible to create a space of inquiry which refused common or good sense as the only direction. As such, I moved away from considering anorexia as actual – individualised, categorised and fixed – and moved towards an interrogation of anorexia and potential in the context of the pre-individual, moving and unfixed event. Within the text that follows I will be working with, and holding in paradoxical tension, anorexia as an 'aspirational lifestyle choice', as it is often conceived in pro-anorexic (or 'pro-ana') spaces online (Dias 2003; Fox et al. 2005), and as a 'biologically based serious mental illness', as it is conceived in medical and psychiatric sense offline within the Diagnostic Statistical Manual (DSM-IV[1]; Klump et al. 2009). In addition to this I will use Deleuze's own paradoxical trope to eat/to speak, to both work with data and to indicate how this might be used to generate ethically reflexive research practice.

The ethnographic sites, which cannot all be explored in this chapter, included both online (B-eat Ambassador network, pro-anorexia sites, YouTube, Facebook) and offline spaces (an eating-disorder prevention project, an intergenerational feminist project, and face to face meetings with a member of the pro-anorexia community). As such, online life and offline life (Markham 1998) are both engaged with in a bid to give a different account of living with, and through, a difficult and complex relationship to feeding the body. The uncertainty and curiosity that reading Deleuze brings about opens us to the idea that we must look to different spaces in the text, the field, the field as text and vice versa (Hine 2000). Rather than expecting to find data about actual anorexia in actual treatment centres, I became motivated to look elsewhere by tracing the flow of ideas, bodies and phenomena to other spaces of difference. I did this not only to develop new and interesting methodological insights but also to engage with the notion of potential as indivisible from the actual – that which is in movement and never ceases to be so. This attention to movement is significant throughout the chapter at numerous levels: ontologically in terms of the way Deleuze disrupts the metaphysics of being through the notion of becoming; the way in which the virtual is mobilised in an attempt to consider the incorporeal dimension *of the body* (Massumi 2002: 5), and also at the practical level of tracing the movements of the phenomenon to different sites (Hine 2000).

In a bid to avoid giving an account of embodiment, or research methodology, which favours either volition or determinism I use the notion of the virtual. This enables a discussion which accounts for potential, movement and becoming. The virtual pertains, at the level of common sense, to online pro-ana spaces. However, this is distinct from, and by no means collapsible into, what Brian Massumi infers by it. He suggests that, following Deleuzian ideas, the virtual is that which is *of the body* – real-and-abstract: incorporeal. The virtual is that which is always already in movement and might most effectively be considered as the potential of the actual – *or* 'as energy is to matter' (2002: 5). Here it is important to note that this movement is not towards a particular or pre-destined actual. As with the Deleuzian ideas it works with, this paper moves away from fixity and predictability. By working with the virtual of the feeling, sensing, moving body, I have a useful way of troubling both the bordered individual who contains mental illness and the intentionality of the autonomous subject who chooses it as a lifestyle.

To paraphrase Massumi (2002), I will be working with 'Anorexia Nervosa' as an object which is an evolving and snowballing differential, not something which is timeless or timelessly true. While some scholars, including Giles (2006), raise the question of whether or not 'ana' and 'anorexia nervosa' can be considered as the same discursive object, in terms of my engagement there are more trenchant questions to be asked, particularly in relation to the petrification of this nominal identity, as this – unintentionally – serves to put anorexia on a 'pedestal'. As such, this chapter will work with the phenomenon, both as an embodied becoming and an object of discourse. Through Deleuze's notion of the event what is at stake is always already connected to multiple interplays: the potential and the actual; corporeality and incorporeality; bodies and language; the individual and that which is pre-individual. Concepts which comprise the event are not independent and isolated. Rather, they are relational and multiply connected to other concepts. As with the people, places and communities our research explores, Deleuze prepares us to be mindful of where we expect to find actual things, be they definitions, objects, bodies or communities.

While Medicine and Psychiatry refer to the 'proper name' 'Anorexia Nervosa', pro-anorexics speak about 'Ana', 'AN', 'ED' and 'wannarexia'. Where 'AN' and 'ED' mobilise medical short-hand and highlight the power of the medical discourse, what is interesting to the paper is an 'improper' name: 'wannarexia'.[2] This pejorative term indicates the desirability of what is considered within good and common sense as a mental illness. By engaging with the pre-individuality of the event I do not deride or pathologise *individuals* with a difficult relationship to feeding the body. Instead I move towards a necessary iconoclasm. Both medical and anorexic notions of anorexia, and the anorexic body, are dogmatic. Therefore speaking back to both philosophically is politically and productive of value to a feminist rethinking of the matter of matter.

Young Women and Anorexia Nervosa

> The ideal little girl incorporeal and anorexic . . . must disengage themselves from their real, voracious, gluttonous or blundering images. (Deleuze 2004: 30)

There exists a significant body of work around eating disorders (Brook 1999; Grosz 1994; Hepworth 1999; Lawrence 1984; Lupton 1996; MacLeod 1981; Malson 1998; McSween 1986; Orbach 1982, 1986; Probyn 2000) which, by engaging with issues of gender, power, knowledge, embodiment and resistance, trouble common sense readings of anorexia as a mental illness or 'bizarre' pathology' (Brook 1999: 73). However; while many of the texts have made significant contributions to developing a feminist understanding of eating disorders, most were published prior to the development of virtual pro-ana communities. Nonetheless, as online life is increasingly acknowledged as part of everyday life (Garcia et al. 2009; Kozinets 2010; Markham 1998), the notion of pro-anorexia is of increasing interest to social researchers (Day 2010; Ferreday 2003; Hammersley and Tresseder 2007; Pollack 2003).

In line with all social networking activities, pro-ana sites have increased during the last decade. Optenet (2008), an international IT security company, reported that between 2006 and 2008 the number of pro-ana websites increased globally by 470 per cent. Whether or not this figure is disproportionately large in relation to other social networking sites is debatable. However, what this does highlight is that anorexia is an issue which is being engaged with in a significant way across virtual (cyber, and real-and-abstract) spatio-temporalities. Indeed, in a study of thirteen- to seventeen-year-old school children, 12.6 per cent of girls and 5.9 per cent of boys claimed to have visited such sites (Custers and Van den Bulck 2009). While these figures are of course open to interpretation, what is significant is the space they create for contesting the capacity of medical and psychiatric sense to fully engage with what they consider 'biologically based serious mental disorders' (Klump et al. 2009). The figures given for those who are at the very least curious about anorexia, how to become anorexic by exploring the tips and tricks sections (Dias 2003), are considerably higher than the figures for those who the Royal College of Psychiatrists suggests 'get' anorexia: according to the medical sense of the DSM-IV (American Psychiatric Association [APA] 2000) actual anorexia is a rarity which affects only seven in one thousand females, and one in one thousand males (Royal College of Psychiatry 2009). What this suggests is that online spaces are one site where researchers might look to find different experiences of anorexia.

The earlier research on eating disorders, particularly the paradox of feminine agency, resistance and conformity, is engaged with by Day in the context of pro-ana sites (2010). She suggests that the websites emphasise the benefits of anorexia as ways of coping and providing support to those who engage in extreme and ascetic bodily practices. She concludes by suggesting that 'what are often regarded as destructive health behaviours reproduce accounts of both "ideal femininity" and "resistance to femininity"' (Day 2010: 246). The paradox that Day engages with leads her to suggest that theorisations must be mindful of either 'celebrating' such resistance as pertaining to women's power, or thinking only through what she terms 'oppressive discourses' which tend towards determinism. In the next section I will begin to work with the incorporeal event in the context of my own research, to trouble this dichotomy between either celebrating or bemoaning anorexia. This will set in motion the idea that although Deleuze's ideas are not easy (they are abstract and far from common sense), they offer important tools for working away from a priori notions of the actual body towards its potential.

Putting Deleuze's Theory to Work

Paraphrasing Deleuze again, the problem with dominant models in cultural and literary theory is not that they are too abstract to grasp the concreteness of the real. The problem is that they are not *abstract enough* to grasp the real incorporeality of the concrete. (Massumi 2002: 5)

As a methodological text the chapter will show the working out and working through of conceptual aspects of the event (the dual and quasi cause, the accident, actualisation and counter-actualisation) in an attempt to productively disrupt good sense understandings of 'Anorexia Nervosa' and 'pro-anorexia'. Here, reinvestments in the notion of *actual* anorexia will be suspended by refusing the ontological certainty of *being* in favour of Deleuze's notion of becoming. This will allow into the frame of engagement that which is *of the body*: 'Of it, but not it. Real, material, but incorporeal' (Massumi 2002: 5).

In evoking Deleuze's language of the event we are afforded a means to consider the reality and the abstractness of bodies *and* language, without setting up a hierarchal relation. In *The Logic of Sense* (2004) language is not subsumed under materiality or vice versa, the surface of language is always already in relation to the depths of bodies in which it subsists. Within the event the nature of the cause is dual. In one direction it pertains to the pre-individual and incorporeal of the body: its potential. In the other direction it depends for its real or actual causes upon mixtures of bodies. In other words, the virtual and actual are no more separable than the individual is from other bodies and from that which is pre-individual and in a process of becoming. Bodies are causes in relation to one another, causes of '"incorporeal entities" . . . not things or facts, *but events*. We cannot say that [events] exist, but rather that they subsist or inhere' (Deleuze 2004: 7, emphasis added). This dual cause is worth bearing in mind for later, particularly in relation to the eating-disorder prevention project which was a significant site within my ethnographic project.

The project of unfixing identities and considering proper names (Deleuze 2004) is particularly important to my research, not least of all because of the investments that pro-ana communities make in 'actual' anorexia, and the fixed ontology of *being* actual anorexics. This approach does not contest the idea of a difficult relationship to feeding the body, a relationship which impacts on life chances ranging from education and employment to access to support networks and bodily potentials. On the contrary, in conceiving of anorexia in relation to the Deleuzian event we move towards an understanding of what is real (and abstract) about it, *prior* to or *outside* of the administration of a diagnostic label (DSM-IV; APA 2000) or the appearance of emaciation. By engaging with the notion of potential, as indivisible from the actual but as that which is *not towards a* determined end point, we allow into the discussion movement and becoming.

Also worth mentioning at this point is another significant way in which Deleuze moves us away from determinism. The event subsists within us, waits for us and mobilises our will to actualise or bring about that which is already waiting, 'that which is already in the process of coming about and never stops coming about' (Deleuze 2004: 242). We are, then, not speaking of an individualised typology. We are not engaging with the notion that pre-destined bodies inevitably move towards fixed or determined points and stay there. Rather, by engaging with the pre-individuality of the event and the virtual *of the body*, we refuse to make individual bodies contain the abject and pathological and instead engender a hopefulness which is valuable to a feminist rethinking of the body, as I explore below.

By acknowledging the abstract as an aspect *of the body* (Massumi 2002: 30), we are working with that which is everyday, but which has no 'everyday language' to make it utterable. Rather, 'everyday language' is a discursive space in which good and common sense too often circulates. As with the event itself, what we are working with is 'beyond the general or the particular' (Deleuze 2004: 169). The event is not about individual, categorised, fixed bodies, nor is it about the actual stripped of the virtual. Instead, it is directed *towards mixtures of bodies and pre-individual potentials*. To accommodate our engagement with that which is not the body, but of the body – virtual – we would benefit from looking away from good and common sense language towards the language of the event – its movements and becomings. In the following section I continue to put Deleuze to work, drawing out some implications for research methodology and highlighting how the concepts I've elaborated so far have inspired both the design and 'doing' of research.

Becoming Curiouser and Curiouser: Putting Real and Abstract Ideas to Work in Research Practice

> Look only at movements – and they will bring you to matter.' (Massumi 2002: 206)

As much as methodology is a procedural concern, it is always already connected to our conceptions of ontology, epistemology and ethics. These theoretical ideas inform the questions we formulate and the spaces, or sites, we take these questions to. The puzzlement and uncertainty that reading Deleuze brings about contributes to an existing methodological literature, particularly in terms of the work of the ethnographer. Geertz suggests that ethnographers' sustained engagement with the field can transmute the strange into the familiar and the familiar to the strange, inducing a productive 'puzzlement'. This occurs through 'displacing the dulling sense of familiarity with which the mysteriousness of our own ability to relate perceptively to one another is concealed from us' (Geertz 1993: 16). Ethnography, as a theoretically informed discipline and method of carrying out and representing research, is not neutral: 'methodological preambles are far from innocent in the construction of ethnographic authority' (Markham 1998: 46). The ethnographers' stories of the field and their object of study, how and why they arrived and what they bore witness to, have less to do with an indubitable account of reality than they do with the descriptive, analytic and interpretive representation the ethnographer serves to their audience to chew over and digest.

Here, I would suggest that one of the most significant contributions Deleuze makes to methodological design, practice and representation is to help us to make the strange, familiar and familiar, strange; 'destroy[ing] good sense as the only direction' (Deleuze 2004: 5). Alongside the disruption of good and common sense Deleuze also helps us to engage differently with the subject, the collective, agency, materiality and language. Concepts which Deleuze operates, such as the quasi cause and the event, are not explicitly defined or found in one place,[3] just as the phenomenon we seek to explore is not immediately available in neat isolation. As with the object of inquiry, we find ideas moving and subsisting with other concepts in the body of the text. The idea that things are not always where we expect to find them opens up an interesting methodological synergy between where we expect to find the 'actual' object of study, and where we expect to find 'actual' definitions of Deleuzian concepts.

For example, Hine notes that 'the sites which we choose to study are often based on common sense understandings of what the phenomenon being explored is' (2000: 58). If good and common sense understandings suggest that anorexia is a mental illness with, *and because* it has, diagnosable criteria (DSM-IV), then we are inclined to set in motion methodological practices, including timely and difficult ethical procedures (Halse and Honey 2007) which gain us access to spaces where 'mentally ill' people reside or are 'treated'. While there are without doubt ill bodies in such spaces, and gaining an ethically accountable story from them is important, there are implications if this is the only space we look to in order to gather data.

In other words, if we engage with the object as individualised, fixed and categorised, not as the snowballing open-ended differential Massumi (2002) speaks of, our work has difficultly accounting for incremental and potential becomings. In terms of my work this would mean reinvesting in actual anorexia as more important than the bodies which fall outside of the category's demands, which may have implications in terms of other objects or nominal identities such as class, race, sexuality or gender. If I invest in the actual as divisible from potential, my research would ignore those bodies which the logic I operate through would produce as improper. I would be complicit in placing anorexia on a pedestal, as one participant in my research suggests:

> I used to believe I WAS a wannabe. I used to believe I merely WANTED to be anorexic and had put it up on a pedestal. Why? Because I was anorexic, was in denial, believed I was still far too huge and ugly to be sick . . . That's all it took for me to look like a flaming raging wannabe to other people. Constantly looking for more to help me learn to be anorexic. Because I didn't think I was. (saccharinescreen)

In questioning the idea of a self-evident actual, by engaging with potential as indivisible from it, I moved from *that which occurs* – the Deleuzian accident – towards *the inside of what occurs* – the event. Here the inside of what occurs is not the psychic interiority of the bordered individual. The event is always already pre-individual – beyond the general and particular – but always already in movement. To bring about, or actualise, that which was always already in movement – but not towards a determined or fixed actual – the event mobilises in us a will. Not a cognitive will, a choice or decision of thought, but an incorporeal will *of the body* – the quasi cause.

Below, I quote Deleuze at length because of the powerful resonance between his argument and the way in which I sensed pro-anas engaged with the idea of 'choosing' anorexia, demonstrated, for instance, in the way in which two participants in my research, 'Cities-in-dust' and 'inbetweendays', feel themselves compelled, or invited, to make a choice which 'is not a choice like you think', or as common sense would understand it.

> To the extent that events are actualised in us, they wait for us and invite us in. They signal us: 'My wound existed before me, I was born to embody it.' It is a question of attaining this will that the event creates in us; of becoming

the quasi cause of what is produced within us, the Operator . . . The event . . . manifests in us the neutral splendour which it possesses in itself in its impersonal and pre-individual nature, beyond the general and the particular, the collective and the private. (Deleuze 2004: 169)

Made a choice to 'become anorexic'? It's not a choice like you think but 'what is a choice?' Is there such a thing? I did not make a choice – I was a little kid. (Cities-in-dust)

I used to think 'I wish I had an eating disorder' but I was already doing and thinking the same shit as I am now. (inbetweendays)

I will now develop Deleuze's paradoxical trope 'to speak/to eat' in relation to this paradox of lifestyle choice and mental illness. I argue that without recourse to an embodied language which can tap into the incorporeality of the concrete, the *actual* body of the speaker 'snaps up' that which is pre-individual: beyond the general and the particular.

From Prevention to Pro-ana: Speaking of Food and Eating Words

My project began by identifying eight pro-anorexia websites by entering the term 'pro-ana' into an internet search provider. Kozinets suggests that for the purposes of research ethics we can 'regard the use of some types and uses of computer-mediated cultural interactions as similar to the use of texts' (2010: 142). As such, during this initial stage of research the sites were considered as textual due to the fact that the only aspect explored were the archived, public-and-private, discussion boards. All of the sites observed had *private* inbox functions which were inaccessible to anyone other than the specific member, as well as *public* or communal discussion boards. Although 'data' was conceived as textual, I remained mindful of issues of anonymity and confidentiality. 'Heavy cloaking' (Kozinets 2010) was therefore carried out. In practice this meant that all data copied and pasted to Word documents for early and provisional analysis were changed from the outset. Names of sites were changed, and all user profile pictures were deleted. Pseudonyms were changed by conflating random words from other discussion threads.

During this preliminary investigation one particular word struck me: wannarexic. It struck me at both a theoretical and practical level. As a word it appeared to introduce the idea that for some individuals anorexia was desirable, thereby contesting taken for granted notions of anorexia as only a 'biologically based serious mental illness' (Klump et al. 2009). Also, the way in which it was mobilised as a pejorative term on discussion boards highlighted that pro-ana spaces were spaces of contestation. Wannarexics were improper, oppositionally defined to actual or 'genuine' anorexics.

> In short for those of you new to the term, stupidly vain (usually teenager) who have the misconception that they can choose to become anorexic or 'ana' at the flick of a switch ... No one can choose to become anorexic, it is a serious mental illness. One with genuine anorexia nervosa never wants to have the illness, they wish they didn't have it at all. (Bonypink999)

Having read *The Logic of Sense*, my noticing the word 'wannarexic' at the surface of language was already in movement. In this book, Deleuze puts the portmanteau words of *Alice in Wonderland* – 'jabberwocky', 'snark', 'mimsy' and 'slithy' – to work in his exploration of the relationship between the surface of language and the depths of bodies. In showing us his method of working through the implications of conflated articulation – 'Jabberwocky', for instance, employs the verb *to jabber* with the adjective *wocur* meaning fruit or offspring – Deleuze invites us to do the same. Wannarexic, as a portmanteau, is a particular order of esoteric word, a contracting word which conflates the closed metaphysics of *being* with the noun or adjective anorexic. As with 'Jabberwocky' the content of 'wannarexia' coincides with its function (Deleuze 2004: 54): it wants-to-be. Wannarexia, by sleight of hand, invests in actual anorexia as distinct and special, not something that happens to just anyone. Here we are reminded of what saccharinescreen wrote in terms of putting anorexia on a pedestal. Through such reverence, anorexia is imbued with special qualities, it is more powerful than the subjects who either desire it or are diagnosed with it.

Returning the question Giles (2006) raises about whether or not 'ana' and 'Anorexia Nervosa' can be considered as the same discursive object, we see here that Bonypink999 operates at the level of what Deleuze refers to as denoting intuition: 'of all of the images associated with a word – with a particular word in the proposition – we must choose or select those which correspond to the given whole. The denoting intuition is then expressed by the form: "it is that" or "it is not that"' (Deleuze 2004: 16). For my purposes, this impetus to fixity – 'it is that', 'it is not that' – is connected to the bordering process of what actual anorexia is, and what actual anorexics are: a logic which produces bodies as excessive and improper. Rather than the idea of the *cognitive choice* to be anorexic which Bonypink999 draws on, and Cities-in-dust perhaps troubles, Deleuzian ideas open a space to consider that something *of the body, real and abstract, incorporeal* is compelled, not to choose, but to bring about that which is always already in a process of becoming.

Returning to the idea of that which is both every-day, yet has no everyday language to draw on, I introduce ana4eva, who makes connections at the surface of language and sense making to the story of Alice in Wonderland:

> If I am nineteen years old, sixty pounds, and eating a carton of yoghurt a day, and it takes me precisely two hours to eat this carton of yoghurt, and I smoke a cigarette every fifteen minutes to prove that I can stop eating, then I will be safe, retaining my dictatorial grip on my body, my life, my world. By contrast, If I so much as taste a bit of unsafe food on my tongue, it will not travel through my body in the usual biological fashion but will magically make me grow, like Alice taking a bite of the wrong cake.

The language ana4eva serves to the reader seems to contain traces of esoteric riddle which would not be out of place in either Carroll's *Wonderland* or *The Logic of Sense*. 'If I am x, y, z: *what am I?*' (Anorexic, Ana, Mentally Ill, Wannarexic, etc., etc.). One could almost imagine the haughty caterpillar, through rings of smoke, or the Cheshire Cat through his disembodied smile, presenting this puzzle to the adventuring Alice. However, alongside this answerless riddle we find in the recipe of ascetic bodily practices something real and abstract, virtual or incorporeal. Ana4ever suggests that there is something other than 'usual biology' at work which can bring about magical growth.

For both Deleuze and ana4eva, there is more to the body than meets the eye. As we have already noted, bodies are causes in relation to one another, causes of '"incorporeal entities" ... *events*' (Deleuze 2004: 7). Here, the language of the event allows us to engage with this idea of magical growth without discounting it as the bizarre or paranoid fantasy of the mentally ill. The tasting body does not cause the (f)actual growth of usual biology; it causes a magical and imperceptible growth which pertains to the incorporeal dimension *of the body*: its potential. To paraphrase Massumi, that which is imperceptible and insensate, but moves through sensation.

In this articulation we have perhaps an awareness of the virtual: the potential *of* the body in movement. However, this movement refuses the final resting place of a distinct emotional state or particular word – relating to both the depths of bodies and the surface of language. Although the extract evokes a process of becoming, of potential, in the last instant this is somewhat tied to the fixity of *being* an actual anorexic. Ana4eva senses the potential *of* the body, yet potential is not amenable to a dictatorial grip. As such, potential must be sutured to a predictable, determined, individualised actual: physical growth. To an obdurate palette, the uncertainty of embodied potential creates an abject taste on the tip of the tongue. The pre-individuality of the event is individualised through a focus on ana4eva's actual body.

Preventing Potential?

Soon after my early exploration of pro-ana sites I became a participant observer in a short-term eating-disorder prevention project. In receipt of twelve months' local authority funding it had been tendered, and awarded, on the basis of a good and common sense understanding of (f)actual or proper anorexia as a serious mental illness. This understanding implied that anorexia was amenable to prevention, diagnosis and therapeutic treatment. However, the feminist youth workers who managed and delivered the project also paid particular attention to a socio-cultural understanding of disordered eating. As such, they saw *the cause* of eating disorders as external to the subject and traceable to the media, patriarchy and the thin ideal. Pro-ana websites were never discussed in team meetings, nor was the desire to be anorexic. 'Wannarexia' and the social spaces in which the term flowed did not figure in the way the problem of the rise in diagnosed eating disorders was considered. However, as I have already indicated, in the refusal to split the actual from the virtual, potential cannot be prevented; it is always already in movement but not towards a predictable or final resting place.

Group work was carried out in schools, youth work and young parent projects. It was delivered to both males and females aged thirteen to twenty-one. As a prevention project it was neither necessary nor desirable that participants were identified, or identified themselves, as 'eating disordered'. This posed a problem in gathering data for the research question, which encouraged me to ask: *'what is the "everyday" experience of having an "eating disorder" and how does it impact on everyday life, including work and education?'* Although the original site didn't lead me to participants, it did lead me to other sites, including a feminist organisation based in the North of England. Through this site a detailed pro forma was sent to potential participants giving details of my research aims and participant's rights to anonymity, confidentiality and ethical treatment. This information was disseminated to a thousand youth workers, feminists and young people. Of the thousand inboxes to receive the email, there was one particularly interesting response from a young woman called Joanne.

During our first face-to-face meeting, as we were served to one another for the first time, we spoke of food and carefully ate one another's words. I asked why she had come forward and suggested that I would like the project to be mutually interesting and if possible beneficial. As I have suggested above, I had been thinking through Deleuze's trope to eat/to speak: 'What is more serious: to speak of food or to eat words? . . . If we then speak of food, how can we avoid speaking in front of the one who is to be served as food?' (Deleuze 2004: 29). In the above quote we see that to speak/to eat pertains to the depths of the body and the surface of language. Not only was this a useful concept when it came to analysing and interpreting mine and Joanne's discussions, it was also relevant to the ethics of the project. I did not want to relate to Joanne as a source of data, encouraging her to speak of a difficult and complex relationship to feeding the body, only to then serve her as food and dine out on the stories. With this abstract idea in mind I began by serving my project to her as an ethical engagement which would require the commitment of both of us over time. I presented outright Joanne's right to anonymity and confidentiality and suggested that after each interview we discuss whether or not she remained satisfied with the project and her involvement in it. I proposed that we both left ample time at the end of our recorded discussions to chew over the more difficult aspects of our talk. I suggested this to ensure that Joanne left the field with feelings as close to those she had entered with as possible.

Joanne committed to the project, agreeing to meet with me at regular intervals to work towards a 'different account of anorexia', which troubled the way that the medical model and the DSM-IV served it in cultural freeze frame (Massumi 2002). In line with the mobile research method, Joanne offered me another way to follow the phenomenon to different sites. Together we acknowledged the abstract and mundane aspects of life online and life offline without subsuming one under the other (Markham 1998). In our first meeting Joanne gave an account of her adolescent experience of anorexia and pro-ana sites. During this meeting what came to the surface of language were 'bits of things' which had already been chewed over. Everything was partially digested, the by-products of prior therapeutic regurgitation. Because talk of food had been in reference to the past, I asked her how she now 'lived differently'.

Living differently was a phrase I had considered before entering the field as a means to both avoid the term recovery and to work with Deleuze's idea of counter-actualisation. Although recovery is often presented straightforwardly as a state distinct from anorexia, there is still debate about what the term actually means (Bardone-Cone et al. 2010).

Institutionally speaking, however, recovery is usually interchangeable with weight gain and consistent eating practices which maintain normative levels of biological functioning. Yet this notion of recovery is often contested by pro-anas (Fox et al. 2005). For example, one participant argued that 'Recovery is a myth' (Violet_Rage), and Joanne was also sceptical. Even though I had explicitly avoided the term when I asked Joanne how she 'lived differently' she responded with 'yeah, erm, technically I'm not totally recovered'.

I was interested in what Joanne might be able to tell me about becoming the 'master of actualisations and causes' (Deleuze 2004: 243). This was important to the politics of the project, a politics of movement which was hopeful of the idea of becoming. Rather than conceiving of an unliveable relationship to feeding the body as the end or beginning of being, becoming moved my thinking away from fixed identities and proper names. The term recovery was thus also avoided as it implied an end point to pathology and a starting point of normalcy. The ethics of the research sought to conceive of anorexia differently. In evoking the term recovery I would be mobilising conservative and good sense which would be incongruent with the methodology's concern with movement and unfixing.

As already suggested, when we speak of the body according to medical sense there is no space to acknowledge its incorporeal or virtual dimension. Potential is severed from, and obfuscated by, the actual. There is no accounting for the ways in which the sense of the event subsists within bodies and is bought about by its incorporeal dimension: the quasi cause. Deleuze's theoretical ideas moved my research question from being focused on *that which occurs*, the accident (weight loss or weight gain), towards questions which attempted to make luminous *the inside of what occurs*, the pre-individual event.

What the event and its dual causality opened the research to was the idea that the will is mobilised to bring about *that which is already in movement*. I found a means of acknowledging volition in anorexic becoming while refusing to conceive of this as a mental choice. Instead I worked with the idea of that which already subsists within the virtual dimension *of the body*. Using the event to think through anorexia challenges the idea of it as a mental illness caused by abnormal biology (Klump et al. 2009) and as a lifestyle choice based on cognitive decisions. Because Joanne saw herself as 'technically . . . not totally recovered' our face-to-face meetings often involved her bringing to the surface of language what she conceived of as *the cause* of her eating disorder. Yet her linguistic emissions were often accompanied by dissatisfaction. As she traced the circumstances of her own life I often sensed that something remained problematically inaccessible. She struggled to make sense, not least of all because her good and common sense conceived the body as bordered, fixed, autonomous and intentional (Brennan 2004).

In the thirteenth series of *The Logic of Sense*, 'The Schizophrenic and the Little Girl', we can see useful parallels in the way that common and good sense language fails Joanne and how something of what she might wish to bring to the surface of language remains within her body. In having no space to conceive of the real and abstract relationship between the body and language, Joanne's dissatisfying articulations are swallowed down and 'snapped up' by the body. Perhaps these remnants, these 'bits of things', contribute to her account of fullness and being 'too big'. Everything is inside and everything is body and corporeal. The pre-individuality of the event, its neutral splendour, becomes the problematic property of the individual.

> Things and propositions have no longer any frontier between them, precisely because bodies have no surface. The primary aspect of the schizophrenic body is that it is sort of a body sieve ... The consequence of this is that the entire body is no longer anything but depth – it carries along and *snaps up everything into its gaping depth ... Everything is body and corporeal. Everything is a mixture of bodies and inside the body, interlocking and penetration.* (Deleuze 2004: 99, emphasis added)

As with ana4eve and her predictable, determined, individualised actual, when Joanne could not fully account for the reason she felt so powerfully compelled by anorexia, fat filled the gap. She restricted her intake because she was too fat; she wasn't a proper anorexic because she was too fat.

> I don't deserve the label of eating disorder, never mind anorexia because of my size and it even feels sort of stupid saying the word anorexia because of my size even though I know I have the exact same behaviours as someone diagnosed with anorexia it just doesn't feel like something that I can say.

While Joanne embodies the wound and operates the sense of the event, her place outside diagnostic criteria engenders a feeling that she is an improper anorexic. In the last instance, as with saccharinescreen, medical and psychiatric conceptions of anorexia are invested in as being more important than their embodied experience.

Deleuze and Methodology: Future Considerations

Throughout the chapter I have engaged with theory which is directed towards being 'abstract enough to grasp the real incorporeality of the concrete' (Massumi 2002: 5). I have worked with the Deleuzian language of the event, which is connected to the real and abstract of the body, its virtual or incorporeal dimension. In doing so, I have been able to approach the object of inquiry differently. In avoiding sense-making which goes in only one direction, and working with the pre-individuality of the event, I have neither celebrated anorexia as a lifestyle choice, nor determined it as a mental illness (Day 2010).

In summarising the implications of the chapter for research methodology, one idea which is of immense value to how researchers conceive the 'research problem' is the *dual cause* – that which is *of the body* or virtual, and requires for its actual causes, mixtures of bodies. This idea opens up and works with the unhelpful binary of volition and determinism: *the quasi cause*, as one direction of the dual cause, as means of disrupting choice as always and only cognitive; *counter-actualisation*, or what Deleuze refers to as 'the freedom by which we develop and lead the event to its completion and transmutation' (Deleuze 2004: 243). Operationalising the event enables possibilities for thinking about both 'anorexia' and 'recovery' as fixed ontological points of 'being' but also as *the accident*. I worked with this idea to suggest that 'what occurs' should not be where inquiry starts or stops. In setting out these ideas my argument has been towards a shift of focus – not only seeing with our eyes, nor making that which is accidental to the event the focus of our engagement. Instead, I suggest that we take the challenge of working with those 'bits of things' – affects, ideas, sensations and movements – which are often disregarded under usual methods of working. With Deleuzian thinking our engagements cease to be *only* about 'individuals', 'structures' and 'constructs' and instead take the challenging, yet necessary, task of working with what is really incorporeal about the concrete, that which is pre-individual and always already in movement.

Referring to Grosz's insight, that 'scientific notions are internalised, if only indirectly, through their absorption into popular culture' (1999: 134), we find in Deleuze a way of avoiding complicity with those ideas and discourses which would imply certain bodies are 'improper'. Through working with these ideas I am more able to ask questions of what 'actual anorexia' implies as well as what 'counter-actual anorexia' might mean. In asking questions of the actual, I can engage more effectively with offline and online observations; for instance, Violet_Rage's assertion that 'recovery is a myth'. Also, if we can acknowledge that there is an incorporeal dimension *of the body*, which is connected to the bringing about of the event, we can begin to reconsider choice, which, to paraphrase Cities-in-dust, is not like you think.

As a final point, through the exposition of my own method, what I would wish others to take away is that although the ideas Deleuze asks us to work with are both difficult and disruptive, they make us curious: willing and waiting to be productively puzzled. In designing and carrying out research, I would suggest that if we fail to interrogate those 'bits of things' and take for granted the 'actual' as more important than the potential, we fall short of what our practice might potentially be. Perhaps, if we do not grasp the real incorporeality of the concrete, we make solid both icons and dogma. With regard to the design and conduct of future research, with Deleuze we have the possibility of holding in tension multiple interplays and paradoxes. In practice, by moving away from the assignation of fixed identities and common sense, we are perhaps afforded a different methodological space in which we might consider the 'research problem'. Here, in daring to question the actual, the fixed and the categorised, we might move towards working with the pre-individuality of the everyday, the embodied and the linguistic as they play out in mixtures of bodies in ways which are beyond the general and the particular.

Notes

1. A. Refusal to maintain body weight at or above a minimally normal weight for age and height (e.g., weight loss leading to maintenance of body weight less than 85% of that expected; or failure to make expected weight gain during period of growth, leading to body weight less than 85% of that expected). B. Intense fear of gaining weight or becoming fat, even though underweight. C. Disturbance in the way in which one's body weight or shape is experienced, undue influence of body shape on self-evaluation, or denial of the seriousness of the current low body weight. D. In postmenarcheal females, amenorrhea, i.e., the absence of at least three consecutive menstrual cycles. (From APA 2000).
2. 'Wannarexia' contracts the words *want to be* and conflates this with anorexic, indicating the desire of the inauthentic subject to be a 'real anorexic'.
3. Although the Twenty-First series of *The Logic of Sense* (2004) is called 'The Event', a thorough reading of it, and the concepts of which it is comprised, comes about through reading elsewhere within the text.

References

American Psychiatric Association (APA) (2000), *Diagnostic and Statistical Manual of Mental Disorders*, 2nd edn, text revision, Washington, DC: American Psychiatric Association.

Bardone-Cone, A. M., M. B. Harney, C. R. Maldonado, M. A. Lawson, P. D. Robinson, R. Smith and A. Tosh (2010), 'Defining Recovery From an Eating Disorder: Conceptualization, validation, and examination of psychosocial functioning and psychiatric comorbidity', *Behaviour Research and Therapy*, 48: 194–202.

Brennan, T. (2004), *The Transmission of Affect*, New York: Cornell University Press.

Brook, B. (1999), *Feminist Perspectives on the Body*, London: Longman.

Butler, J. (1990), *Gender Trouble*, London: Routledge.

Butler, J. (1997), *The Psychic Life of Power*, Stanford: Stanford University Press.

Butler, J. (2004), *Undoing Gender*, London: Routledge.

CAPSAID (2011), 'Campaign to Abolish Psychiatric Diagnostic Systems such as ICD and DSM' <http://www.criticalpsychiatry.net/?p=527> (accessed 13 September 2011).

Custers, K. and J. Van den Bulck (2009), 'Viewership of Pro-anorexia Websites in Seventh, Ninth and Eleventh Graders', *European Eating Disorders Review*, 17: 214–19.

Day, K. (2010), 'Binge Drinking: Conformity to damaging ideals or New Resistant Femininities', *Feminism and Psychology*, 20(2): 242–8.

Deleuze, G. (2004), *The Logic of Sense*, trans. M. Lester with C. Stivale, London: Continuum.

Dias, K. (2003), 'The Ana Sanctuary: Women's pro-anorexia narratives in cyberspace', *Journal of International Women's Studies*, 4(2): 31–45.

Ferreday, D. (2003), 'Unspeakable Bodies : Erasure, embodiment and the pro-ana community', *International Journal of Cultural Studies*, 6(3): 277–95.

Fox, N., K. Ward and A. O' Rourke (2005), 'Pro-anorexia, Weight-loss Drugs and the Internet: An "anti recovery" explanatory model of anorexia', *Sociology of Health and Illness*, 27(7): 944–71.

Garcia, A. C. et al. (2009), 'Ethnographic Approaches to the Internet and Computer-Mediated Communication', *Journal of Contemporary Ethnography*, 38: 52–84.

Geertz, C. (1993), *The Interpretation of Cultures*, London: Fontana.

Giles, D. (2006), 'Constructing Identities in Cyberspace: The case of eating disorders', *British Journal of Social Psychology*, 45: 463–77.

Grosz, E. (1994), *Volatile Bodies: Towards a Corporeal Feminism*, Indianapolis: Indiana University Press.

Grosz, E. (1999), 'Space, Time and Bodies' in J. Wolmark (ed.), *Cybersexualities: A Reader on Feminist Theory, Cyborgs and Cyberspace*, Edinburgh: Edinburgh University Press, pp. 119–35.

Halse, C. and A. Honey (2007), 'Rethinking Ethics as Institutional Discourse', *Qualitative Inquiry*, 13(3): 336–52.

Hammersley, M. and P. Treseder (2007), 'Identity as an Analytic Problem: Who's who in "pro-ana" websites?', *Qualitative Research*, 7: 283–300.

Hepworth, J. (1999), *The Social Construction of Anorexia Nervosa*, London: Sage.

Hine, C. (2000), *Virtual Ethnography*, London: Sage.

Klump, K.L., C. M. Bulik., W. H. Kaye, J. Treasure and E. Tyson (2009), 'Academy for Eating Disorders Position Paper: Eating disorders are serious mental illnesses', *International Journal of Eating Disorders*, 42(2): 97–103.

Kozinets, R. (2010), *Netography: Doing Ethnographic Research Online*, London: Sage.

Lawrence, M. (1987), 'Education and Identity: The Social Origins of Anorexia' in M. Lawrence (ed.), *Fed-up and Hungry: Women, Oppression and Food*, London: Women's Press Limited, pp. 207–25.

Lupton, D. (1996), *Food, the Body, and the Self*, London: Sage.

MacLeod, S. (1981), *The Art of Starvation*, London: Virago.

McRobbie, A. (2009), *The Aftermath of Feminism: Gender, Culture and Social Change*, London: Sage.

MacSween, M. (1986), *Anorexic Bodies*, London: Routledge.

Malson, H. (1998), *The Thin Woman: Post structuralism and the Social Psychology of Anorexia Nervosa*, London: Routledge.

Markham, A. (1998), *Life Online: Researching Real Experience in Virtual Space*, Oxford: AltaMira Press.

Massumi, B. (2002), *Parables for the Virtual: Movement, Affect, Sensation*, Durham, NC: Duke University Press.

Optenet (2008), 'International Internet Trends Study', <http://www/optenet.com/mailing/pdfs/TrendReport.pdf> (accessed 25 May 2009).

Orbach, S. (1982), *Fat is a Feminist Issue 2*, London: Hamlyn.

Orbach, S. (1986), *Hunger Strike: The Anorectic's Struggle as the Metaphor for Our Age*, London: Faber.

Pollack, D. (2003), 'Pro-Eating Disorder Websites: What should be the feminist response?', *Feminism and Psychology*, 13: 246–51.

Probyn, E. (2000), *Carnal Appetites: FoodSexIdentities*, London: Routledge.

Royal College of Psychiatry (2009), *Eating Disorders: Key facts from the Royal College of Psychiatrists*, <www.rcpsych.ac.uk> (accessed 14 June 2010).

Chapter 9

Classification or Wonder? Coding as an Analytic Practice in Qualitative Research

Maggie MacLure

Preamble

When it comes to analysing their data, many qualitative researchers find themselves doing something called 'coding'. Broadly, this involves looking for pattern or order in a body of data – such as interview transcripts or field notes – by identifying recurring themes, categories or concepts. However although widespread, the practice of coding is not unproblematic. In this chapter I begin by discussing various ways in which coding offends, particularly against some of the key tenets of poststructural and post-humanist research, before sketching out some alternative engagements with data that are not bound by the structures and strictures of coding. Yet I do not conclude that coding should be abandoned as an analytic practice. I argue that there is a languorous pleasure and something resolute in the slow intensity of coding – an ethical refusal to take the easy exit to quick judgement, free-floating empathy, or illusions of data speaking for itself. More importantly, when practised unfaithfully, without rigid purpose or fixed terminus, the slow work of coding allows something other, singular, quick and ineffable to irrupt into the space of analysis. Call it wonder.

The critique of coding developed here is influenced by the work of Deleuze in that it prioritises movement, becoming, difference, hetero-geneity and that which exceeds 'capture' by language. In particular, the critique is animated by Deleuze's *The Logic of Sense* (2004), which pursues strange relations among language, bodies, things and ideas, and unsettles the orderly relationship between words and world posited by linguistics or by Platonic philosophy. More generally, the argument that unfolds below is influenced by Deleuze's critique of *representation* (e.g. 1994, 2004) – i.e. of that form of thinking that DeLanda paraphrases as 'typological' (2002: 18). Representational thinking categorises the world and establishes hierarchical relationships among classes – genus and species, category and instance, and so on. This is the same logic that regulates research coding, as I discuss below. Following Deleuze, I do not deny that the logic of representation is culturally and politically significant, and therefore a proper object of qualitative research. The logic of representation is, after all, 'the structuring process that constructs a liveable world around us … [producing] stable meaning and stable subjects to exchange it' (Lecercle 2002: 60). But I also recognise the movements of another logic identified by Deleuze, in which the world is not held still and forever separate from the linguistic or category systems that 'represent' it. This other logic is the logic of *assemblage*, in which objects, utterances, institutions, bodies and fragments relate in 'unholy mixture' (Lecercle 2002: 53) rather than orderly hierarchy. 'In assemblages', Deleuze wrote, 'you find states of things, bodies, various combinations of bodies, hodgepodges; but you also find utterances, modes of expression, and whole regimes of signs' (2007: 177). Later in the chapter I discuss some examples of the entanglement, or unholy mixture, of language and materiality, drawn from field notes made during a recent research project, a poem by Meredith Quartermain, and two fragments from the well-known Preface to Foucault's (1973) *The Order of Things*. I use these examples to build a concluding argument for coding as a particular kind of experimental assemblage, namely the construction of a cabinet of curiosities.

Coding

It should be noted that coding is not tied to one particular qualitative methodology. As an analytic practice, it can be found in approaches as disparate as grounded theory, multimodal analysis, critical discourse analysis, content analysis, and many different forms of ethnography. However, most versions of coding, whatever their provenance, involve: (a) a body of 'data' (interviews, field notes, responses to questions, documents, personal narratives, 'naturally occurring interactions', visual images, etc.); (b) a search for recurrence and pattern, through (c) naming and collecting (categorising); and (d) reduction of complexity through the assembly of data into superordinate categories or concepts.

It might be helpful at this point to include an example of conventional research coding. The following diagram shows the codes that were used in a study of women's narratives of their experiences of disability.

In this study, women's narratives of disability, in the form of transcribed interviews, were cut up into segments, compared for

(Duggan et al. 2008: 981)

resemblance to or contrast with other segments, collected together and renamed under codes, and rearticulated as 'nodes' in a structure of successively more general or higher-order categories. So, for example, the comment 'The way I get along with my life is I don't try to think about it' was coded as 'coping strategy-emotion focused' (node 3.4.1) (Duggan et al. 2008: 984). I have introduced this study here, not in order to do justice to its contents or arguments, but to highlight the structure that typically underlies and regulates coding. This example makes particularly clear the tree-like or 'arborescent' structure of coding, a point that is significant in my argument below.

It should also be noted that I am dealing specifically in this chapter with coding as practised within qualitative research. I sometimes refer to this as 'research coding' to distinguish it from other usages. I do not consider, except in passing, the important treatment of codes and coding in the work of Deleuze and Guattari (2004a, 2004b; also Deleuze 1971), in which coding is associated with *territorialisation*. Coding in this broader sense is characterised by Deleuze and Guattari as a matter of cutting into flows of difference and intensity to produce systems of meaning and order – systems that are never culturally or politically innocent, and which are by no means restricted to human or intentional activity. Deleuze and Guattari note that something, however, always exceeds or evades the action of coding, remaining illegible and unrecognisable by the prevailing code, and thus presenting a threat to order and stability. While I do not engage this broader, Deleuzian notion of coding directly, it is implicit in the arguments that unfold below, particularly at the points where I discuss that which escapes coding.

The Offences of Coding

I want to turn now to a critique of conventional research coding, and to consider how such coding conflicts with some key tenets of post-structuralist research approaches. Poststructuralism is a contested term which is resistant to definition or generalised description (Stronach and MacLure 1997).[1] However, by way of a thumbnail sketch, post-structuralism could be characterised in terms of an opposition to the rationalist, humanist worldview that is the (continuing) legacy of the seventeenth-century 'Enlightenment'. Poststructuralism anchors itself in a critique of reason, as the faculty that regulates the social and moral order, and challenges belief in progress as the inevitable result of scientific and philosophical rationality. Theorists reject the idea of universal truth and objective knowledge, asserting that truths are always partial, and knowledge always 'situated' – in other words, produced by and for particular interests, in particular circumstances, at particular times. Poststructuralism is also associated with the 'crisis of representation', in which language is no longer held to represent or reflect a pre-existing reality, but is inextricably implicated in the fabrication of realities. Finally, poststructuralism decentres and dis-assembles the humanist subject – the thinking, self-aware, truth-seeking individual ('man'), who is able to master both 'his' own internal passions, and the physical world around him, through the exercise of reason.

For poststructuralism, coding offends on a number of fronts. First, it positions the analyst at arm's length from 'her' data, encouraging illusions of interpretive dominion over an enclosed field, and making a cut between a centred humanist subject and the docile objects of her attention. Coding also undermines an ethics of responsibility, since it establishes and protects the 'panoptic immunity' of the liberal subject who is entitled to interrogate and dissect the lives and business of others, while preserving the privacy, intactness and autonomy of his (or her) own, 'secret' self (Miller 1988: 162).[2] Researchers code; others get coded.[3] In other words, coding does little to prevent the arrogation of interpretive mastery to the analyst, or to disturb the essentially colonial relation of researcher to subject – problems that have troubled qualitative inquiry for decades.

Coding assumes, and imposes, an 'arborescent' or tree-like logic of hierarchical, fixed relations among discrete entities (Deleuze and Guattari 2004a: 18; Barthes 1977). This tree structure can clearly be seen in the example from Duggan et al. (2008) above. This is the basic logic of coding, even if it is not always explicitly displayed in the form of a tree diagram. It could take the form of a table, a grid, or even just a list of themes. The logic can be applied to almost any phenomenon. So although the most common forms of data in qualitative research are written texts such as interview transcripts and field notes, anything can be coded – images, sounds, happiness. Even tears: Nelson (2000) classified adult crying into types such as 'healthy crying', 'crying for no reason' and 'prolonged or frequent crying associated with depression', together with types of 'inhibited crying' such as 'healthy tearlessness' and 'detached tearlessness', relating these to attachment styles and symptoms of clinical disorders. Barthes (1977) identified classificatory tree structures in some strange places: in the organisation of St Ignatius Loyola's *Exercises*; in the passions (810 of them) classified by the nineteenth-century utopian socialist Charles Fourier; and in the Marquis de Sade's rules for the orchestration of libertine practice – an 'erotic grammar' which Barthes describes as 'analogous to the diagrammatic "trees" proposed by our linguists: in sum . . . the tree of crime' (1977: 29).

This is part of the problem with research coding – the fact that the 'grammar' always pre-exists the phenomena under investigation. Things are condemned always to contract the same sorts of relationship to one another – genus to species, category to instance, general to particular, disposed according to relations of identity, similarity, analogy or opposition (Deleuze 1994). This is the logic of representation, which works, in Olkowski's words, to 'subsume all differences under the one, the same and the necessary' (1999: 185). Within the schema of representation, things are frozen in the places allotted to them by the structure that comprehends them – in the double sense of enclosing them, and of rendering them comprehensible. Coding does not allow that things might (will) deviate and divide from themselves to form something new. It cannot cope with difference in itself – as movement, change and emergence (Deleuze 1994). Instead, difference can only be 'represented' in terms of static relations among already-formed entities. Relatedly, the arborescent structure of coding designates all elements that are at the same level or node as of equal weight or significance; and unchangingly so. Coding does not recognise changing speeds and intensity of relation, or multiple and mobile liaisons amongst entities.

Coding also tends to take you 'away' from the data – from their detail, complexity and singularity. Indeed this is one of the primary aims of coding, as is spelled out in one methods textbook: 'Coding takes you away from the data – "up" from the data to more abstract ideas or categories. Coding will also take you "down" from the idea to all the material you have linked to it' (Richards and Morse 2007: 115). The data are sacrificed, offered up to the ruling idea. This is essentially a Platonic operation, as Deleuze describes it, of bringing things under the 'action' of the Idea (2004: 4). Coding exemplifies one of two 'dimensions' identified by Plato – the dimension of 'limited and measured things, of fixed qualities, permanent or temporary which always presuppose pauses and rests, the fixing of presents, and the assignation of subjects' (Deleuze 2004: 3). Coding is an operation, then, that drags fixed, hierarchical structure from the proliferated surface of life, cutting its flows into 'limited and measured things', and hanging them in bunches under their ruling Ideas. 'Limited things lie beneath the Ideas', Deleuze writes. But he also notes that something – a 'mad element' in language – always eludes the embrace of the Idea (2004: 4). I return below to consider this 'mad element' and how it might manifest in research coding.

For the moment, and continuing with this litany of offences: coding renders everything that falls within its embrace *explicable*. Barthes locates this obsession with meaning and explication deep within Western textual practices: 'the West moistens everything with meaning, like an authoritarian religion which imposes baptism on entire peoples' (1982: 10). Difference, chance and alterity struggle to free themselves from the clammy coating of causes and effects, reasons and hierarchy applied by Western rationality. Stewart, endorsing this statement by Barthes, argues that the appetite for meaning inherent in the 'ethnographic code' has affinities with the bourgeois code imposed by social workers and health professionals upon clients, such as the participants in Stewart's ethnography of a former coal-mining community in West Virginia.

She describes the ethnographic code as one that 'deploys practices of classifying, mapping, and interpreting meaning to imagine its object as a bounded symbolic whole with readable meanings and discoverable causes and explanations' (1996: 69). She is troubled by the similarity between her ethnographic 'discipline' that provides her with a 'safe distance' from her subjects, and the 'defensive disengagement' of social workers from their clients. Stewart wonders whether the ethnographic code and the social work code are both manifestations of a Western 'decontaminated mode of critique that inhabits a stable center of certitude by imagining itself above or outside its "objects"' (1996: 69–70).

Both codes, she suggests, involve a *forgetting* of cultural specificity, singularity, and the dense texture of things and words that are fabricated in people's everyday encounters with one another. However Stewart also notes that people have resources for evading or disrupting the disciplinary rage for meaning, by exploiting that which exceeds the grasp of rationality and its codes, to open a 'space of excess in which the physicality of cultural politics (vocality, tactility, touch, resonance) exceeds the rationalised clarity of "system" and transcendent understanding' (1996: 130). Stewart recommends, and enacts, an ethnographic practice of *unforgetting*. Such a practice involves attention to the excess and resistance of 'the anecdotal, the accidental, the contingent, and the fragmentary' (1996: 11).

Finally, and implicit in all of the foregoing: as an act of renaming, coding recodes that which is *already* coded by language, culture, ideology and the symbolic order. Massumi, after Deleuze, argues that these are all 'stop-operations' – secondary and derivative mechanisms for arresting the processual indeterminacy of movement and matter so that meaning, structure and order may transpire (2002: 7). As Massumi notes, this does not mean that coding and signification are false; or that social determination is a fiction. 'Grids happen', he remarks, continuing: 'social and cultural determinations feed back into the process from which they arose'. It is not a matter, then, of choosing process over position, or structure over change. These are 'inseparable', though movement and indeterminacy are ontogenetically prior, as 'the field of emergence' from which positions and codes emerge (2002: 8).

Coding can therefore be very effective (though this is not always so in practice) in charting the circuits of power, culture and knowledge through which order will have been produced out of difference. But it handles poorly that which exceeds and precedes 'capture' by language, such as the bodily, asignifying, disrupting (and connecting) intensities of affect. The unavoidably linguistic nature of coding – its trade in signs

– ignores the entanglements of language and matter, words and things. Materiality is endlessly deferred in a relay of signs (see Barad 2007; Hekman 2010).

'Rebel Becomings' (Deleuze)

I want to suggest that qualitative method needs greater attention therefore to that which coding misses – movement, difference, singularity, emergence, and the entanglements of matter and language. Deleuze, invoking Plato, glimpsed a second, non-representational dimension or tendency subsisting in language, hidden by the tremendous power of representation to cut into the flow of difference to bring forth stable referents, meanings and speaking subjects. As noted above, he calls this other tendency a 'mad element' or 'wild discourse' that slides over its referents and transcends its own limits, restoring language to the open potential of becoming. He asks:

> might there not be *two* languages and *two* sorts of 'names', one designating the pauses and rests which receive the action of the Idea, the other expressing the movements or rebel becomings? Or further still, is it not possible that there are two distinct dimensions internal to language in general – one always concealed by the other, yet continuously coming to the aid of, or subsisting under, the other? (Deleuze 2004: 4, emphasis added)

This wild discourse does not mediate anything. It does not refer outside of itself, or build towards some already-foreseen, higher, ideational fulfilment. And it does not emanate from, or attach itself to, an already-formed, phenomenological subject. It does not represent.

Analysis (if we want to continue to call it that) might dwell in those 'rebel becomings' that evade coding's capture and resist 'elevation to generality' (Smith 1995: 27). In the spirit of Stewart's (1996) practice of 'unforgetting', this would mean attending to those phenomena that qualitative research often prefers, or needs, to forget: for instance, fragments of 'data' that refuse to settle under codes or render up decisive meanings. Or speech-acts that obstruct the serious work of analysis, making it hard to break things up into categories and boil them down into themes – problematic acts such as mimicry, mockery, jokes, lies, insincerity, irrelevance, self-contradiction. We could focus on the irruption into data of those emissions that lie on the boundary of language and body, such as laughter, tears, snorts, shrugs or silences – not in order to recruit these to meaning and purpose within codes and categories, as in the study of crying mentioned above, but to note their disjunctive belonging to *both* language and body. In place of the cerebral comforts of ideas and concepts, or as well as these, we could acknowledge those uncomfortable affects that swarm among our supposedly rational arguments – moments of nausea, complacency, disgust, embarrassment, guilt, fear and fascination, that threaten to undo our certainty and our self-certainty by, again, allowing bodily intensities to surge up into thought and decision making. These gut feelings point to the existence of embodied connections with other people, things and thoughts, that are far more complex than the static connections of coding.

All these phenomena are unsettling – both in the field, where they often make us feel uncomfortable, and at the point of analysis and coding, if we can't find rational ways of accounting for them, other than counting them out as superficial or as accidents. It might be more useful, though, to treat these problematic phenomena as hot-spots – moments of productive *disconcertion*, to use Michael Taussig's (1993) term, that undermine the analyst's imperial self-assurance.

What might such moments of disconcertion look like? And, perhaps more significantly, what do they *do* to the basic economy of representation and coding? It may be helpful to consider some disconcerting moments that my colleagues and I experienced during a classroom ethnography of young children and 'problem' behaviour.[4] The aim of the research was to try to understand how and why some children earn a reputation as a 'problem' in their first year at school. The project was based in one reception class (4–5 year olds) in each of four schools in and around Manchester, in the North of England. The project team worked closely with teachers and other staff, visiting each school regularly, and making written and video observations of all aspects of school life, from the daily minutiae of classroom and playground activities to assemblies, concerts and parties (see MacLure et al. 2011).

Not infrequently, we were at a loss to know what to 'make' of an incident or a piece of data. One instance, which we have written about elsewhere, concerned Hannah, aged 5, who would not, or could not, utter her name during the morning ritual of taking the register (MacLure et al. 2010). Hannah's silence (but was it 'hers'?) sparked a kind of rage for explanation and meaning, as everyone sought to know *why* Hannah remained mute; what might have *caused* her silence; what it *meant*; whether or not it was *intentional*. The disconcerting force of Hannah's silence seemed to move outward in concentric circles to affect all those in her ambit – class teacher, classmates, other school staff, parents, and of course we too as researchers. The undecidable nature of Hannah's silence, hanging in some threshold between language and something else, brought interpretation to a standstill in a blizzard of unanswered questions.

We noticed this dynamic many times in the course of the project: a point at which interpretation seemed to falter or stutter, turning the rage for explanation back on itself in a kind of vibrating immobility. Or *impassibility*, to use Deleuze's word (2004: 109). Another instance concerned a child who had started to vomit each day as lunch time approached. Again, the school staff, and we ourselves, attempted to bring the vomiting, and the child, into the scheme of representation, assuming that it, or she, must 'mean' something. Everyone wanted the vomiting to be codable – a sign of something else: 'attention seeking'; 'immaturity'; 'lax parenting'; 'timidity' . . . But like Hannah's silence, the vomiting remained a point of indetermination between the materiality of the body and the abstraction of meaning, refusing to offer itself up either as signification or as 'mere' bodily process (see also MacLure 2011).

Moments of disconcertion such as these, where bodily matters resist translation into codes and significations, but at the same time seem to demand this, reveal the routine machinations of representation in education and research. They show how children's actions and affects are coded as instances of something more abstract – such as 'behaviour'. But these moments also allow us to think of the limits of rationality's reductive explanations of children, and to consider how the external world impinges on children, as on all of us, in ways that do not necessarily pass through language.

I have referred to these moments as 'disconcertion', but the affects that they sparked in us as researchers might equally be described as fascination, or exhilaration, even if none of these words seems quite right. Perhaps they are better caught in Massumi's (2002) lexicon of affect – as incipience, suspense, or intensity. Or even, though it seems self-aggrandising to describe it in this way, as the 'passion' of the event, which Deleuze describes as 'a sort of leaping in place of the whole body' (2004: 170). At any rate, we learned to welcome and pause at these moments, which could not be planned for, but emerged unpredictably in project meetings, or as surprises at the point of writing papers and articles. They were almost literally hot-spots, experienced by us as intensities of body as well as mind – a kind of glow that, if we were lucky, would continue to develop (cf. MacLure 2010: 282).

I would suggest that the act of dwelling in such moments and watching-making them grow like crystals, outwards from the edges (Deleuze 2004: 12), is part of an ethical obligation to relieve research subjects – especially, for our research, children – from the banality and the burden of the ethnographic and other codes that hold them in place (MacLure et al. 2011). The art historian Mieke Bal writes of the refusal to honour 'the fleeting pace that generates indifference' (1999: 65). It is imperative to slow down the facile machinery of interpretation so that it catches on the snags, the 'lucky finds', the marginalia and the odd details that fascinate the researcher and draw her into the weave of discourse, instead of allowing her to rise above it.

Nevertheless . . .

I do not conclude from all this that coding should be abandoned. This could never be possible in any case since, as I have suggested, all language, in its conventional, representational 'dimension', shares the fixative ambitions of coding. More than this, though, and despite all the foregoing, I want to argue in favour of coding as an analytic practice. Firstly, coding demands immersion in, and entanglement with, the minutiae of 'the data'. Even though the ultimate aim conventionally is to move 'away' from the data through abstracting, reducing or generalising, nevertheless, the entire architecture is built on a long, slow, familiarisation with the details. This involves a kind of experimentation or crafting as one sorts, labels and disposes items that – even allowing for the prior determinations of discourse, discipline or ideology – never fully pre-exist their formation *as* 'examples' of categories that are themselves still being shaped.

Moreover I think there is, or can be, a languorous, and not wholly cerebral pleasure in giving oneself over to the data. Maybe it's just me, but I enjoy that part of the research process that involves poring over the data, annotating, describing, linking, bringing theory to bear, recalling what others have written, and seeing things from different angles. I like to do it 'manually' too, with paper and pen, scribbling a dense texture of notes in margins and spilling onto separate pages. There's something about embodiment in all this, which turns me away from computer-assisted qualitative analysis programs such as nVivo, though I would not want to suggest that things have to be done in the old ways.

The process of coding is both active and passive – a matter of actively *making* sense yet also of accommodating to something ineffable that is already 'there'. The researcher is at this point a live conduit wherein the materiality of things, the struggle for concepts, one's 'shared entanglement' (Bal 1999: 30) with others, and with the uncut and unbounded totality of the data, can be *felt*. This recalls Deleuze's characterisation of coding as the cutting off of flows, mentioned above. Persons, according to Deleuze, are 'interceptors' of flows that precede and exceed their own predicament, and thus are operators (as well as products) of coding. 'A person is always a cutting off [*coupure*] of a flow ... a point of departure for the production of a flow, a point of destination for the reception of a flow, a flow of any kind; or, better yet, an interception of many flows' (Deleuze 1971).

It is only after one has come 'out' of the flow of coding, moved away and up from the data into the rarefied atmosphere of abstractions and generalities, that the humanist subject appears as fully and fatally cut off from 'the data' that she has cut up, and is therefore able to contemplate it as if it were laid out on/in a table. As long as one is 'inside' the *process* of coding, folded into movement and becoming, there is the possibility of a very different kind of engagement with data from the distanced contemplation of the table that is the arrested result of the process. The question of what one brings 'out' of the process will depend on how far one is committed to the overarching project of including all the data within an abstracting structure of categories and levels; in other words, how far one is willing to ignore the stuff that does not fit. In my own case, I usually stop well before a point of seeming 'saturation'. During the process of coding, some things gradually grow, or glow, into greater significance than others, and become the preoccupations around which thought and writing cluster.

Uncanny Taxonomies: The Logic of Assemblage

Coding is haunted by that 'mad element' that subsists in language. In order to produce its themes and meanings, coding necessarily attempts to suppress difference and alterity, inserting intervals between things that, prior to the insertion, did not exist individually and separately as such. The gaps between elements in the structure of coding are thus uncanny spaces where excess and disorder may be glimpsed and exploited to creative effect. Foucault memorably described the disturbing effects of taxonomic disorder in the preface to *The Order of Things*, in his much-quoted discussion of Borges' Chinese encyclopaedia, which categorised animals as:

> (a) belonging to the Emperor, (b) embalmed, (c) tame, (d) sucking pigs, (e) sirens, (f) fabulous, (g) stray dogs, (h) included in the present classification, (i) frenzied, (j) innumerable, (k) drawn with a very fine camelhair brush, (l) *et cetera*, (m) having just broken the water pitcher, (n) that from a long way off look like flies. (Foucault 1973: xv)

This is the groundless taxonomy of the heterotopia, where 'monstrosity' lurks alongside 'wonderment' (or perhaps they are the same thing) in the 'interstitial blanks' between categories, in an impossible (non) space that is completely other to the levels and structures of representation. This is 'a ceremonial space', Foucault writes, 'overburdened with complex figures, with tangled paths, strange places, secret passages, and unexpected communications' (1973: xix). The heterotopian space does not allow us the distance of contemplation: we are caught in its tangled paths and secret passages. It cannot be mastered or viewed in its totality from on high, as if laid out on an 'operating table'. Foucault exploits here the double sense of 'operating table', as the sterile and shadow-less place of analysis lit by a glassy sun, and also the *tabula*, the classificatory table that 'enables thought to operate upon the entities of our world, to put them in order, to divide them into classes, to group them according to names that designate their similarities and their differences' (1973: vxii). In other words, to code them.

Foucault suggests that heterotopias 'secretly undermine language', and that this is the source of their power to disturb.

> [Heterotopias] shatter or tangle common names, because they destroy 'syntax' in advance, and not only the syntax with which we construct sentences but also that less apparent syntax which causes words and things (next to and also opposite one another) to 'hold together' . . . heterotopias . . . dessicate speech, stop words in their tracks, contest the very possibility of grammar at its source; they dissolve our myths and sterilize the lyricism of our sentences. (1973: xviii)

This is, in other words, the 'mad element' that dwells in and alongside the order that language and coding produces – an uncanny order that allows language and matter to assume strange relations, in the absence of the linguistic glue that holds words and things together and apart. Many poets and artists have recognised the creative potential for disorder that insists in taxonomies. Consider for example André Breton's list of the kinds of objects that interest surrealists, which seems haunted by intimations of desire:

> a wild child's museum, knickknacks from insane asylums, a collection belonging to a consul made anemic by the Tropics, broken, mechanical toys, burned milk, steam organs, the odor of priests, corsets of black silk with leafy patterns, and glass bouquets of the flowers referred to in Shakespeare. (Breton quoted in Durozoi 2002: 1–2)

Breton's collection has a dream-like quality. It is a 'hodgepodge' of objects and fragments that one might not expect to find in the same 'table', mixing the organic and the inorganic, things and words. It is also synaesthetic, mingling smells, textures and colours.[5] It obeys the logic of assemblage, which Lecercle paraphrases as 'the logic of AND rather than INSTEAD OF', and which he associates with dreams and non-sense (2002: 60).

Meredith Quartermain's poem, *Matter 9: To Texture to Verb*, tangles with taxonomy too – in this case with the six basic categories from which Roget's great Thesaurus unfolds, of Abstract Relations, Space, Matter, Intellect, Volition and Affections. In Quartermain's poem, matter, words and ideas contract strange relations that shatter syntax and disarrange parts of speech.

Matter 9: To texture to verb

beached on the coast of specific gravity
at sea with fancy and sand for judgment
wonder steps on clams and mussels of metaphor
to skull and jaw, employing language to preposition.

To part in speech chalk and cheese, a dock
and a daisy – how very like a whale –
the moths, beetles, flies of Matter flutter
to harlequin Abstraction. Or vamp
the moods and tenses of Intellect. Then fidget Space
to veer, jibe, sidereal Volition
and shimmer Affection's galaxy of spasms.

Suppose to patchwork world, hands wings fins
hook in peculiar loops the arteries of eggs in nests,
the spawn of the frog in water
the stripes on the cub of a lion,
the spotted chicks of blackbirds –
hook the framework's splanchnology.

Suppose the tissue of matter is the change of matter,
its cleavage and strata – suppose we know what changes
changes sense.

It's touch and go with the cat-tribes and plumage of stuff,
this disparate desperate otherwise.
Yes, we know means eyes and antennae
weave tooth
or grain a home-spun woolly cotton.

To text, to specify –
a whole without coherence
to sprinkle terrain, a world-thing mixed –

pregnant with alloy, laced with entanglement,
and haunted with purity.

(Quartermain 2008: 26, permission to quote the poem in full kindly granted by Quartermain)

In the poem, classifications and distinctions such as abstract and concrete, noun and verb, body part and part of speech, matter and idea, animate and inanimate, text and tissue do not hold together by keeping themselves apart, according to the usual taxonomic discipline. Matter-words are clouds of flying creatures, bothering the other five capitalised, loftiest categories that preside over Roget's massive taxonomy (Affection, Abstraction, etc.) – fluttering, vamping, jibing and shimmering them in barely-grammatical fashion. Syntax is fractured and names are tangled in a manner that recalls Foucault's description, above, of the heterotopia. Nouns act like verbs for instance, as in the title of the poem, where 'verb', usually a noun, takes on the grammatical function of a verb. 'Fidget', 'veer', 'vamp' and 'shimmer', usually intransitive verbs, seem here to take direct objects. And it is not clear whether 'harlequin', verb-like, is harassing 'Affection', or whether, adjectivally, it is qualifying it – i.e., bestowing qualities upon it. Body parts, plants, invertebrates, insects, mammals, birds, geological formations, organs, sensuous surfaces and innards[6] are laced and tangled with words, clichés, and abstract ideas. This, again, is the logic of assemblage, where words do not uncomplicatedly represent things through the god-like administration of grammar.[7] Nor does the poem appear to invite a reading as *metaphor* – another hierarchical ruse of representation, in which one thing stands for or replaces another. While unexpectedly grand entities such as Affection, Space or Intellect are the objects of small, jumpy movements – jibing, veering, fluttering, etc. – we do not seem to be invited to read these metaphorically, as figures of something else. Not representation, then, but the 'unholy mixture' of assemblage: 'pregnant with alloy, laced with entanglement'.

Despite (or because of) its refusal to represent, a slippery sense moves in the poem. The repeated occurrence of the infinitive form of the verb ('to verb', 'to preposition', 'to veer', 'to patchwork', etc.) is also significant here. Deleuze associates sense with the infinitive form, as 'that which is not yet caught up in the play of grammatical determinations – an infinitive independent not only of all persons but of all time, of every mood and every voice' (2004: 245). Sense, for Deleuze inheres in propositions and is an attribute of states of affairs, but is not reducible to either of these 'sides'. Rather, sense is 'the boundary between propositions and things' (2004: 25). Things and propositions, bodies and words: taxonomies are supposed to keep these apart. But it is sense that traces the 'line-frontier' between them. Quartermain's poem spools out along that frontier, calling attention to the edgy vibrations of words and matter that are usually concealed by the structures of representation.

In *The Logic of Sense*, Deleuze often discusses things and propositions in terms of *eating* and *speaking*: 'things or propositions, to eat or to speak' (2004: 75). Speech issues from the depths of bodies, from the same organs that are involved in eating – the gut and the palate, the moist air of the lungs and the meat of the tongue – and is emphatically material. Yet as the incorporeal stuff of propositions, speech is ideational (cf. MacLure 2011). There is a striking example of a taxonomy where speaking and eating, words and things resonate to 'disconcerting effect' in another paragraph from Foucault's Preface to *The Order of Things*, one that is much less frequently quoted than the Chinese encyclopaedia:

> 'I am no longer hungry,' Eusthenes said. 'Until the morrow, safe from my saliva all the following shall be: Aspics, Acalephs, Acanthocephalates, Amoebocytes, Ammonites, Axolotls, Amblystomas, Aphislions, Anacondas, Ascarids, Amphisbaenas, Angleworms, Amphipods, Anaerobes, Annelids, Anthozoans. . . .' But all these worms and snakes, all these creatures redolent of decay and slime are slithering, like the syllables which designate them, in Eusthenes' saliva . . . It was certainly improbable that arachnids, ammonites, and annelids should one day mingle on Eusthenes' tongue, but, after all, that welcoming and voracious mouth certainly provided them with a feasible lodging, a roof under which to coexist. (1973: xvi)

Foucault considers this example to be more familiar and less 'monstrous' in its disconcerting effects than the Chinese encyclopaedia, since the latter has no conceivable 'ground' that could accommodate all its heterogeneous categories of animals, while Eusthenes' mouth provides a 'feasible lodging' for all the conjured creatures. Yet I would suggest that there is something distinctly disconcerting about the meeting of dictionary entries and their referents in Eusthenes' mouth – an uncanny effect that Foucault actually intensifies in his account of snakes and syllables slithering together in the saliva in Eusthenes' 'welcoming and voracious mouth'.

The data examples that I discussed above have this same quality of calling attention to the problematic of language and materiality that coding conceals. A child's silence that weighs nothing yet hangs heavy in the air with the solidity of a reproach; a child's stomach contents that issue from the mouth but cannot speak; yet are consulted, like an oracle, for signs; the gut feelings that slither in the dry affectual space of the research interview. It is not necessary to abandon coding to glimpse stranger relations than those of the tree or the table, because these strange relations are coding's uncanny 'other'.

Conclusion: The Wonder of Coding

Rather than working under the auspices of metaphors such as tree, matrix or table, perhaps we could think of coding as the ongoing construction of a cabinet of curiosities or *wunderkammer* (wonder cabinet). Assembled across sixteenth and seventeenth-century Europe, the cabinet of curiosities was a room or cupboard built to hold and display the collections of princes, merchants, scholars, apothecaries and priests. Crammed with the fruits of exploration, imperialism, technological advancement, scholarship, medicine and mercantile adventures at the edges of the known world, the cabinets held natural history specimens, optical instruments, mechanical toys, artworks, precious gems, maps, fragments of sculpture, strange objects, the stuffed carcases of exotic animals and anatomical anomalies (see further MacLure 2006). The cabinet of curiosities exhibits, then, the logic of assemblage, which the art historian Lugli defines as 'a syntax of unanticipated associations' (2000: 30).

Standing at the threshold of modernity and scientific rationality, such cabinets were 'liminal objects' (Mauriès 2002), informed both by the waning Gothic world of miracles, magic and relics, and by the growth of humanism and scientific reason. They bear witness, according to Lugli (1986), to collection as a form of *inquiry* – an open-ended experimentation with, and receptivity to, bodies of knowledge whose contours and sub-divisions were constantly shifting and expanding, and therefore always eluding the collectors' encyclopaedic ambitions. Stafford calls it a form of 'experiment with order and disorder' (2001: 7). In other words, the cabinets were attuned *both* to classification and to wonder, system and secret.

As with Foucault's Chinese encyclopaedia, the cabinet's contents were not laid out for contemplation at a distance, but were concealed in nested drawers, shelves, niches and boxes. Visitors were obliged to enter into this nested topography in order to answer the invitation to 'handle' its contents. Stafford argues that this compartmentalisation, concealment and framing of the contents created a multi-sensory experience in the user that she calls *intensification* (2001: 7). As a kind of exhilaration of the senses, intensification is affectually complex: learning, enchantment, perception, cognition and seduction are caught up in each other.

Perhaps we could think of coding, then, as just such an experiment with order and disorder, in which provisional and partial taxonomies are formed, but are always subject to change and metamorphosis, as new connections spark among words, bodies, objects and ideas. Such a conceptualisation would recognise coding, not as a static representation or translation of a world laid out before us on the operating table of analysis, but as an open-ended and ongoing practice of *making* sense. It would also recognise that the gaps and intervals that we make as we cut and code the flow of difference are possible openings for wonder. We need therefore to learn not to look away or to fear that which we can scarcely comprehend, or bear to comprehend, when 'subjects' refuse to submit to the discipline of coding, since those occasions might be the ones that open onto wonder.

This is an ethical as well as a methodological issue, since wonder necessarily disrupts the boundaries of power and knowledge that allow coders to maintain the enigma of their own self-certainty by rendering others legible. Wonder is a liminal experience that confounds boundaries of inside and outside, active and passive, knowing and feeling, and even of animate and inanimate. If I feel wonder, I have chosen something that has 'already' chosen me. Wonder is in this sense indissolubly relational – a matter of strange connection. It is moreover simultaneously Out There in the world and inside the body, as sensation, and therefore is distributed across the boundary between person and world. 'The experience of wonder', writes Greenblatt, 'seems to resist recuperation, containment [and] ideological incorporation' (1991: 17). Yet it connects and opens. Recognising the potential for wonder in the work of coding might therefore allow some temporary point of indecision on the threshold of knowing, from which something unexpected might issue.

Notes

1. Poststructuralism is associated with founding names such as Lacan, Derrida, Butler, Deleuze, Kristeva and Foucault. However, as noted, there is considerable contestation over who 'is' and 'is not' a poststructuralist, and there are very substantial theoretical differences among the various 'names'. The work of Deleuze would not, for instance, fit with certain aspects of the thumbnail sketch I have given. For discussions of poststructuralism, with particular reference to qualitative research methodology, see Stronach and MacLure (1997); St. Pierre and Pillow (2000); Lather (1991); MacLure (2003).
2. Miller was not referring to coding, but to the nineteenth-century novel and its role in producing the liberal subject of modernity.

3. One can of course code oneself. For instance Peshkin identified six different 'I's in a 'subjectivity audit' of his responses during fieldwork in a high school. The fact that one's 'data' is oneself does not disturb the essentially hierarchical relation between coder and data/subjects (1988: 18).
4. 'Becoming a Problem: How and Why Children Acquire a Reputation as "Naughty" in the Earliest Years at School'. Funded by the Economic and Social Research Council, ref: RES–062–23–0105
5. Foucault's reference, above, to the 'operating table' as the place where 'the umbrella encounters the sewing machine' (1973: xvii) itself invokes a surrealist assemblage. Foucault is here re-citing a celebrated phrase by Lautréamont, which Breton and the surrealists considered the perfect definition of the surrealist notion of objective chance: 'the chance encounter between an umbrella and a sewing machine on an operating table'.
6. 'Splanchnology' is apparently the science of the viscera.
7. 'I am afraid we are not rid of God because we still have faith in grammar' (Nietzsche 1982: 483).

References

Bal, M. (1999), *Quoting Caravaggio: Contemporary Art, Preposterous History*, Chicago: University of Chicago Press.

Barad, K. (2007), *Meeting the Universe Halfway: Quantum Physics and the Entanglement of Matter and Meaning*, Durham, NC: Duke University Press.

Barthes, R. (1977), *Sade, Fourier, Loyola*, trans. R. Miller, London: Jonathan Cape.

Barthes, R. (1982), *Empire of Signs*, trans. R. Howard, New York: Hill & Wang.

Best, S. and D. Kellner (1991), *Postmodern Theory*, New York: Guildford.

DeLanda, M. (2002), *Intensive Science and Virtual Philosophy*, London: Continuum.

Deleuze, G. (1971), 'Capitalism, Flows, the Decoding of Flows, Capitalism and Schizophrenia, Psychoanalysis, Spinoza', Cours Vincennes, 16/11/1971, <http://www.webdeleuze.com/php/texte.php?cle=116andgroupe=Anti+Oedipe+et+Mille+Plateauxandlangue=2> (accessed 14 September 2011).

Deleuze, G. (1994), *Difference and Repetition*, trans. Paul Patton, New York: Columbia University Press.

Deleuze, G. (2004), *The Logic of Sense*, trans. M. Lester with C. Stivale, London: Continuum.

Deleuze. G. (2007), 'Eight Years Later: 1980 interview', in *Two Regimes of Madness: Texts and Interviews 1975–1995*, revised edition, trans A. Hodges and M. Taormina, Paris: Semiotext(e), pp. 175–80.

Deleuze, G. and F. Guattari (2004a), *A Thousand Plateaus*, trans. B. Massumi, London: Continuum.

Deleuze, G. and F. Guattari (2004b), *Anti-Oedipus*, trans. R. Hurley, M. Seem and H. R. Lane, London: Continuum.

Duggan, C. H., K. J. Albright and A. Lequerica (2008), 'Using the ICF to Code and Analyse Women's Disability Narratives', *Disability and Rehabilitation*, 30(12–13): 978–90.

Durozoi, G. (2002), *History of the Surrealist Movement*, trans. A. Anderson, Chicago: University of Chicago Press.

Foucault, M. (1973), *The Order of Things: An Archaeology of the Human Sciences*, New York: Vintage Books.

Greenblatt, S. (1991), *Marvellous Possessions: The Wonder of the New World*, Oxford: Clarendon Press.

Hekman, S. (2010), *The Material of Knowledge: Feminist Disclosures*, Bloomington: Indiana University Press.

Lather, P. (1991), *Getting Smart: Feminist Research and Pedagogy With/in the Postmodern*, New York: Routledge.

Lecercle, J-J. (2002), *Deleuze and Language*, Basingstoke: Palgrave Macmillan.

MacLure, M. (2003), *Discourse in Educational and Social Research*, Milton Keynes: Open University Press.

Lugli, A. (1986), 'Inquiry as Collection', *Res* (Autumn): 109–24.

Lugli, A. (2000), *Assemblage*, Paris: Adam Biro.

MacLure, M. (2003), *Discourse in Educational and Social Research*, Buckingham: Open University Press.

MacLure, M. (2006), 'The Bone in the Throat: Some uncertain thoughts on baroque method', *Qualitative Studies in Education*, 19(6): 729–45.

MacLure, M. (2010), 'The Offence of Theory', *Journal of Education Policy*, 25(2): 277–86.

MacLure, M. (2011), 'Qualitative Inquiry: Where are the Ruins?', *Qualitative Inquiry*, 17(10): 997–1005.

MacLure, M., R. Holmes, E. Jones and C. Macrae (2010), 'Silence as Resistance to Analysis. Or, on not opening one's mouth properly', *Qualitative Inquiry*, 16(6): 492–500.

MacLure, M., L. Jones, R. Holmes and C. MacRae (2011), 'Becoming a Problem: Behaviour and reputation in the early years classroom', *British Educational Research Journal*, DOI:10.1080/01411926.2011.552709.

Massumi, B. (2002), *Parables for the Virtual: Movement, Affect, Sensation*, Durham, NC: Duke University Press.

Mauriès, P. (2002), *Cabinets of Curiosities*, London: Thames and Hudson.

Miller, D. A. (1988), *The Novel and the Police*, Berkeley: University of California Press.

Nelson, J. K. (2000), 'Clinical Assessment of Crying and Crying Inhibition Based on Attachment Theory', *Bulletin of the Menninger Clinic*, 64(4): 509–29.

Nietzsche, F. (1982), 'Twilight of the Idols' in W. Kaufmann (ed.), *The Portable Nietzsche*, Harmondsworth: Penguin.

Olkowski, D. (1999), *Gilles Deleuze and the Ruin of Representation*, Berkeley: University of California Press.

Peshkin, A. (1988), 'In Search of Subjectivity – One's Own', *Educational Researcher*, 17: 17–21.

Quartermain, M. (2008), 'Matter 9: to texture to verb', in *Matter*, Toronto: Bookthug, p. 26.

Richards, L. and J. M. Morse (2007), *Read Me First for a User's Guide to Qualitative Methods*, 2nd edn, London: Sage.

Smith, R. (1995), *Derrida and Autobiography*, Cambridge: Cambridge University Press.

Stafford, B. M. (2001), 'Revealing Technologies/Magical Domains' in B. M. Stafford and F. Terpak (eds), *Devices of Wonder: From the World in a Box to Images on a Screen*, Los Angeles: Getty Publications, pp. 1–109.

Stewart, K. (1996), *A Space on the Side of the Road*, Princeton: Princeton University Press.

St. Pierre, E., and W. Pillow (2000), *Working the Ruins: Feminist Poststructural Theory and Methods in Education*, London: Routledge.

Stronach, I. and M. MacLure (1997), *Educational Research Undone: The Postmodern Embrace*, Milton Keynes: Open University Press.

Taussig, M. (1993), *Mimesis and Alterity*, London: Routledge.

Chapter 10

Activating Micropolitical Practices in the Early Years: (Re)assembling Bodies and Participant Observations

Mindy Blaise

Deleuze's ontology is not a resting place; it is not a zone of comfort; it is not an answer that allows us to abandon our seeking. It is the opposite. An ontology of difference is a challenge. To recognize that there is more than we have been taught, that what is presented to us is only the beginning of what there is, puts before us the greater task of our living. We have not finished with living; we are never finished with living. However we live there is always more. We do not know of what a body is capable, nor how it can live. The alternatives of contentment *(I have arrived)* and hopelessness *(There is nowhere to go)* are two sides of the same misguided thought: that what is presented to us is what there is. There is always more. (May 2005: 172)

Recently, some in the field of early childhood have been inspired by the philosophies of Gilles Deleuze and Félix Guattari because they open up opportunities for inventing new ways of thinking about childhood, teaching and learning. This is significant because the dominant discourse in the field is rooted in developmentalism, which represents childhood, teaching and learning in overly simplistic ways. Instead of making room for the complexities of childhood, developmentalism reduces these to an either/or way of thinking. For example, children's gender/sexuality is seen as either masculine or feminine, children's play is understood as either concrete or abstract, and early childhood teaching is thought of as either developmentally appropriate or inappropriate. Instead of being curious about childhood and difference, developmentalism encourages teachers to determine, know and 'fix' what goes on in the classroom. Deleuze's ontology and philosophical concepts are useful resources for rethinking this over-simplification and restoring the complexities and nuances of child gender/sexuality.

Liselott Mariett Olsson (2009) and Hillevi Lenz Taguchi (2010) are two scholars who draw from the post-humanist philosophies of Deleuze and Guattari (1984, 1987) to offer new possibilities for early childhood. Their work is of significance because they connect post-humanist ideas with early childhood practices in order to challenge current ways of teaching and researching. They show how Deleuze's ontology of difference provides alternatives for understanding the field, and, as May asserts, 'there is always more' (2005: 172). Deleuze and Guattari's philosophy and concepts are central to Olsson's work. In her research with early childhood teachers she uses these ideas to challenge dominant ways of thinking about practice. She shows how movement and experimentation are already taking place in early childhood settings, and how they afford new possibilities for change in a field that works hard at evaluating children and their learning according to predetermined developmental standards. Lenz Taguchi's work is also influenced by Deleuze and Guattari, but she combines this with theories from feminist physicist Karen Barad (2007, 2008) to introduce what she calls an 'intra-active pedagogy'. Lenz Taguchi's research expands our understandings of the relational field by shifting our attention to the force and impact of the material world. Instead of focusing just on the relationality between humans, Lenz Taguchi's work illuminates intra-active relationships, those relationships that exist between all living organisms and the material environment.

Deleuze and Guattari's strange and at times counter-intuitive concepts help us to develop a postdevelopmental logic that recognises 'the world (is) composed of fields of difference' (May 2005: 115). Postdevelopmentalism is a term I have used to describe those practices that contest the narrowness of developmental discourses in early childhood by highlighting new ways to attend to the politics of difference (see Blaise 2005, 2009a, 2009b, 2010). This chapter continues to expand postdevelopmentalism by working with Deleuze and Guattari's philosophical concepts, as well as considering the material as an active agent in the construction of difference and reality. This chapter begins by experimenting with two new ideas, namely 'segmentarity' and 'micropolitics', for understanding research with young children as taking place in a relational field where connections are constantly made, remade and blocked.[1] Next, room is made for considering the material or nonhuman elements that compose the web of research encounters, the ways that these reveal gender/sexuality discourses and the implications this has for activating micropolitical research practices in the early years. This experimentation echoes Mazzei and McCoy's (2010) work, allowing me to rethink encounters with difference and the kinds of knowledges I created when conducting research in the early years.

While Olsson (2009) uses micropolitics and segmentarity to work with preschool teachers' efforts to regain movement and experimentation in their practice, I am curious how these concepts might ignite new potentials in gender/sexuality research, perhaps opening up the possibility of collective and intensive experimentation with difference. Using a Deleuzo-Guattarian-inspired postdevelopmental logic might change how we research child gender/sexuality. My experimentation begins by revisiting qualitative data from an evaluative study on multi-age grouping conducted with twelve early childhood professionals across three community-based childcare centres located in an urban Australian city (see Edwards, Blaise and Hammer 2009). This project aimed to determine different stakeholders' understandings of multi-age grouping and its associated issues. Data was sought that reflected the experiences and understandings of key participants involved in programme delivery, including parents, children, teachers and administrators. A variety of qualitative research methods were utilised to generate data, including focus groups, interviews, participant observations and photographic documentation. Teacher research was also employed as a key strategy for accessing the understandings of children and families. The study was conducted over an eleven-month period and included a five-month exploratory field investigation into multi-age grouping. These field investigations were carried out by early childhood professionals and they were supported by the research team through research workshops and field visits. I was the researcher who conducted these field visits. Not only did these visits provide participants with an opportunity to share their data and initial analysis with me, but I also used them to conduct participant observations of multi-age grouping. Whilst the focus of this project was on multi-age pedagogies and not children's emerging subjectivities, the following data shows how encounters with child gender/sexuality are always present while conducting research as a participant observer.

Encountering Gender/Sexuality: Child-bodies, Boobs, Hair, Earrings and Shoes

The following research vignette is presented at length because I am attempting to challenge rigid segmentarity (a Deleuzo-Guattarian concept discussed later), or the ways in which qualitative research is often re-presented. Usually, research vignettes are re-presented in small, discreet segments, followed by an analysis. Whilst this is a common methodological practice, it often limits rather than encourages different understandings or engagements with data, and in this case gender/sexuality.

An older (four-year-old) girl child-body is standing on a wooden plank that is approximately 80 cm off the ground and is preparing her body to jump towards the ground. I watch from the sidelines as the girl child-body bends her knees, clenches her hands into two fists while holding them by her side, and scrunches her face as she jumps up and then lands firmly with both feet on the tanbark. She begins to turn her girl child-body back towards the plank, but stops when she notices me. She slowly approaches me, pointing to my notebook, and asks, 'What's that?' I tell her that it is my field notebook and that I am writing down things that I see and feel. I invite her to look through it with me. Like a teacher, I point to the words and read aloud what I've been writing. I soon find out that this girl child-body is named Amanda and then ask her the names of the other child-bodies I've been observing. While pointing, Amanda says, 'That's Zoe, Madeline and Roland. Zoe is my little sister.'

A few minutes pass and seemingly out of nowhere, Amanda's girl child-body is standing at the side of my sitting woman adult-body. I wonder, where did she come from and how long has she been standing here? She is now leaning against my right arm and shoulder. She pushes her girl child-body closer to my woman adult-body. Soon her entire girl child-body is pressed against the side of my arm. She puts her hand on my shoulder and leans in close to my face. I keep my woman adult-body very still and my breathing slows down. If I turned my woman adult-body towards her, our faces would touch. Keeping my woman adult-body still, I carefully write down in my field notes, 'I am being looked at and this feels very odd.' Then, I jot down, 'Teachers? Parents?' I am wondering where the other teacher and parent adult-bodies are and what they might be thinking if they saw this. Did anyone notice this uncomfortable encounter between bodies, or is this just an everyday interaction that goes unnoticed by non-researching adult bodies?

While still studying my face, Amanda inches her girl child-body even closer, pressing one hand down on my shoulder while quietly asking, 'What's your name again?' Suddenly her eyes move towards my ears. She notices my red dangling earrings and takes her hand reaching for one them. My woman adult-body flinches and I am uncertain about what to do. I hold my head very still because I am not too sure about this four-year-old girl-body touching my earring. I am keenly aware of how quickly a gentle touch can turn into a tug, or worst a firm pull, ripping the earring down and through my earlobe. Amanda takes her index finger, and pokes my earring, making it swing back-and-forth. I can feel a slight tug on my ear lobe as the earring gently swings. I feel my woman adult-body slowly relaxing. Without turning my head, I move my eyes and catch Amanda's gaze with a smile. Amanda quickly looks away from me and focuses her attention back to the earring. She smiles at the earring and then gives it another poke. She looks at me, leans her girl child-body close to my face and softly says, 'I like them. They are pretty. You know, my mum has earrings.' I scoot my body away, trying to put some distance between our bodies and tell her again that my name is Mindy.

Zoe, Amanda's younger sister, appears and she too becomes fascinated with my earrings. Even though I have shifted my woman adult-body away from the girls, they have moved their sister child-bodies closer. All three bodies are touching. My woman adult-body is draped with sister child-bodies. Zoe moves her sister child-body to my other side. I am now trapped by two child-bodies, one on my left and the other on my right side. Like her sister Amanda, Zoe becomes fascinated with my earring and uses her finger to gently poke it. While keeping a hand on my shoulder, she pokes and watches the earring. Next, Zoe leans her girl child-body towards me, pushes my hair away from my face and tucks it behind my ear. Then, while cupping both of her hands together, she leans close to my ear and whispers, 'I like your earrings.'

Both sister child-bodies are still standing on the left and right sides of my sitting woman adult-body, and they are looking at me. My legs are stretched out and I tap my feet together, making a loud noise with my shoes. Zoe quickly turns and looks at my feet. She reaches towards them, but can't quite touch my shoes so she moves her child-body closer to my left foot. She squats, while reaching her hand out until she can just touch my shoe. She moves even closer and begins stroking it, as if it were a pet, saying, 'Nice shoe'. She looks at me, smiles and laughs. I let out a small laugh and smile back at her. At the same time, Amanda's girl child-body is leaning against my right shoulder, arm and side. She is asking me a series of questions about my earrings, such as, 'Where did you get them? Did your mum buy them for you? Did your boyfriend buy them?' She then starts stroking my hair, while saying in a soft voice, 'I really like your hair.'

Roland has now joined us. He pushes his boy child-body past Zoe's girl child-body, and grabs my breast. My researching woman adult-body quickly reacts by tensing and moving away. I push his hand away while saying, 'Hey!' When my woman adult-body moves, Amanda's girl child-body wobbles. She holds on tightly to my shoulder. I react by pulling my shoulder back, away from her hand, while saying, 'Ouch, that hurt!' At the same time, I am looking up from the floor, trying to see if there are any teacher and parent adult-bodies watching. For a slight moment I feel panicky. In my field notes I write, 'heart is racing'.

Micropolitics

In order to think differently about researching gender/sexuality in the early years, I am first going to focus on Deleuze and Guattari's concept of micropolitics and how this frames research within a relational field. A relational field includes what Deleuze and Guattari call 'transversal' connections, between bodies, ideas and the material, that allow for different rhythms and movements. It is through these encounters and connections that a micropolitics of difference is activated. Micropolitics are about the beliefs of both society (macro) and the individual (micro) and how these flows of desires produce difference. The molecular and molar, like the micro and the macro are not separate entities. A developmental logic wants us to separate the relationships between large and small-scale politics and claim the large-scale is more significant than what might be happening locally at the micro level, between researchers, those they research and the material. A micropolitics considers the small, everyday encounters as significant to the processes of change; as I will show later, even touching an earring can be significant. Just because a movement, action or encounter is small, does not mean it is insignificant. Taking a micropolitical stance has the potential to destabilise existing power relationships, and in the case of early childhood this is the dominance of developmental discourses. To act in a minor way is not to oppose the macro or political system, but to work within the local, or the early years classroom.

Understanding the early years environment as a relational field, where micropolitics occur, is not easy because it requires teachers and researchers to move away from a dominant developmental logic that persists in fixing gender in terms of binaries; locating children as innocent and naive, creating a linear relationship between sex-gender-sexuality and representing difference as negative. In order to challenge this very limiting way of understanding child gender/sexuality and to bring the relational field to life, a postdevelopmental logic is needed. Deleuze and Guattari challenge us to consider that we are all a part of the relational field and are composed, either individually or as groups, of various lines, which are in a constant state of movement. This dynamic rather than static understanding of the relational field forces us to move away from familiar ways of recognising and re-presenting children in terms of what kind of gendered or sexual being they are, to instead pay attention to the child-subject as a process of becomings that are enmeshed in active processes. Therefore, it is necessary to rethink the role of the participant observer from being someone who simply recognises and re-presents child gender/sexuality to someone who extends and opens-up child-subject becomings. One way this might be done is by engaging with these processes and recognising how micropolitical practices are embedded within them (Olsson 2009). This means that the researching female adult-body must *connect with* these processes, rather than working hard to document them, dismissing them as insignificant or shutting them down. Although the research vignette shows how I was beginning to wonder about my researching female-adult body, I was not connecting with micropolitical practices. Micropolitical practices begin with a radical rethinking of the researching space and the role of the researching female adult-body. To explore this, I will look at Deleuze and Guattari's concept of segmentarity, which is useful for pushing us beyond observing just individual, developmentally bound bodies by challenging us to rethink the social and relational field in ways that are not easily recognisable.

Lines, and Living a Segmented Life

Using the philosophical concept of segmentarity brings forth an understanding of child gender/sexuality and research in this field different to that suggested by a developmental approach. Deleuze and Guattari (1987) write about segmentarity in relation to the social, material and spatial when they examine how everyone and everything is structured, or segmented, from different directions and in different spaces. While they explore the superficiality of dominant segments, they develop this concept further by examining how binary, circular and linear modes of segmentarity function. Their examination of these modes allows for a different understanding of the social child (and adult) to emerge. Segmentarity is neither a static behaviour, nor does it imply that something is waiting to happen. Instead, binary, circular and linear segments are interactive and function in both rigid and supple ways. Through their interactions, they can become entangled or bound up with one another. And yet, these different modes can quickly change direction, force or intensity according to one's perspective. As the following sections show, these modes challenge us to rethink gender/sexuality in the early years classroom.

Binary Segments

A binary segment is found within the common dualistic frameworks of social identities, such as gender, race, social class, etc. In the early years classroom the social field is segmented by age (adult-child), gender (male-female), roles (researcher-researched), body size (big-small), mobilities (walkers-crawlers), relationality (human-nonhuman), activities (outdoor play-indoor play), etc. They are rigidly segmented when these categories are understood as fixed. For instance, child-bodies are allowed to jump-off the plank because the activity occurs outdoors, adult-bodies do not use the play equipment because it is built for small child-bodies. This rigidity becomes supple when markers or segments blur, such as when the girl child-body jumps off the play equipment, an activity usually done by boy child-bodies. Although there seems to be a clear distinction between the rigid and supple, they actually coexist by overlapping, mixing with each other and becoming entangled. Deleuze and Guattari name these lines of rigid segmentarity 'molar' (macro), and all other lines 'molecular' (micro). The molecular lines are part of the micropolitical and they work in detail, operating in small groups. It is underneath the rigid lines, drawn by positivist science, that 'lines of flight' can be found. The early years classroom is criss-crossed by lines of flight and it is on these lines where something new, including the acceptance and production of difference, can be made. These lines of flight happen through the everyday encounters children have with each other, and with ideas, materials and adults. While researching gender/sexuality in the early years, multiple encounters with difference occur between researching female adult-bodies and girl and boy child-bodies and it is through these encounters that an embedded and embodied subjectivity is made possible (Braidotti 2006).

Circular Segments

Life is also segmented in a circular fashion. This concept recognises that we are not fixed beings, but instead belong to several larger groups, and are part of different networks. These networks change depending on the circumstances, which opens up new possibilities for connecting with others. For instance, the multi-age childcare centre is made up of child-bodies of different ages. Although age, particularly within education, has been considered a rigid binary line, at this centre children are not separated (or segmented) by age. Instead, other factors, such as siblings, personalities or availability are used to determine how child-bodies are grouped. The Wombat room is made up of baby, toddler and five-year-old child-bodies. These child-bodies are grouped this way because there might be sister bodies, who are two and four years of age, or three-year-old child-bodies who use the service only on Tuesdays and Thursdays. Depending on the time of day or the curricular activity, a child who is part of the Wombat room might have opportunities to play with other children from the Goanna and Koala rooms. In other words, although Amanda and Roland are segmented by different ages and families, they are also part of the childcare centre and part of room-groupings within that. If they live in the same neighbourhood, then they might belong to yet other segments. Even though Amanda and Zoe are different ages, they are segmented in a circular fashion because their bodies might be physically located at the same time in the Wombat room. However, in the morning, Zoe may find the finger painting interesting or she might want to play with the girls who are already stringing beads at the table. Outside, Amanda's four-year-old girl-body interacts with baby and toddler-bodies that are crawling, falling, wobbling and sitting. Some bodies are white, and others are brown. These circular segments intersect with each other, and also with binary segments. Segmentary lines provide various opportunities for bodies, ideas or materials to connect. It is when and how these lines connect that open up possibilities for collective experimentation between bodies, ideas and materials.

Linear Segments

The final segmentary is the linear segment, indicating a unidirectional movement from one segment to the next. Research encounters I have with children happen on the chronological line. Each segment on this line is an encounter I have with children and, in turn, a matching segment on another line is an encounter they have with me. The philosophical concept of segmentarity, including the various lines and arrangements that are possible, is helpful for thinking differently about the relational field. As we bear in mind that all of these lines are intersecting and cutting-across each other, these concepts help us consider the complexity of this researching space. It is through these movements that multiple desires and differences are connected as well as blocked. Circular and linear segments can begin to blur, as well as collapse into binary segments. One of the problems with binary segments, as Deleuze and Guattari would see it, is that they have become overcoded, or had too much attention paid to them, thereby losing their dynamic ability to quickly come together and move apart. 'Lines of flight', however, are considered the most interesting kind of line because they move across boundaries, making new connections and carrying with them the possibility of creating something different (Deleuze and Guattari 1987; Renold and Ringrose 2008).

Trying to locate and identify these lines once and for all is not the spirit of working with Deleuze and Guattari's philosophy and concepts. Instead they provide resources for rethinking the social world in which we research and live with others, and in this case how my researching female adult-body researches and coexists with various child-bodies.

As a researcher, it is easy to document and state what is, but it is more difficult to move towards grasping the 'more' that May refers to, and these philosophical concepts are useful resources for appreciating that. Engaging with a Deleuzo-Guattarian concept of segmentarity is just one way in which we might begin to consider the multiplicities of actions in the relational field, rather than reducing this (developmentally) to one story about what is going on. It is an intentional move away from reductive representations of what is happening while researching, directed instead towards a different understanding of reality, an opening up of possibilities, rather than a closing down of what is, and helping us become comfortable with the uncertainty of *the more*.

As my encounters with gender/sexuality in the field will show, micropolitical movements are already happening in the early years. Practising a micropolitics involves scrutinising the lines that make up the relational field, focusing on their capabilities, and noticing their interventions (Houle 2005). However, appreciating the processes of lines might not be enough to activate micropolitical practices that can productively engage with difference. A different kind of research process is needed and, as MacLure suggests, this might be found in research methods that work with materiality and engage 'with new forms of relationality that makes for diversity, affect, and conflict' (2010: 5). The following section shows how making room for the material, the nonhuman and affective physicality is possible and might be one way of engaging with relationality and difference while researching child gender/sexuality.

The Material, the Nonhuman and Affective Physicality

Recent criticisms claiming that poststructural research focuses primarily on language and discourse for knowledge production, while neglecting material or nonhuman forces, have encouraged a different way of attending to gender/sexuality (Alaimo and Hekman 2008). Scholars who are beginning to include the nonhuman in their research include Lenz Taguchi (2010) and Hultman and Lenz Taguchi (2010), as they work with an intra-active relational materialist approach in order to understand how the field of early childhood includes relations with the nonhuman. A relational materialist approach takes into account the material and nonhuman and understands the child as emergent in a relational field. Post-humanist concepts, such as difference, differenciation, intra-activity, the in-between, etc., open up new options for showing how nonhuman forces contribute to children's becomings (Hultman and Lenz Taguchi 2010). Their analysis of photographic images from a preschool playground inspired me to revisit data, attending to material and nonhuman forces, including my researching female adult-body.

Several examples of the material or nonhuman are found in the data presented above, including the plank that child-bodies used for jumping, a field notebook utilised to record observational notes, or my hair and shoes. Revisiting the data with an intentional focus on the material – my 'breasts' and 'hair' as parts of my segmented researching female adult-body; those red dangling earrings – reveals different understandings of the relational field. I am curious how bodies, gender/sexualities, and the material are activating a micropolitics of difference, either separately or all at once. Encounters with difference cannot usually be planned, although we sometimes try to provoke them, and they occur when you least expect it. I did not wear the red earrings with the intention of enticing girl child-bodies to make contact with my female adult-body. Nor did I plan for a boy child-body to grab my breast. These were unpredictable and awkward moments, and yet to many who work in early years settings they are considered common or mundane interactions with children. Rather than letting these encounters pass unnoticed, they can be thought of as in-between spaces where lines of flight and emergent becomings are possible. Both my breasts and earrings, at different moments, were constitutive forces that sparked molecular moments or micropolitical practices.

Neither my breasts nor earrings have agency on their own. But these material or nonhuman differences offered certain possibilities in relation to several child-bodies. The material or nonhuman provoked children's desires, including Amanda's and Zoe's potentially quite different desires for femininity. For example, the red earring sparked conversations about boyfriends, and my hair and shoes caused a physical response. Roland's desire to engage in a form of sexual masculinity, might have been provoked by child- and woman-bodies in different ways, as we notice that Amanda's child-body was ignored, but my woman-body was grabbed. Some might argue that these forces or encounters with gender/sexuality are found within the hegemonic heterosexual matrix (Butler 1999), especially when we consider the kinds of femininities that Amanda and Zoe seemed to be desiring or the masculine discourse that Roland appeared to be enacting in relation to my female adult-body. However, this way of thinking tends to conceptualise desire as negative, rather than a productive force. Instead of considering Amanda and Zoe's interest in the red earrings based on wanting to imitate a particular 'adult'-like form of femininity and sexuality, we can reconsider their desires as an effect of material, human and nonhuman bodies connecting (Deleuze and Guattari 1987). From this perspective, it is through connections with different bodies that difference and desires are produced, and in this case the girl child-body. In other words, both the red earring and my female adult-body offer possibilities for collective experimentation with difference through these encounters with the girl and boy child-bodies.

Although these desires might constitute one line of flight, there are others we can find. For instance, when Amanda's girl child-body was standing beside my sitting woman adult-body and leaning against my right arm and shoulder, my body remained still. My body neither reacted by scooting away nor did it turn towards and embrace the girl child-body. Field notes indicate that I was uncertain about what moves to make and wondered about the gaze of other adults. These thoughts were related to a moral-panic discourse that is a reality for adults working in early childhood. As others have written (Tobin 1997; Johnson 2000), the discourses of child development, childhood innocence and sexuality impact on the ways in which adults physically engage with children. In that moment of uncertainty, I could feel the moral-panic discourse working as it prevented me from acting. Amanda could have walked away, but instead she presses her girl child-body against my researching female adult-body *and* then puts her hand on my shoulder *and* leans in close to my face, *and* studies my face, *and* inches her girl child-body closer, *and* presses down on my shoulder, *and* then quietly asks, 'What's your name again?' We are engaging with difference, but it is Amanda's curiosity, rather than mine, that is keeping this line of flight alive.

Another line of flight is made possible through the overlapping of multiple bodies, the nonhuman and the material. For instance, the red earrings keep the girl child-bodies engaged as they repeatedly return to them, even after I have shifted my adult-body away. It is possible that I have physically moved my female adult-body away as a strategy for escaping flows of desires, which were making me uncomfortable. It is gender/sexuality, as encapsulated in the earrings, shoes and hair, that opens up the relational field as the girl child-bodies continue their micropolitical acts. My uncomfortableness with these multiple child-bodies, and in particular the boy child-body, is blocking lines that have the potential for creating something new. Interestingly, it is the girl child-bodies that are most persistent. My female adult-body strongly reacts to the boy child-body's display of masculine sexuality, which has power due to the macropolitical processes of male adult-bodies in society. Overall, a developmental perspective would probably fail to consider these encounters as related to difference or gender/sexuality.[2]

And in failing to do so, the potentialities of these encounters and what they might produce are missed.

Although the encounters between my researching female adult-body and the boy child-body are a manifestation of age and gender/sexuality, a postdevelopmental logic would see them as encounters of reactive and active forces driven by desires. First, the engagement with gender/sexuality is not just between my female adult-body and a boy child-body. Other girl child-bodies are part of the social and relational field. The boy child-body uses male sexuality to push past Zoe's girl child-body and grab my breast. The moment when adult/child and female/male bodies meet is when active and reactive forces collide. But in this relational field, it is impossible to know for certain how these forces might impact on other child-bodies. For instance, what are Amanda and Zoe learning about gender/sexuality or what desires might have been ignited? If active forces have the potential to affirm, rather than block, productions of difference (Deleuze 1983), then how might a micropolitics take active forces on board? Instead of relying on a developmental logic that would instantly assume the older and bigger researching adult-body is the only active force capable of activating a micropolitics, it might be more productive to appreciate how small child-bodies can affirm difference. It now becomes important to remember that a micropolitical practice includes making room for not just the material and the nonhuman, but for *the more*, including all bodies in the relational field.

Considering bodies as constitutive forces changes how we understand the teaching and researching space. Instead of an adult researcher interacting with children, or children becoming distracted by earrings or breasts, the material brings together different lines and forces, and different connections are made within and between humans and non-humans. The material helps us to understand *the more* in the relational field, rather than simply what is. I hadn't in any way foreseen Amanda and Zoe's interest in the earring. Since there is no way of predicting absolutely the limits of what the earring or my female adult-body can do or makes possible, it is important to engage with these bodily intensities long enough so we can see what might happen. The moment contact happens, between humans and the nonhuman (in this case my breasts and earrings), a different kind of knowing is produced, and this is done collectively. Amanda's interest in and engagement with the earring troubles the traditional division between humans and the nonhuman, between Amanda and the earring, between the earring and me, between the researcher and the researched. In other words, the material has the potential to blur the boundaries between researcher/researched, human/

nonhuman, gender/sexuality and makes room for something *more*, such as new connections and becomings.

Attending to the material would be one element in a postdevelopmental logic that begins to disrupt binary and dualistic thinking. However, by missing, ignoring or reacting to the material, we fall back into developmental understandings of difference. This was most evident when a boy child-body encounters the researching female adult-body. It was the negative difference between adult/child, femininity/masculinity, gender/sexuality that caused me to react to the boy child-body. Deleuze (1994) considers negative difference as a product of dualistic or binary thinking, and proposes a difference without an opposite or negative. Developmentalism is built on these negative differences. I would argue that bringing both segmentarity and the material into the discourse disrupts dualistic and binary logic, which is a product of developmentalism. This is not to say that anyone, particularly women, must let themselves be touched freely. Rather, it is about being aware of how our reactions, whatever they are, are part of the micropolitics of that space.

Activating Future Experimentations

Although my researching feminised adult-body provoked child-bodies, it was the child-bodies that activated micropolitical practices. For instance, Amanda and Zoe's encounters with my body, including when they leaned on me, tucked my hair behind my ear, patted my shoes and poked my earring, were turning me into the researched. The earring seemed to activate several micropolitical practices, but instead of working with them, I was reluctant to follow this line of flight. My reluctance might have blocked some lines, but these girl child-bodies were capable of turning this over *and* over *and* over. It was girl child-bodies who kept the flows of desires moving, not my researching female adult-body. These micropolitical acts, initiated and carried out by child-bodies, are another example of disrupting developmentalism because this perspective does not consider young children capable of such movements. Molar and molecular lines met when girl child-bodies were researching my female adult-body. The researching girl child-bodies were segmenting my body as they examined, leaned on, touched and poked separate parts of or extensions of my body. In these encounters, segmentary lines were functioning in both rigid and supple ways and it was the girl child-bodies, in relation to the nonhuman and the material, that were turning the binary rigid segment upside down.

My experimentation with segmentarity, micropolitics and materiality has helped me consider how researching child gender/sexuality in the early years can be enacted in ways that appreciate and engage with difference from a postdevelopmental stance. Working with Deleuze and Guattari's philosophical concepts is useful for rethinking bodies not as discrete and separate entities, but as processes that are constantly on the move and never complete. Examining bodies as processes shifts the focus of participant observations from the body towards relations 'in-between' bodies and linkages between different kinds of bodies. This shift helps reconfigure adult- and child-bodies by challenging common developmental boundaries placed around the body, such as adult/child, boy/girl, older/younger, researcher/researched, etc. These boundaries are blurred further by experimenting with participant observations while researching child gender/sexuality. For example, if it is always the micropolitical that produces or erases difference, it seems important to consider how bodies are always in process through lines, connections and linkages in the relational field. Whilst there are several micropolitical practices at play in the above vignette, one that is useful to consider is the moment when I encountered Amanda's curiosity in my body. Her curiosity overturned the researcher/researched relationship in her close examination of my body, femininity and materiality and in her questioning of my actions. Amanda activated a micropolitical practice and I could have extended it by seeing what possibilities it suggested. I could have asked, 'What do you need from me right now? Do you have other questions?' Another example of micropolitical practices occurred when my researching female adult-body was sitting on the floor, leaning up against the wall, and girl child-bodies were standing on my right and left side, draping their girl child-bodies on top of mine. Although I wrote about my anxieties, I wonder what these encounters were like for Amanda, Zoe and Roland. I could have activated a micropolitics by asking them what it was like to drape their girl child-bodies over mine. Was it intense, comforting or nice? I might share with them that it made me uncomfortable, which would then generate a new line of flight. I might have missed that moment, but I believe that the act of revisiting these encounters with gender/sexuality can be a belated way of activating a micropolitics of difference. If my aim is to work with difference in a way that allows for lines of flight and a politics of becomings, then I will need to (re)assemble bodies within participant observations. In doing so, different kinds of moves or practices will be required of me, other participants and materials.

Enabling the conditions for such experimentations means first rethinking how we understand the social and relational field of researching, and the role of bodies in this work. A micropolitics enables singular and local connections (Surin 2005), while also encouraging a different style of thinking. It produces further differences and further worlds. These encounters with gender/sexuality are contingent and productive. However, we never know the eventual outcomes of our encounters or relations, but Deleuze and Guattari suggest that our curiosity and willingness to think differently could transform our research and teaching practices, and the molar and molecular politics that accompany them.

Notes

1. It should be noted that I began writing this chapter with the intention of limiting the number of philosophical concepts I would explore. However, I soon realised that this is an impossible task because each concept leads into many others *and* connects with another *and* another *and* another. In *Dialogues*, Deleuze comments on how the conjunction 'and' can be used to produce an expansive way of thinking rather than a more closed, either/or logic (Deleuze and Parnet 2002).
2. Valerie Walkerdine's (1990) earlier research shows how preschool children and their teachers are produced through gendered power relations. In particular, her research illuminates how child-centred pedagogy and developmental notions of childhood sexuality render teachers powerless. We see this when two four-year-old boys rely on patriarchal discourse to constitute their female teacher and a three-year-old girl as powerless objects of male sexual discourse. This was one of the first empirical studies that questioned developmental logic and the role it plays in making childhood sexuality invisible.

References

Alaimo, S. and S. Hekman (2008), 'Introduction: Emerging models of materiality in feminist theory' in S. Alaimo and S. Hekman (eds), *Material Feminisms*, Bloomington: Indiana University Press, pp. 1–19.

Barad, K. (2007), *Meeting the Universe Halfway: Quantam Physics and the Entanglement of Matter and Meaning*, Durham, NC: Duke University Press.

Barad, K. (2008), 'Posthumanist Performativity: Toward an understanding of how matter comes to matter' in S. Alaimo and S. Hekman (eds), *Material Feminisms*, Bloomington: Indiana University Press, pp. 120–54.

Blaise, M. (2005), *Playing it Straight! Uncovering Gender Discourses in the Early Childhood Classroom*, New York: Routledge.

Blaise, M. (2009a), 'Revolutionising Practice by Doing Early Childhood Politically' in S. Edwards and J. Nuttall (eds.), *Professional Learning in Early Childhood Settings*, Rotterdam: Sense Publishers, pp. 27–47.

Blaise, M. (2009b), 'What a Girl Wants, What a Girl Needs: Responding to sex, gender, and sexuality in the early childhood classroom', *Journal of Research in Childhood Education*, 23(4): 450–60.

Blaise, M. (2010), 'Creating a Postdevelopmental Logic for Mapping Gender and Sexuality in Early Childhood' in S. Edwards and L. Brooker (eds), *Engaging Play*, Buckingham: Open University Press, pp. 80–95.

Braidotti, R. (2006), *Transpositions: On Nomadic Ethics*, Cambridge: Polity Press.

Butler, J. (1999), *Gender Trouble: Feminism and the Subversion of Identity*, 2nd edn, New York: Routledge.

Dahlberg, G. and P. Moss (2009), 'Foreward' in L. M. Olsson, *Movement and Experimentation in Young Children's Learning: Deleuze and Guattari in Early Childhood Education*, New York: Routledge, pp. xiii–xxvii.

Deleuze, G. (1983), *Nietzsche and Philosophy*, trans. H. Tomlinson, New York: Columbia University Press.

Deleuze, G. (1994), *Difference and Repetition*, trans. P. Patton, New York: Columbia University Press.

Deleuze, G. and C. Parnet (2002), *Dialogues II*, trans. H. Tomlinson and B. Habberjam, London: Continuum.

Deleuze, G. and F. Guattari (1984), *Anti-Oedipus: Capitalism and Schizophrenia*, trans. M. Seem, R. Hurley and H. R. Lane, Minneapolis: University of Minnesota Press.

Deleuze, G. and F. Guattari (1987), *A Thousand Plateaus: Capitalism and Schizophrenia*, trans. B. Massumi, Minneapolis: University of Minnesota Press.

Edwards, S., M. Blaise and M. Hammer (2009), 'Beyond Developmentalism: Early childhood teachers' understandings of multi-age grouping in early childhood education and care', *Australasian Journal of Early Childhood*, 34(4): 55–63.

Houle, K. (2005), 'Micropolitics', in C. J. Stivale (ed.), *Gilles Deleuze: Key Concepts*, Montreal: McGill-Queen's University Press, pp. 88–97.

Hultman, K. and H. Lenz Taguchi (2010), 'Challenging Anthropocentric Analysis of Visual Data: A relational materialist methodological approach to educational research', *International Journal of Qualitiative Studies in Education*, 23(5): 525–42.

Johnson, R. (2000), *Hands Off! The Disappearance of Touch in the Care of Children*, New York: Peter Lang.

Lenz Taguchi, H. (2010), *Going Beyond the Theory/Practice Divide in Early Childhood Education: Introducing an Intra-active Pedagogy*, New York: Routledge.

MacLure, M. (2010), 'Qualitative Inquiry: Where are the ruins?' Keynote presentation to the New Zealand Association for Research in Education Conference, University of Auckland, 6–9 December 2010.

May, T. (2005), *Gilles Deleuze: An Introduction*, Cambridge: Cambridge University Press.

Mazzei, L.A. and K. McCoy (2010), 'Introduction: Thinking with Deleuze in Qualitative Research', *International Journal of Qualitative Studies in Education*, 23(5), 503–9.

Olsson, L. M. (2009), *Movement and Experimentation in Young Children's Learning: Deleuze and Guattari in Early Childhood Education*, New York: Routledge.

Renold, E. and J. Ringrose (2008), 'Regulation and Rupture: Mapping tween and teenage girls' resistance to the heterosexual matrix', *Feminist Theory*, 9(3): 313–38.

Surin, K. (2005), 'Micropolitics', in A. Parr (ed.), *The Deleuze Dictionary*, Edinburgh: Edinburgh University Press, pp. 162–3.

Tobin, J. (1997), *Making a Place for Pleasure in Early Childhood Education*, Yale: Yale University Press.

Walkerdine, V. (1990), *Schoolgirl Fictions*, London: Verso.

Chapter 11

Researching the Pedagogical Apparatus (*Dispositif*): An Ethnography of the Molar, Molecular and Desire in Contexts of Extreme Urban Poverty[1]

Silvia M. Grinberg

> The great ruptures, the great oppositions, are always negotiable; but not the little crack, the imperceptible ruptures, which come from the south. We say 'south' without attaching any importance to this. We talk of the south in order to mark a direction which is different from that of the line of segments. But everyone has his south – it doesn't matter where it is – that is, his line of slope or flight. (Deleuze and Parnet 1987: 131–2)

The end of the century has taught us to conceive of our life as a torrent of crisis and change, uncertainty and instability: subjects and institutions are dismantled and disappear; hypotheses of de-subjectivation and de-institutionalisation serve to define that which, by its very nature, escapes definition. Crisis, uncertainty and change have become the organising statements of our lives in the world to such a degree that, at present, they constitute the most certain aspect of our lives. The call to change, to become subjects in a permanent state of transformation and adaptation are the specific and most stable features of the society in which we live. Indeed, in recent years we have become so accustomed to speaking of crisis and uncertainty that they have come to seem like objective data about a given reality. Here, with Deleuze and Guattari, we understand that 'given' reality to be a sort of displacement and codification of the flows of desire that capital both creates and fears. It is in this context that I will discuss the results of ethnographic research on what Deleuze called our actuality. That is, the current. As Deleuze so rightly pointed out, '*the current* is not what we are but rather we are in the process of becoming' (1992a: 164). And this is where the notion of apparatus offers a particular way of studying the present, in so far as it entails an attention to both sedimentation and actualisation:

> apparatuses, then, are composed of the followings elements: lines of visibility and enunciation, lines of force, lines of subjectification, lines of splitting,

breakage, fracture, all of which criss-cross and mingle together, some lines reproducing or giving rise to others, by means of variations or even changes in the ways they are grouped. (Deleuze 1992a: 162)

Significantly, an interrogation of the current entails a vision that veers away from universals in order to approach apparatuses as multiplicities in which processes in formation operate. Thus, the study of *dispositifs* – here of the pedagogical apparatus – means an analysis of series, of lines that come together but also come apart, collide, escape. And it is these series that we encounter in our fieldwork. After years of crisis and reform, in empirical work we often come upon situations that we do not know how to respond to or describe (Deleuze 2005), but that are increasingly palpable. These situations call for a vision capable of approaching this un-known. That means giving up any attempt at or pursuit of universals that might explain and suture our interrogation. Instead, what interests here are these folds, juxtapositions and splittings: the unexpected, that which challenges understanding. It is not only a question of assuming a theoretical commitment with an author, of looking for Deleuzian concepts in the field, say, but of embracing a vision that offers ways of grasping the current. In the words of Mazzei and McCoy, the challenge 'is not merely to "use" select metaphors presented by Deleuze and Guattari (e.g., nomadism, rhizome, lines of flight, smooth and striated spaces) and to illustrate these metaphors with examples from data, but to think with Deleuzian concepts in a way that might produce previously unthought questions, practices, and knowledge' (2010: 504).

In this framework, this chapter will discuss these dynamics in terms of the research being conducted from a poststructuralist ethnographic perspective (Jung-ah Choi 2006; Youdell 2010) in contexts of extreme urban poverty in the Buenos Aires Metropolitan Area. I propose, with Deleuze, an approach to the empirical that relinquishes the universal without that implying any sort of relativism. Indeed, it is the universal 'which needs to be explained . . . The One, the All, the True, the object, the subject are not universal, but singular processes' (Deleuze 1992a: 162). And that singularity is precisely what is of interest to ethnographical work. The singular in the empirical is not the individual, but the event, the case, such that the processes of making a political map of an individual, a group or a society are, at core, not that different since an individual is that field of singularities (Deleuze and Parnet 1987). So it is in this framework that I will describe, through the notion of the pedagogical apparatus, the way the State regulates these territories as well as uncodified flows, the molar as well as the molecular. It is in the space between these two terms that subjects, especially young people at school, inhabit their concerns and desires and, to use the words of Deleuze and Guattari, the process of reterritorialisation takes place. Thus, the event is the making of history in the present, which is not the same thing as lived experience, which drowns young people in a universal and/or makes them into discrete individuals. The ethnography I propose here consists of the study of the form events assume in this configuration, and hence their detours and broken historicity. Ethnographic fieldwork in this frame enables us to approach the apparatus in its singularity: the process of regulation, the conduct of conduct as well as the lines of fissure and fracture, taking account of the molar, the molecular and the desire.

Thus, on the basis of an empirical investigation, I intend to describe the lines that, since the late twentieth century, have characterised the pedagogical apparatus in contexts of extreme urban poverty in the framework of what Deleuze called 'societies of control'. What matters here is to understand the torrent of permanent crisis as the very logic of capitalism (Deleuze and Guattari 2004a). The concept of 'management societies' (Grinberg 2008) is used to refer to the logics that characterise the actual rationality of the government of populations (Foucault 2006; Rose 1999; Rose, O'Malley and Valverde 2006), beyond the logic of discipline described by Foucault. We live in societies where subjects and institutions have been called upon to manage themselves in order to become innovative and responsible, as well as adaptable and flexible, where change is the constant of existence in the world.

Deleuze has been a point of theoretical and methodological departure as well as arrival. The Deleuzian framing opens research to something different that would not otherwise be possible. I embarked on this fieldwork after years of work on government documents (Grinberg 2008). Working with documents has a number of peculiarities, among them a certain degree of coherence when it comes to analysis, which vanishes instantly when it comes to fieldwork. In the daily practice of this research what I have come upon is traces of that which is in the process of becoming. The territory is constituted between uncodified flows and the regulation and organisation of those flows. Thus, after months in the field, when everything seems to be an ungraspable tangle, Deleuze and Guattari have enabled an approach to understanding 'reality' that is, in fact, multiple and hence does not allow for univocal or binary readings. Doing research means experiencing striated, discordant and/or juxtaposed realities that take the form of rhizomes. And just when it seems that one has come to grasp a process, a new line opens up, problematising it. If this is true of research in general, it is, as we shall see over the course of this chapter, particularly true of research in contexts of extreme urban poverty. So, doing ethnographic research requires interrogating processes of subjectification, the dominant as well as the little cracks, the imperceptible ruptures, the emerging forms of knowledge, the rationalities that manage to take hold as well as the struggles and resistances experienced on a daily basis, with their complexities and multiple contradictions. It requires interrogating the ways that these processes are experienced, finding the various depths, logics and layers that social life entails. This means exploring the multiplicities and folds of daily life and work, of how people live, operate and generate life; the heterogeneous, diffuse, contradictory and juxtaposed forms that take shape and intersect in the field and that come before us like a puzzle that it is impossible to complete.

Here, I will specifically address schools located in the neighbourhoods of the Buenos Aires Metropolitan Area commonly called shantytowns. I will discuss the pedagogical apparatus in hyper-degraded urban territories (Davies 2007), paying particular attention to processes of subjectivation and resistance. It is important, then, to describe forms of State regulation as well as uncodified flows of desire as they appear in these urban territories. In the words of Tamboukou, 'resistance is immanent in *dispositifs* of non-juridical models of *power ... lines of* flight and *becoming* are immanent in *agencements*' (2010: 693). It is, then, crucial to heed the life force of the population, the ways the subjects of the neighbourhood – especially the young people – inhabit and exist in these neighbourhoods and institutions, and their concerns and desires, as well as the regulation and codification of these urban flows. In other words, what I will attempt to provide is a cartography of processes of deterritorialisation and reterritorialisation (Ringrose 2011). Finally, while this research focuses heavily on the school and, hence, the pedagogical apparatus, it is my belief that it would be possible to draw a similar political map of any other institution.

Studying the Pedagogical Apparatus: The Methodological Relevance in Deleuze's Terms

The first issue that arises when working in situations as complex as these is the impossibility of finding a single way to understand the manifold school processes as they take place in educational institutions in shantytowns. Hence, I would like to begin by recounting something that I experienced during my first visit to one of these schools.

I start out greeting the principal, who speaks of the problems that the school faces: 'The problem with this community is that the students only come to school to get the certificate that gives them access to subsidies and welfare plans; their parents don't look after them.' At this moment, a teacher walks in and says, 'The school is like a daycare center.' She goes on: 'These kids couldn't care less; they have no interests, poor things, they get no stimulation at home.'

Minutes later, while standing in the schoolyard at recess, a fourth grader asks me suspiciously, 'Who are you? What are you doing here?' I answer, and in turn I ask her, 'And what are you doing here?' She stands right in front of me, looks me in the eye and, with an expression that seems to say 'I don't understand the question', shrugs and says, 'I'm here to learn.' (Field notes 2011)

In the field of education, much work has been done on modes of domination. Many studies speak of how teachers' disdainful images and assessments of students from underprivileged sectors anticipate expulsion from school.[2] The situation described above could be understood in terms of that reading; indeed comments like those fit nicely with many studies in the field of the sociology of education. But, here 'the question is not whether a particular concept is "true", but whether it works, and whether it opens up the range of possibilities in a given situation' (Hickey-Moody and Malins 2007: 2). So, what is interesting here are not the teachers' and administrators' disdainful characterisations but the response of the nine-year-old girl.[3] Her words suggest that there is something else that is crucial: power relations, and the creation and transformation of the pedagogical apparatus, of practices of creativity and struggle. Yet, as stated above, reality is juxtaposed, and it is not a question of placing blame or allocating responsibility. The school acts as a place of multiple and intersecting demands that exceed both the task of the teachers and the task of the students. The disjunctures that take place in schools every day are what condition the very possibility of pedagogical bonds and, therefore, the ability of this girl to do what she has come to school to do: learn.

Thus, after that visit something became clear: it was not going to be enough to evidence the workings of practices of domination. I had come upon (and I continue to come upon) a nine-year-old girl with desires and interests. So a first issue arose: what was at stake was the unexpected. Every day teachers come upon this 'unexpected' element that questions the categories with which they think about and approach students and their families. This is precisely where a Deleuzian vision enriches the ethnographic reading. It is in the complexity of the everyday, particularly in the banality of the everyday (Deleuze 2005), that the work of Deleuze is capable of grasping the unexpected, not only by providing concepts that allow us to begin to understand what is and/or is not in the process of becoming, but also by inviting us to create concepts (Deleuze and Guattari 1997). This is because the unexpected always appears alongside the creation and the actualisation which, as Deleuze points out, all apparatuses entail. And this is one of the most striking things about doing research with Deleuze in mind. Precisely where nothing is expected of students and their families, or of teachers and indeed these schools in general, is where we come upon desiring machines. We come upon a viscous reality, a reality juxtaposed with lines of force, practices of codification as well as decodification. This reality must be read as multiple on a theoretical level and comes before us as a set of multiplicities. In Deleuze's texts, there is a tension between the forces of stratified power relations and the forces of what is in the process of becoming, of subjects in action, in struggle. The molar force as well as the molecular force: lines of sedimentation as well as lines of actualisation (Deleuze 1990).

Studying pedagogical apparatuses means approaching forces in a constant state of tension. And in relation to all apparatuses (*dispositfs*) it is important to distinguish between what we are and what we are becoming, the current.[4] Thus, there are lines of sedimentation but also 'lines of breakage and fracture. Untangling these lines within a social apparatus is, in each case, like drawing up a map, doing cartography, surveying unknown landscapes' (Deleuze 1990: 155). As Ringrose points out, Deleuze and Guattari 'also recast the meanings and possibilities of human desire complicating the psychoanalytic theory of lack via symbolic laws . . . toward a corporeal theory of action and becoming for "mapping" cartographies of flows and particles energy that disrupt repressive regimes' (2011: 614).

Although there could be a number of different explanations for the situation at the school, what is most relevant here is a discussion of the terms of the research being performed. Specifically, a discussion of the difficulties related to the theoretical and methodological problems confronted in trying to study schooling processes, working with subjects who come together and yet fail to come together. Doing research in education is particularly complex when it attempts to evidence not only processes in the making, but also a set of processes that are open *per se*, that constitute a wager, like the act of shooting an arrow in a certain direction so that someone else might pick it up and shoot it in another direction (Deleuze 1998). This is the ethical and political force of Deleuzian research to think differently (Hickey-Moody and Malins 2007; Ringrose 2011). And this is because educating means coming upon life forces, wills, the lines of creativity and actualisation, but also the archive, of which Deleuze speaks in his discussion of the notion of the apparatus. It is a sort of surplus value, as Deleuze would say, that is subtracted from the statements that are made in these schools every day. Indeed, if there are lines of sedimentation, it is because there are other lines that escape and create. When the nine-year-old girl says 'I'm here to learn', it can be understood as one of the micro-ruptures, the small fissures, of which Deleuze speaks.[5]

What matters, then, is mapping these lines of subjectivation: the processes as they are experienced and/or produced by subjects, the lines of force in a territory, understanding that differences are not produced between the macro and the micro,[6] but rather between 'distinct systems of reference, depending on whether it is an overcoded segmented line that is under consideration or the mutant quantum flow' (Deleuze and Guattari 1987: 221). It is not a question of great movements, but of ruptures that intersect and combine, some of them giving rise to others through variations or even mutations in the *dispositifs*. Subjects are not just standing around waiting for what has been planned for them to happen. 'Everywhere there are mix-ups to sort out: the productions of subjectivity escape from the powers and forms of knowledge [*savoir*] of one social apparatus [*dispositif*] in order to be reinserted in another, in forms which are yet to come into being' (Deleuze 1992a: 157).

Desire and Abjection: Mapping Molecular and Molar Forces

The Urban Flows

Urban life constitutes one of the clearest examples of the crystallisation of management logics. In Deleuze's description of control societies, he states that, 'It is true that capitalism has retained as a constant the extreme poverty of three-quarters of humanity, too poor for debt, too numerous for confinement. Control will not only have to deal with erosions of frontiers but with the explosions within shantytowns or ghettos' (Deleuze 1995: 181). In this context, education has ceased to be a space for the normalisation of conducts to become a space for clustering homogeneous populations. In the shantytowns of regions like Latin America, we come across these frontiers, these flows from the outskirts of the city, on a daily basis. These are urban flows that, as we shall see, cross the borders of the shantytown and generate nuclei of instability as well as the constant molar search for regrouping and territorialisation.

Undertaking fieldwork from a Deleuzian perspective exposes certain power relations immersed in other power relations: sets of microdeterminations, attractions and desires. 'Good or bad, politics and its judgments are always molar, but it is the molecular and its assessment that makes it or breaks it' (Deleuze and Guattari 1987: 222). First off, though, it is important to bear in mind the exponential growth of shantytowns after years of social and economic crisis.[7] Indeed, in the late 1970s, the area that is described here was practically uninhabited. By the end of the twentieth century, this vast area was already densely populated, and in 2001,[8] as a result of yet another crisis of flexible capitalism, the population grew dramatically. As part of these processes a new subject appeared in the city and in schools – *cartoneros* – one who would take to the streets to rummage in the trash in search not only of food but also of materials like paper, cardboard and/or metals that could be sold.

In just a few months' time, approximately[9] 40,000 *cartoneros* began circulating around the city. Significantly, the mass media used the word 'invade' to describe this situation.[10] From one day to the next, people who lived in shantytowns came out with their carts in tow and *invaded* the city. It was no longer a question of the unrest that might occur in the shantytowns; they were now in the city streets. In this context, the *tren blanco*[11] which made it possible to enact a form of order was created. This train put an end to a situation where the *cartoneros* with their carts full of trash would travel alongside common passengers. It also served to allocate a territoriality to the *cartoneros* who, by definition, wander through the city.

It is in this context that, during a discussion of the various possible topics that could be addressed in a documentary video on daily life in the neighbourhood, a thirteen-year-old student who during the day goes into the city to *cartonear*, states:[12] 'We could make one about cartoneros, about the bullet train. . .'. In response to my startled look about the possible connection between a bullet train and his daily life, he says, 'that's right . . . tren blanco *is a bullet train*'.[13] Significantly, at the time of this discussion amongst the students there was much talk in the mass media about the creation of a high-speed train service, a 'bullet train,' which would entail, among other things, a multimillion-dollar investment. Thus, this young man's ironic comment not only suggested a possible topic for the video but also an unexpected image of what he experiences on a daily basis. Furthermore, his idea gave the video a political slant through the use of humour. Indeed, this humour is highly threatening, or even provocative. As Deleuze and Guattari point out, the axiomatic always has to face these provocative flows even while it codes molecular lines and renders escape apparent.

Desire and Abjection at School: Always Being at the Border

Starting in the late twentieth century, the schools located in these urban contexts – many of which were created during those same years as a result of the growth in the shantytowns' populations – became centres that served a wide range of purposes. Under management logic, they have to act like NGOs, formulating projects to raise funds. This is because, like the neighbourhoods in which they are located, the schools in these urban territories display signs of urban decay and poverty, and to meet the needs of school administration like building maintenance and the procurement of teaching materials they must seek their own sources of funding in the form of social plans and programmes, and so forth (Grinberg 2011).

The school buildings are highly precarious due to a combination of poor original constructions and quick deterioration. One group of students commented that 'last year we painted the school . . . with money from our parents'. There is evident deterioration of the infrastructure – walls, windows and chairs, etc. – that seriously compromises the teaching and learning experience of which the nine-year-old girl spoke. Furthermore, fixing the building depends on the parents' good will. Thus, the community's molar and already sedimented form of empowerment (Rose 1999) has left the schools at the mercy of an impossible circle of civic virtue. The school, in this sense, is a direct effect of these times of community virtuousness and empowerment.

After weeks of meetings with various organisations active in the neighbourhood, a committee decides to organise a week-long campaign geared towards keeping the block in which the school is located healthy. Specifically, in this campaign the students, along with the neighbours, will collect the trash on the street in order to demonstrate what it would be like to live on clean streets. Significantly, the school is located on a dirt road and, even when it has not rained for several days, it is muddy. (Field notes 2011)

This is why school life is a constant back-and-forth whose administration is akin to a juggling act (Grinberg 2011). Things are just allowed to carry on until a fire is started or someone starts yelling very loud.

There is grave institutional inadequacy when it comes to dealing with the vast range of problems, conflicts and needs that appear on a daily basis. The fate of the neighbourhood, of the schools, staff, students and their families, depends on individual will and on what the sum of those wills is capable of doing. This is not due to the absence of the State, but rather to the ways that it makes itself felt in these urban spaces. The territory entails a multiplicity of lines of force that converge, split and collide. Public utilities in these territories are irregular: trash collection, for instance, which in the rest of the city happens daily, here requires the active involvement and management of the neighbours, even though this neighbourhood is part of the same city, and exists under the same government. School 'improvement' is also 'irregular'.

At the beginning of the school year, a construction project to improve the school building gets underway. After two months of construction, the computer lab is still unusable. Now, it is up to the principal to get angry enough so that the construction company in charge of the project returns to the school to finish its work. Meanwhile, neither teachers nor students can use that room, and they have no idea when they will be able to. (Field notes 2011)

Thus, what began as the State fulfilling its obligation to maintain and improve the school premises has become a sort of whirlpool of new and ever greater responsibilities to be assumed by individual subjects. A Deleuzian vision is crucial to re-reading these situations, away from simple binaries like health-disease or presence-absence towards perceiving the ways in which the State is present at a distance and to interrogate how undertaking school, when always on the border, might actually happen.

In these neighbourhoods, the shift of tasks and responsibilities onto individual subjects generates a response that ranges from virtuousness to powerlessness. But when powerlessness sets in, the school space quickly becomes a territory of dispute between teachers, students and families. The attitude of teachers often ranges from a sort of militant devotion to abject fear,[14] expressed as complaints about the deficiencies of students and their families.

I know and have worked with a lot of teenagers from shantytowns. Many of them get out because, as I have said, they decide to study, to stay at home and study instead of going out to play or drinking on the corner. You know what I mean? And those kids have a future. I know a lot of people who used to live in shantytowns and are now businesspeo-ple, teachers; they have gotten out. And they have nice cars and houses. (Teacher at the school, 52 years old)

Teachers often find it difficult to communicate with their students, whether in informal dialogues or in the classroom. This means classes are often riddled with confusion that sometimes leads to listlessness, disputes and/or refusals to participate. Indeed, it often means the molar negation of the interest of students and their families, but also of the teachers and classes where, for all intents and purposes, students do not perform any of the tasks requested of them.

The teacher writes an exercise on the blackboard and tells the group what they have to do. At that very moment, some of the students take their notebooks out of their backpacks, others turn around to ask a classmate what they have to do, others stare out the window and so . . . the hour is up and only two have actually been doing the work; others have been talking to their classmates or sitting there silently with their notebooks closed, not doing anything. The teacher answers a question from a student while telling another kid to sit down and, in the midst of all this, an assistant comes in to bring the snack that they have at recess. Towards the end of the hour but before recess, the teacher starts to say that those who have not done their work cannot go out during recess. The students look at her and laugh. (Fifth grade class, fifteen students in the classroom)

Of course, there is no reason to be upset about not getting to go out for recess, since this class was recess and the next one will be as well. A first and simple reading would maintain that this is the case because the students don't take an interest in anything; it would codify these flows as a simple manifestation of the students' indifference. A Deleuzian approach challenges this interpretation (interpretosis). It offers an alter-native way to see flows and to understand the generalised listlessness which often seizes the classroom. The conditions in which school life is undertaken – living on the border – the fact of having been left to one's own devices, puts teachers as well as students in very delicate situations where, in the age of management, school life operates according to a logic of letting do.[15] Indeed, it is common for students in the classroom to go from doing nothing to actively participating. For teachers, these situations are very difficult to resolve or even to understand, and they end up being read in terms of abject fear.

Thus, the vision of these urban spaces as abject, no-go spaces (Rose and Osborne 1999), spaces that should be avoided entirely, is also applied to the school and its students. In terms of the students, it is expressed in the words of the teachers like those cited above when they come to deem teaching itself impossible. It is likely that the loneliness the teacher refers to in statements like 'Parents send their kids to school but don't take care of them', and 'They are home alone all day', reflects what the adults in these schools feel and experience on a daily basis as well, adults who have endured processes of change, crisis and reform that have rendered their task unclear and made it very difficult to approach and establish bonds with students. This is expressed in multiple and contradictory statements like 'Let's do something for these kids', 'Nothing can be done with these kids', 'These kids cannot be taught ... they won't participate,' etc. Though they may seem contradictory, these statements aptly characterise the pedagogical apparatus and the way teachers inhabit these urban spaces. Words that vacillate between euphoria and depression (Erehnberg 2000) should come as no surprise, since the working conditions of teachers form an integral part of this anguish. A teacher told us that she once got the days of the week mixed up and took the wrong bus. After travelling for almost an hour, she ended up at the school she was supposed to be at the following day.[16] This sort of disorientation constitutes an integral part of this sense of 'always-being-on-the-border' that characterises the pedagogical apparatus in these urban spaces in the age of management.

The question now is how these readings of need operate. Deleuze and Guattari challenge the seeing and interpreting of this as simply negative deficit and abjection where we understand desire as negative and lack. The abject, as Deleuze and Guattari point out, is not a molar need in the subject but 'the *molar organization* [that] deprives desire of its *objective being*' (2004: 34, italics in the original). This is a significant point. Nihilism and need are the privileged terms used to describe (not only, but especially) young people who live in shantytowns. 'A total lack of enthusiasm', one teacher says. If that phrase is considered in the terms proposed by Deleuze and Guattari, need and total absence could be read in relation to molar organisation, to capitalism: need is organised, prepared.[17]

Faced with images of apathy, laziness and the negation of the future, these students speak of their interests and aspirations as well as their doubts; they know the conditions in which they live and how those conditions are an obstacle to realising their desires. Yet, all of these students consider school a means of escape, a place that offers a promise for the future. Below is a fragment of an informal conversation with four students from the school:

Y: I'd like to become a teacher, a nursery school teacher.
R: What about you, Horacio?
H: I want to be a chef.
R: And did your brothers and sisters finish school?
H: The only brother I have who is at the university now is studying law. He went to school here. He finished and he is at the university in Drago . . .
Y: You see, here we are now saying we are going to go to the university, and then when we are older we are going to be in the street. I don't have that much self-confidence. I don't have so much faith in myself.
R: Why don't you have faith in yourself if you have never once had to repeat a year?
Y: I have heard so many people, so many kids say that they were going to study and they never had the chance . . . They don't have enough money to study. Maybe tomorrow I won't have enough money to be able to study . . .
I: I say I would like to do this, that, and the other but who knows what I'll be up to tomorrow, right? I might not have enough money to study . . . And I don't have that much faith in myself. That's why I'm not so interested in all that. That's why I just listen, because I have seen people, kids, who say, who said, that they are going to study to be a teacher or whatever, and when they are older they are living in the street or something. They don't have enough money to study, that's why I am not all that interested.
R: So you would like to but you are afraid of being disappointed?

Viewed through the Deleuzian understanding of desire, there is nothing in the students' words that makes us think of laziness or a lack of interest. Indeed, in their hopes of finding in education the possibility for a future, they renew the modern promise of education. This vision of a better future does not imply denying the conditions in which they live, but rather figuring out how to balance their lives today with their desires and aspirations. As Deleuze and Guattari state, there is no fear of need but rather concrete recognition of the difficulties faced in order to realise desires. Desires whose hope for realisation Western societies have placed in the educational system since the nineteenth century.

Hence, readings of nihilism and need can be understood in terms of the notions of the apparatus, the lines of light which distribute the visible and the invisible, and affirmations (énoncés) over which differential positions are distributed (Deleuze 1992b); in others words, practices geared towards the overcodification of threatening flows and, therefore, of subjects denied any ability to desire. Nonetheless, the young people born in these urban spaces work through their hardships differently, and this is a central part of the analysis of the apparatus. The words of these young people cannot be confined to a space between negation and need. They involve something extra and, in my view, crucial because issued from another perspective, one that revolves around neither romantic woe nor disenabled desire. Subjects with hopes, desires and aspirations are read as abject. As Ringrose points out (2011), through the molar organisation of desire in this assemblage, subjects are constituted as lacking, depriving them of the legitimacy of their desires.[18] So, what is it that defines the apparatus' lines of actualisation? Desiring machines, we could respond quickly, on the basis of our experiences with these young people. By emphasising the affirmative and productive nature of desire, Deleuze and Guattari not only take issue with psychoanalysis but also construct a conceptual support that allows us to think of desire not as what is yielded by repression but as a productive force in and of itself. They state that 'If desire is repressed, it is because every position of desire, no matter how small, is capable of calling into question the established order of a society: not that desire is asocial, on the contrary' (Deleuze and Guattari 2004: 121). If these descriptions speak not only of these young people and their needs but also of the negation of them as subjects with desires, it is because that desire is disturbing. But they are also the object of abjection. It is not a question of denying the difficulties these young people face, but of inhabiting desire. In a twofold operation, they express their aspirations and affirm life and the neighbourhood in which they live without falling into romantic readings of a reality that, as they themselves point out, undermines their hopes. In other words, we find ourselves with lines of affirmation that constitute tiny, sometimes imperceptible, breakages, where desire becomes threat and object of the dynamic of the molar, of nihilisation. Thus, in the face of a management logic that leaves schools in an unanchored back-and-forth, the struggle of the students and even, with all their ambivalence, the teachers, consists of insisting, in the face of nihilisation and abjection, that they steadfastly keep searching, keep desiring.

Closing Notes

If, as Deleuze (1992b) says, we belong to certain apparatuses and operate within them, then what we have spoken of in this chapter are lines of sedimentation and actualisation, or lines of creativity, as they are manifest and intersect on a daily basis in schools in contexts of extreme urban poverty. Through Deleuze, I have approached the study of the pedagogical apparatus on the basis of the ethnographic as a means to grasp the current. Studying the pedagogic apparatus means entering a field that involves both the sedimentation and the disruption of power relations. The molar and the molecular are not binary poles. I have suggested that the abject negation of the other as desiring subject, within the political conditions of school life, mean that these schools, like the neighbourhoods in which they are located, always exist at the border. I have also attempted to demonstrate how even there, on the border, where nothing is expected, we find subjects who do hope and desire, and participate in any activity that might become a vehicle for expression or self-expression.

When everything melts away, the struggle is to remain, to be present, to put stock in an institution that constitutes something more than an isolated individual. In times when crisis has become the most stable component of life, we find a struggle to wager on schools, to find a place in them, with students who get angry and fight and, above all else, desire. Before the image of abjection that is often imposed on these neighbourhoods, an image that includes diagnoses of apathy and calls for resilience, we find young people determined to continue to attend school and place their aspirations for the future in it; young people who do not passively accept the negation that falls on them and who refuse their status as subjects with no future. In the face of abject fear, it is crucial for these students to make visible situations in their lives that are unspoken; and we find subjects with a wealth of desires and aspirations that escape the nihilism of which they are accused as well as the abject negation of the neighbourhoods in which they were born.

A Deleuzian approach to the study of the pedagogical apparatus as it is experienced in schools on a daily basis means opening up a set of lines, of bifurcations and ruptures; it means approaching multiple situations of collapse and construction. Such ethnographic work entails addressing the multiple forces at play, in this case, in the daily workings of schools in a context of urban poverty. Other approaches quickly lead to binary readings that blame teachers and/or students for poor school performance or that idealise situations in which community virtue is the only way of dealing with the problems of daily life in the age of management, the age of letting do. With Deleuze, I have ventured other ways of addressing this field. That means approaching the empirical as the history of the present and addressing the political map, the daily life of institutions and/or individuals. I have discussed ways of addressing *the little crack, the imperceptible ruptures*, and how, through them, events change course. It is no longer, then, a question of the indifference of these young people and their unwillingness to learn, but of the complexity of their desires, the hints of affirmation as well as the tensions that they express when they say 'I want'. The always latent question continues to be to what degree these bifurcations are able to resist or transform current forms of domination. Once again with Deleuze (1990), we can say that the only way to resolve antinomies is to dissolve them. In any case, these flows of desire continue to do their work.

Notes

1. I have been able to carry out my research thanks to the following subsidy: *La escuela en la periferia metropolitana: escolarización, pobreza y degradación ambiental en José León Suárez* (Buenos Aires Metropolitan Area), CONICET 2010–12.
2. See, among many others, Rosenthal and Jacobson (1971); Bourdieu and San Martin (1988).
3. Indeed, her response and attitude brought me to a question that grew in intensity: with what concepts could I approach the fieldwork, given that reproduction and domination (Baudelot and Establet 1971; Bowles and Gintis 1981) were insufficient. This is because, among other things, the social never appears in this cut-and-dried fashion, with domination neatly separated from transformation.
4. Foucault's *Discipline and Punish* is a clear example but there are many more, from texts on the history of education to those that address the current transformations of educational policy and its design (Ball 2008; Popkewitz and Brennan 1998; Grinberg 2008). There are fewer works that address the actual, the daily workings of these apparatus, but see, among others Grinberg 2010.
5. In Deleuze and Guattari's terms, 'there is rupture in the rhizome whenever segmentary lines explode into a line of flight, but the line of flight is part of the rhizome. That is why one can never posit a dualism or a dichotomy, even in the rudimentary form of the good and the bad. You make a rupture, draw a line of flight, yet it is still a danger that you will encounter organizations that restratify everything, formations that restore power for a signifier, attributions that reconstitute a subject' (1987: 9).
6. Regarding the macro-micro distinction, I understand, along with Deleuze, that 'the differences do not pass between the individual and the collective, for we see no duality between these two types of problem: there is no subject of enunciation, but every proper name is collective, every assemblage is already collective' (Deleuze and Parnet 1987: 107).
7. Other works (Grinberg 2010 and 2011) contain a detailed description of the growth of these neighbourhoods.
8. While shantytowns first came into existence in the early twentieth century, they began to grow quickly towards the end of the century (Grinberg 2011). The financial crisis in Argentina in 2001 was unleashed by the restriction on withdrawals of cash from banks by means of a measure called the *Corralito*. This measure provoked widespread protests and the resignation of President Fernando de la Rúa in December 2001. Most of the people who participated in those protests took to the street spontaneously; they were not members of political parties or social movements. Thirty-nine people were killed by police and security forces during the protests; nine of them were under the age of eighteen.
9. I use the word 'approximately' as there are no official figures on how many *cartoneros* there are or how many people live in shantytowns.

10. One of the largest newspapers in the country said: 'Some 40 thousand *cartoneros* invade Buenos Aires night after night. Only about one quarter of them are classic hobos. The rest are people who lost their jobs or were never able to find work in the first place. And so they embark on a trade that has been saturated by an excess of workers.' See <http://edant.clarin.com/suplementos/zona/2002/10/27/z-00215.htm> (accessed 13 September 2012).
11. For a documentary on the train used to transport the *cartoneros* every night, see <http://www.cinenacional.com/peliculas/index.php?pelicula=3438> (accessed 13 September 2012).
12. For an array of reasons, in Argentina high schools operate during three 4-hour shifts (morning, afternoon and night), and students and their families decide which one to attend.
13. This is a pun: the Spanish word *blanca* (white) used in the name of the train for the *cartoneros* is very similar to the word for bullet (*bala*).
14. In keeping with Deleuze and Guattari: 'Desire, then, becomes the abject fear of lacking something. But it should be noted that this is not a phrase uttered by the poor or dispossessed' (2004: 29).
15. For more on these aspects of school life, see Grinberg (2011). Due to space limitations, they are only mentioned here.
16. Many public secondary school teachers in Argentina work in a number of schools in order to make ends meet.
17. 'The deliberate creation of lack as a function of market economy is the art of a dominant class. This involves deliberately organizing wants and needs (manque) amid an abundance of production; making all of desire tether and fall victim to the great fear of not having one's needs satisfied; and making the object dependent on a real production that is supposedly exterior to a real desire (the demands of rationality)' (Deleuze and Guattari 2004: 28).
18. 'Systems of power would emerge everywhere that re-territorializations are operating, even abstract ones. Systems of power would thus be a component of assemblages. But assemblages would also comprise points (*pointes*) of deterritorialization. In short, systems of power would neither motivate (*agenceraient*), nor constitute, but rather desiring-assemblages would swarm among the formations of power according to their dimensions' (Deleuze 1995: 7).

References

Ball, S. (1994), *Educational Reform: A Critical Post-structural Approach*, Philadelphia: Open University Press.

Ball, S. (2007), *Education plc. Understanding Private Sector Participation in Public Sector Education*, New York: Routledge.

Baudelot, Ch. and R. Establet (1971), *La escuela capitalista en Francia*, México: Siglo XXI.

Bourdieu, P. and M. de San Martin (1998), 'en Propuesta Educativa', 9(19), *FLACSO* Argentina: Buenos Aires Ediciones Novedades Educativas.

Bowles, S. and H. Gintis (1981), *La instrucción escolar en la America capitalista*, Buenos Aires: Siglo XXI.

Choi, J. (2006), 'Doing Poststructural Ethnography in the Life History of Dropouts in South Korea: Methodological ruminations on subjectivity, positionality and reflexivity', *International Journal of Qualitative Studies in Education*, 19(4): 435–53.

Davies, M. (2007), *Planeta de ciudades miseria*, Madrid: Foca.

Deleuze, G. (1990), *The Logic of Sense*, trans. M. Lester with C. Stivale, New York: Columbia University Press.

Deleuze, G. (1992a), 'What is a Dispositif?' in T. J. Armstrong (ed.), *Michel Foucault Philosopher*, New York: Routledge.

Deleuze, G. (1992b), 'Postscript on the Societies of Control', *OCTOBER*, 59 (Winter): 3–7.

Deleuze, G. (1995), *Negotiations 1972–1990*, trans. Martin Joughin, New York: Columbia University Press.

Deleuze, G. (1998), *Nietzsche y la filosofía*, España: Editorial Anagrama.

Deleuze, G. (2005), *La imagen-movimiento*, Buenos Aires: Paidós.

Deleuze, G. and C. Parnet (1987), *Dialogues*, trans. H. Tomlinson and B. Habberjam, New York: Columbia University Press.

Deleuze, G. and F. Guattari (1997), *¿Qué es la filosofía?*, España: Editorial Anagrama.

Deleuze, G. and F. Guattari (1987), *A Thousand Plateaus: Capitalism and Schizophrenia*, trans. B. Massumi, Minneapolis, University of Minnesota Press.

Deleuze, G. and F. Guattari (2004), *Anti-Oedipus: Capitalism and Schizophrenia*, Minneapolis, University of Minnesota Press.

Ehrenberg, A. (2000), *La fatigue d'être soi: depression et société*, Paris: Odile Jacob.

Foucault, M. (1996), *Vigilar y castigar. Nacimiento de la prisión*, México: Siglo XXI.

Foucault, M. (2006), *Seguridad, territorio y población*, Argentina: Fondo de Cultura Económica.

Grinberg, S. (2008), *Educación y poder en el siglo XXI. Gubernamentalidad y Pedagogía en las sociedades de gerenciamiento*, Buenos Aires and Madrid: Miño y dávila Editores.

Grinberg, S. (2010), 'Schooling and Desiring Production in Contexts of Extreme Urban Poverty: Everyday banality in a documentary by students', *Gender and Education*, 22(6): 663–77.

Grinberg, S. (2011), 'Territories of Schooling and Schooling Territories in Contexts of Extreme Urban Poverty in Argentina: Between management and abjection', *Emotion, Space and Society*, 4(3): 160–71.

Hickey-Moody, A. and P. Malins (2007) (eds), *Deleuzian Encounters: Studies in Contemporary Social Issues*, London: Palgrave Macmillan.

Mazzei. L. and K. Mc Coy (2010), 'Thinking with Deleuze in Qualitative Research', *International Journal of Qualitative Studies in Education*, 23(5): 503–9.

O'Malley, P. (2009), 'Resilient Subjects: Uncertainty, warfare and liberalism', Economy and Society, 39(4): 488–509.

Popkewitz, T. and M. Brennan (1998), *Foucault's Challenge: Discourse, Knowledge, and Power in Education*, New York: Teachers College Press.

Ringrose, J. (2011), 'Beyond Discourse? Using Deleuze and Guattari's schizoanalysis to explore affective assemblages, heterosexually striated space, and lines of flight online and at school', *Educational Philosophy and Theory*, 43: 598–618.

Rose, N., P. O'Malley and M. Valverde (2006), 'Governmentality', *Critical Social Policy*, 2: 83–104.

Rose, N. (1999), *Powers of Freedom: Reframing Political Thought*, Cambridge: Cambridge University Press.

Rose, N. and T. Osborne (1999), 'Governing Cities: Notes on the spatialisation of virtue', *Environment and Planning D*, 17(6): 737–60.

Rosenthal, R. and L. Jacobson (1971), *Pigmalión en el aula. Estudio de las expectativas del profesor sobre el rendimiento de los alumnus*, Madrid: Editorial Marova.

Tamboukou, M. (2010), 'Charting Cartographies of Resistance: Lines of flight in women artist's narratives', *Gender and Education*, 22(6): 679–96.

Youdell, D. (2011), *School Trouble*, London, Routledge.

Chapter 12

Lost in Data Space: Using Nomadic Analysis to Perform Social Science

David R. Cole

'Flexibility', 'nomadism' and 'spontaneity' are the very hallmarks of management in a post-Fordist, control society. (Fisher 2009: 28)

This chapter will use the nomadology of Deleuze and Guattari (1987) as a basis for social inquiry, and not a form of 'new management'. In *A Thousand Plateaus*, the nomad exerts force beyond the specific historical reality of the thirteenth-century Mongol nomadic invasions in Europe. This is because the nomad is treated by Deleuze and Guattari as a concept that has political, affective and social realities. In this chapter, I will take this concept of the nomad and use it to analyse qualitative data. The claim is that nomadic analysis serves to demonstrate a new way to perform social science that is non-sedentary. The concept of the nomad, and the resulting analysis, is given content through an Australian government-sponsored research project on the voices shaping the perspectives of young Muslim Australians. I was part of a team from the University of Technology, Sydney, which researched the voices that shape the opinions of young Muslims in Australia (2009/10). We looked, for example, at the religious, secular, community and peer influences on Muslims in Australia, and how they shaped the perspectives of the youth. It was clear that the questions concerning this research would, for the researchers, touch upon many levels, from the deeply personal to the global and political. For example, what was our political position as university-backed social researchers? Were we merely working for the government as part of an information sweep through Muslim communities? How should we deal with controversial issues, such as those concerning security and conflict?

I was given the responsibility of examining the qualitative data that the research methods generated, and this amounted to analysing large quantities of interview and focus-group transcripts for dominant

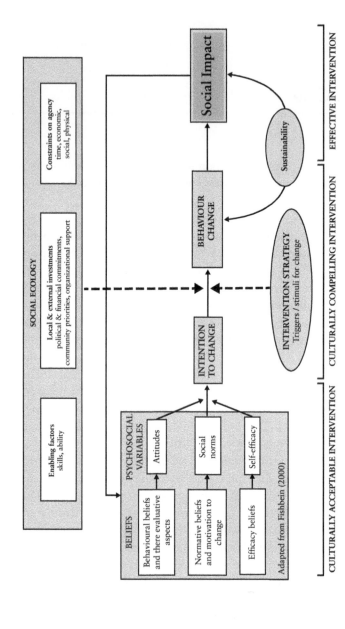

Figure 1. *After:* Panter-Brick et al. 2006: 2813.

themes. The government had asked us as part of the tender to describe the social ecology of the voices of influence on young Muslims in Australia. Social ecology refers to the ways in which social changes happen. The example that was chosen for the research plan concerned intervention to prevent the spread of malaria (see Figure 1).

The model of social ecological change in this diagram comes from medical literature about how to intervene in order to prevent malaria. The team employed this model as a means to explain the social ecology of young Muslims in Australia, and how it could change. The model of social ecology was chosen to represent social change, as it is a clear, scientific schema for intervention. However, the use of the model led me to ask questions such as: Does the social ecological perspective mean that we are preventing some kind of 'disease' during the research, as the malaria prevention model suggests? Who is doing the intervention with respect to young Muslims, and how can one be sure that the intervention and social change are well-intentioned? Who gets to decide what is a well-intentioned and/or appropriate intervention? Working in social inquiry with qualitative data can create irresolvable incongruities between research questions, data fields and analysis. For example, questions about social ecology that have been important to the research aims may become irrelevant given new understandings from data sets; or the rational analysis of dominant qualitative themes may create artificial boundaries between research zones that are not reflected in changing data. This chapter claims that nomadic analysis, which is a focused research and writing application of the nomadology of Deleuze and Guattari, offers a solution to the movement between contradictory pivots and conflictive points in qualitative social research. Nomadic analysis rests on the philosophy of immanent materialism that Deleuze and Guattari articulated in *A Thousand Plateaus*. This chapter will explain and exemplify nomadic analysis and immanent materialism with reference to the research project outlined above.

My Name is David

It is not often that one has to consider one's personal identity as a result of doing social inquiry, or as part of a government-sponsored project (although feminism has long advocated such a move). Yet this happened when I was constructing case studies as part of my designated role in researching the voices that influence young Muslims in Australia. I had been taken to Lakemba, the Muslim district in Sydney, by a local contact, who showed me around the area and introduced me to several young Muslims. One of these individuals was called Mohammed,[1] who worked in a cybercafé on Lakemba High Street. I spoke to Mohammed in the café while he was working, so our interviews were frequently interrupted. Despite these interruptions, I was beginning to understand the voices that were shaping his perspective, until a large man dressed in a traditional *djellaba* came into the cybercafé and started to shout at us. I am represented in the dialogue by the symbol, ®, Mohammed is (M):

> Man interrupting: Yes . . . So if you need something to talk about Islam, there is a people . . . there is actually sheikh available to tell you everything you want to know or you can talk to me. I made at least two hundred video on Islam, I actually I run the only Islamic TV in Australia. *Ahl al-Sunna al-Jamma* TV . . . Ahl al-Sunna means people of the way . . .
> (M): It's not about religion it's about . . .
> ®: It's about voices that influence young Muslims in Australian . . .
> Man interrupting: That's again. Now there is Islam, it means a submission, the one who submitted himself . . . see this child over there, he's a Muslim. You know I'm telling you . . . there's a perception that people have so Shias are not Muslims. Ninety five percent, it's us who are Muslims.
> ®: Right.
> Man interrupting: And there could be five percent of them who you consider Muslims and they consider themselves Muslims, so that's it, now we just got attacked again by you David (reference to ®) . . . Islam it's something else, Islam it's a belief from Allah and by our *Rasoul* shown the way how to do it. So that's something not he thinks I think. You know, these people, do you know much, there was great Imam *Abu Hanifa* who started the first school of jurisprudence and then Shias they wanted to discuss something with him so he came to them and he took his shoes inside and they told him, why did you take your shoes inside. He said because during Prophet, Shias used to steal the shoes. They told him, you lie, because during Prophet there was no Shias. He said well there is no need to discuss.

Above is a section of the transcript that was recorded just after the 'man interrupting' had appeared. The 'man interrupting' had previously asked about my name, and therefore knew that I was called David. To my surprise, I had been unexpectedly thrust into the Arab-Israeli conflict through my proper name and involvement with the social research project. This incident made me ask questions such as: Who am I? What am I *really* doing in this Muslim-dominated area of Sydney? The point here is that this individual experience is suggestive of rupture points in the lives of young Muslim Australians that cannot be represented by government reports due to their impersonal tone, bias towards facts, and 'smoothing' of the contradictions. Mohammed was a young Muslim from Pakistan who had come to Australia in order to study and to further his future career. He lives and works in Lakemba, and was therefore exposed to voices such as the one represented above by the 'man interrupting' on a daily basis. In contrast to Mohammed's empirical evidence, which included contradictory and multiple experiences, the final qualitative section of the Report called: 'Voices Shaping the Perspectives of Young Muslim Australians' divided the data into the following categories:

1. Identity – Individual and peers
2. Social networks of bonding and bridging – Family, community and society
3. Aspiration and inspiration – Individual, family and society
4. Safety and belonging – Individual, community and locality
5. Displacement – Individual, family and peers
6. Racism, prejudice and discrimination – Community and Society
7. Media and representation – Community, society and global
8. Sustaining youth programs – Society

(Collins et al. 2010: 79)

The section of the transcript above did not fit neatly into just one of these eight qualitative categories. At the very least, the evidence about the voices influencing Mohammed could be seen as involving the categories of identity; safety and belonging; and racism, prejudice and discrimination. But there was so much qualitative transcript evidence generated by the research that this episode did not make the final cut. This decision was taken because the verbal interchange above was too messy (see Law 2007), too conflictive, too 'mad' and potentially extreme. Yet of all the experiences that this year-long project generated, this was, for me, the most personally transformative because it made me question who I was and what I was doing in that situation. I suggest that the fact that this evidence was hard to categorise matters less than the potential impact it could have on transformations of the self (see Foucault 1977). At this point, I would like to turn to explaining nomadic analysis in order to more fully understand what happened to me in the cybercafé in Lakemba, and how any long-term effects may resonate through transformation and agency. To do so, it will be necessary to explore the notion of immanent materialism further, in order to build a robust conceptual unit for use in nomadic social inquiry (cf. Anyon 2009).

The Immanent Materialism of Nomadic Analysis

Nomadic analysis is a position for social inquiry derived from the work of Deleuze and Guattari. In *A Thousand Plateaus*, Deleuze and Guattari articulate a new type of materialism through specific historical moments and corresponding intellectual investigations relating to psychoanalysis, geology, linguistics, semiotics, the body without organs, etc. The nomad appears in the '1227: Treatise on Nomadology: The War Machine'. The purpose of this plateau is to describe the ways in which the modern state has emerged from feudalism and latterly merged with the war machine, which appeared in the thirteenth century on the Eastern horizon of Europe in the shape of the Mongol invasions. This critical crossing point in European history is played out today via political tensions between the nomadic and the sedentary; for example in immigration issues, particularly the lives and status of travellers and gypsies; in crafts and practices of metallurgy that have led to developments in electronics and computers (see De Landa 1991); and in the ways in which the state nurtures and uses science. This last complex point regarding nomadology is of particular relevance to nomadic analysis and how such a practice might frame the study of voices that influence young Muslims in Australia. This is because nomad science involves becoming, unstable identities, the questionable middle ground between participants and researchers (see Braidotti 2000), being lost and in-between research aims, methodology and executing the write up (e.g. McCoy 2010). Nomadic science differs from royal science that sets up stable identities, fixed categories and divisions between the researched and the researcher:

> What we have, rather, are two formally different conceptions of science, and ontologically, a single field of interaction in which royal science continually appropriates the contents of vague or nomad science while nomad science cuts the contents of royal science loose. (Deleuze and Guattari 1987: 367)

Nomad science acts as a platform for nomadic analysis. This is in turn part of the immanent materialism of *A Thousand Plateaus*, which encapsulates the moving fluxes or virtual multiplicities that Bergson (1965) had theorised in time. The idea behind immanent materialism is that history gives us a connection between specific confrontations and resolutions in material force and resources, such as the nomadic versus the sedentary, and the multiple flows of materiality that pass through these points – including thought and desire. Deleuze and Guattari mobilised an integrated philosophical system in order to connect these historical moments with temporal flows of materiality, a system made up of aspects of Bergsonian vitalism, Spinozism, Nietzschean will to power (becoming) and Marxian analysis of capital. The resulting perspective has been characterised as a type of panpsychism after Whitehead (1933), in that the temporal matter flows extend the mind into matter and vice versa. The move to panpsychism, however, invites empirical criticisms such as have been recently articulated by Ray Brassier:

> the celebrated 'immanence' of Deleuzean univocity is won at the cost of a pre-Critical fusion of thinking, meaning, and being, and the result is a panpsychism that simply ignores rather than obviates the epistemological difficulties [about the real]. The claim that 'everything is real' is egregiously uninformative – and its uninformativeness is hardly palliated by the addendum that everything is real precisely in so far as it thinks since, for panpsychism, to think is to differ. (2011: 48)

Brassier is pointing to the philosophical problem with immanent materialism and the real. There are no fixed boundaries between the real and the unreal according to Deleuze and Guattari. It is therefore impossible to distinguish between imagined and true data. This is a serious counterargument to the nomadic analysis of this chapter, if one wants to align it with royal or empirical science. How can one analyse the real and non-real voices of influence in the data? How can one avoid conceptual vagueness and a messy analytical connection between theory and data? These problems, however important their resolution is to royal science, are an integral part of the processes of nomadic science. This is because nomadic analysis 'is entirely oriented towards an experimentation in contact with the real. The map does not reproduce an unconscious closed in upon itself; it constructs the unconscious' (Hodgson and Standish 2009: 323). Nomadic analysis involves a social cartography that extends and plays with the forms of the real. This does make the real unstable, and this will be a problem for realists, yet the point is not to take away the grounds for common sense perceptions of the real, but to enable social inquiry to delve into conjoined material flows. These flows cross back and forth between the real and the unreal, for example, in sexual fantasy. This point may be illustrated through the current study, in which the voices that influence young Australian Muslims are analysed and categorised into themes as shown above (Collins et al. 2010). What this process misses out on are the subtle crossing points connected to power and any aspects of rupture – even with respect to negative themes. Nomadic analysis opens up questions to do with the voices that influence young Muslims in Australia by following messy and often vague fault lines in the data. Brassier is correct when he states that this process does not tell us much about the real, yet nomadic analysis does determine a different way of performing social inquiry, and this difference opens up new paths to the real, including a questioning of the real and the often unaccounted for multiplicities of the real. In the current study, this approach helps us to understand the complicated reality for young Muslims living in Australia through engagement with critical markers in their collective unconscious. This understanding of data is a rigorous practice that leads to precepts of nomadic analysis.

Precepts of Nomadic Analysis

The aim here is not to introduce a dualistic division between the way in which the qualitative analysis was carried out in the final governmental report and the proposed nomadic analysis. Rather, the two approaches are complementary – nomadic analysis adding a new dimension to social inquiry. To explain this position further, I will outline the precepts of nomadic analysis with a focus on the unconscious:

- This type of analysis takes forward previous work in the field of feminist nomadic inquiry (e.g. Braidotti 1994). This is because nomadic analysis interrogates between the gaps and through the lines of normatively determined debate about qualitative data, to reveal how subjects are explained unconsciously, from the inside, and in time.
- The nomad adds the necessity of movement and the apprehension of speeds in thought. This augmentation of cognition is based on the philosophical work of immanent materialism, which maps flows of matter in context, and therefore invites the construction of nomadic politics.
- The middle ground between the object and subject is navigated through nomadic analysis. This grounding and going 'back and forth' in the 'relationality' of research does not obviate subjects or objects, but attends to the power concerns that might arise during social inquiry. This attention to power concerns gives the researcher the freedom to articulate institutional, governmental, personal or tribal issues as they are presented during investigation.
- Space is put under pressure through nomadic analysis. For the nomad, any type of containment, whether physical or psychic, is an anathema, and produces a longing for the open steppe. For a university-trained researcher, this fact equates to sensitivity for spatial dynamics as well as restless curiosity and thought outside of institutionally determined norms.
- This pressure on space leads to the practice of deterritorialisation. Concepts, language and the ways in which concepts and language

relate to one another are henceforth exploded through nomadic analysis. The explosion of thought results in asymmetrical explorations of ideas and language in the data field, and away from sedentary approaches to the data.

- The explosivity of nomadic analysis includes giving attention to asignification in contrast to normative overcoding (see Masny and Cole 2009) that avoids meaninglessness. Asignification is not nonsense in the terms of nomadic analysis, but denotes the ways in which the subject escapes subjugation or crosses over in unexpected ways and therefore relates to agency.

- The position of the researcher is continually rethought according to nomadic analysis. Such a rethinking involves participating *with* the research data, and accepting that contact with qualitative data fields changes the researcher in accordance with the material flows that are discovered during research (see Cole 2007). These changes should be included in any research report.

- Beneath the 'skin' of nomadic inquiry lies the principle of multiplicity, or the ways in which research can burrow through the surface effects of the data and attend to multiple assumptions in the research project. The principle of multiplicity may be enacted through differentiating between finer and finer points in the research; these points may be perspectival, linguistic, conceptual or ideological. The principle of multiplicity is complementary to the research founding of difference in kind or as ontology (see Deleuze 1994), which nomadic analysis aims towards though not as subjectivity.

These precepts of nomadic analysis define a purposeful way of working with qualitative data in social inquiry (or war machine). Nomadic analysis complements positivist, psychological and sociological schemas for understanding data and the representation in data. It does not undermine alternative approaches to data handling, but provides another option, one that results in new ways to understand and write about qualitative data within, in this case, the constraints of a governmentally determined project. This research method is a perspective that requires the researcher to thoroughly interrogate his or her shifting relationships with the data field and how this field is represented.

'They Poison Us With Their Faces'

Young Muslims face a paradox with respect to living in Australia. This paradox may be summarised through the statement that Australia is a prosperous country, with a liberal, democratic and open political system that encourages diversity and the freedom of worship, yet concurrent with this surface effect is the history of colonialism and racism that was enacted by the British Empire. On top of these competing realities is the fact that Australia has recently embraced global consumer society, and this can be at odds with the religious tenets of Islam (see Schmidt 2004). The qualitative section of the Report submitted to the Australian government suffered when describing this reality. The data was broken up into themes that tended to isolate and categorise the ways in which the reality of the participants was discussed, and consequently did not get beyond a segmented analysis of the influence of voices on the young Muslims. This process of categorisation and segmentation also happens without the actor(s) inside these processes being fully accounted for. As a result, the thematic qualitative analysis handled a lot of rich data without drilling down into any troubling aspects of the information or discussing what this data meant beyond the categories. In contrast, and in line with nomadic analysis, I will include a short extract from a transcript of an interview with a young Muslim woman called Zain (Z), a twenty-two-year-old fourth-year student in my primary English cohort. The research project at a certain point during the data collection offered $50 gift cards as an incentive for participants, and Zain agreed to be interviewed about the voices that influence her perspective in my office on the university campus. Zain spoke confidently and at length about the voices that influence her perspective:

> (Z): I don't feel that it [discrimination] affects me badly or stops me from doing anything. For example, I'm playing Oztag with friends as a sport, with a bunch of girls in a team. But I read a couple of days ago in the media that FIFA had banned the Iranian women's soccer team because a girl had been strangled by her scarf. But then we had a sports boss in Australia coming out and saying that this wouldn't happen in Australia because that's discrimination. Look, you know this could happen to anyone and it's not the fault of the religion. So I feel pretty lucky living in Australia and the fact that people here are so open minded and they accept different religions. There is racism here, and I have experienced it, but no, I don't think that it's stopped me from doing anything.
>
> ®: Could you tell us a little about this experience?
>
> (Z): We were just walking in the street and someone looked at us as if they were going to *poison us with their faces*. One time someone came up to us and told us to go back to our country. I was like hold on I was born here,

I've been here all my life, then they react with, my God, they can speak English, do you know what I mean, they don't have that expectation of you. So I gave them a funny look and they walked away.
®: Was this an older or younger person?
(Z): Older, yes they were racists.

This dialogue about racism was included in the governmental report under the category of racism, prejudice and discrimination, as it was evidence of discrimination. Yet the report only categorised the data, and leaves the reader to interpret the actual circumstances. According to the nomadic analysis of this chapter, the poison in the faces of the Australians is more than a metaphor or example of discrimination. The 'poison' is a marker or rupture point for the ways in which material forces flow through Australian society. This circulation of antipathy may come to the surface through anti-Muslim sentiment, expressed for example by opposition MPs at election time when Islamic Schools apply for planning permission to build a new college, or, indeed, simply when people identified as Muslims walk down the street. Zain is a quiet, respectful woman, who hardly spoke up during the ten-week English course. Yet when I gave her the opportunity to discuss her experiences of being a young Muslim in Australia, she was articulate and passionate. Zain has taken on board the 'poison in their faces', and this sits in her unconscious to mark her out as 'other'. The power of the experience of being stared at with hatred is augmented by superstitions and beliefs in the Middle East about conjuring an 'evil eye' by looking at another person with sufficient loathing. One might rationally deny this influence, yet in the maelstrom of the unconscious, where the real is mixed up, actions and language can take on synthesised meanings, and the evil eye can have a major influence. Nomadic analysis focuses on the unconscious, not to make everything confusing, but to give beliefs such as the 'evil eye' their due influence in society. The point is not that Zain thinks about the 'poison in their faces' all the time, or that the poison has been magically secreted into her being, but that the poison signifies a marker of unconscious forces that flow through her memories and settle in forms of otherness. The nomadic analysis of this study joins this poison with my being marked out during the research as 'David', signifying more than my proper name. These two experiences demonstrate how the self may be questioned, and agency extended from the rational analysis of cause and effect. The result of nomadic analysis is that being 'called David' or being 'looked at with poison in their faces' are set free from their contextual groundings and given an augmented position in

the findings (cf. Tamboukou 2004). This augmented position has consequences for qualitative social inquiry in terms of meaning and affect.

One of the consequences is that the meaning of 'they poison us with
their faces' takes on new life according to nomadic analysis. This 'life'
is not an artificial or subjective decision on the part of the researcher,
but signifies a following of the material flows through the research
process. The 'poison in their faces' hints at a crack in normative or
accepted language, where the meanings that one might surmise from the
expression spread out and construct a plane of becoming or immanence
connected to 'no-sense'. One may understand this action of change via
Deleuze's (1997) and Badiou's (2003) analysis of Beckett, wherein they
'take advantage of this situation [language not making sense in Beckett]
to sketch a theory of the Other as a possible world, whose only point
of contact with the world of our reality is the Voice that no longer
makes sense' (Leclercle 2010: 149). The consequences of the poison for
Zain constitute otherness, as I was othered in Lakemba through being
publically named as David. Otherness is akin to inhabiting another
world, where meanings are mixed up and action can be misinterpreted
or ignored (see Cole 2008). Nomadic analysis is a passage to this other
place, in order to commune with the other, and to unravel the voices that
articulate the poison or the naming. In the case of Zain, the people who
had looked at her, told her to go back to her country and were aghast
when she spoke, are named through nomadic analysis. In my case, the
'male interrupting' has been located as the Voice that designates the
passage to another world of conflict and violence. Nomadic analysis
does not simply paint these othering agents in moral colours of black
and white, but invites an understanding of the world of the other, and
the voices of otherness. This writing, which deploys nomadic analysis
and immanent materialism to understand social data, is an exploration
of the factors of otherness.

Reflections

One of the professors leading the voices research project set up a new
website during the research cycle, which he called *The Institute of
Cultural Diversity*. I was invited along to the launch in downtown
Sydney, where the professor had assembled an impressive array of academics, state bureaucrats, politicians and other interested parties. I was
particularly struck by a young Muslim woman, who spoke eloquently
on the stage as part of the launch. I approached her after the show to
ask if she wanted to take part in the research project. She readily agreed,

and we arranged to meet in the city offices of my university. Sala (S) is a University of Sydney graduate, with driving ambition and the desire to make a difference in the world. Sala had been involved with many youth programmes and NGOs, including a magazine called *Reflections*:

> (S): Well I mean one of my experiences has been working with *Reflections* magazine, which was a young Muslim woman's magazine. It was developed based on the idea that young Muslim women need a voice and need to speak for themselves because it's often that they're spoken about and spoken on behalf of but they're never given the opportunity to air out their concerns.

The nomadic analysis of Sala's transcript is not as straightforward as that of Mohammed or Zain. This is because there were less rupture points or clear connections to otherness in Sala's narrative. She had successfully navigated her way out of Lakemba, and she was now set for a career in the Foreign Service or with the United Nations. She was an extremely articulate and forthright young woman, who spoke confidently on the research topics that related to the ways in which voices were influencing her perspective. In philosophical terms, her being 'is' grounded in 'becoming', in that she has enacted the will to power; difference was flowing through her in demeanour, conversation and poise – and through her career. Sala was on the way to a great future, as her ambition was matching achievement. Her parents, professionals who had emigrated from Lebanon in the 1970s, set up a corner shop to sustain their growing family, and had suffered racial discrimination and prejudice in Australia so that their children might prosper. This story lies embedded in Sala, and is a gateway to her nomadism, which may be more fully appreciated by deploying a strategy from the work of Elizabeth St. Pierre: 'The space of the aside contains more data, if you will, but data that may escape the violent coercion of manipulation, narration, and interpretation – but only if you wish them to' (St. Pierre 1997: 376). One needs to look for the asides in Sala's data, the data that escapes state science, or the kind of qualitative categorisation as was performed for the Australian government and listed above (Collins et al. 2010). The use of asides is important to the Deleuzian inspired nomadic analysis of this chapter, as it coincides with the rupture points in the narratives, and the ways in which the subjects change. St. Pierre's work is a useful addition to the argument here, as she has demonstrated the application of asides in her nomadic analysis of Georgian women in the United States.

The aside came in an instant when I was interviewing Sala in the city university tower. I suddenly realised the paradox in her story. This happened after I had turned the microphone off and had stopped recording the words. I had told her my story of going to Lakemba, and my experiences of dealing with the local cleric at the Mosque, the 'man interrupting' and a Muslim Youth association. In effect, she informally sided with my position of otherness. I was othered because I am a white, university-backed researcher, working on a project that had been funded by the government. Certain members of the Lakemba community treated me with distrust, and frankly, in the present climate of fear, I was not surprised. Sala, a young Muslim of Lebanese ancestry, had left Lakemba behind, and was now associating with politicians, academics and government officials (often white). She was also in the process of being othered, but by her roots. This change had left her in a potentially ambiguous position with respect to the practice and preaching of Islam as they took place in Lakemba. Sala hid this contradictory reality through her positive attitude and future orientation. Yet such idealism may catch up with her, as the desire to help young Muslims through securing a position of social power propels her away from the community that she wishes to aid. Sala's position had begun to resemble academics who investigate social activism and experience an internal rupturing and distancing between social action and the praxis of academic achievement (see Cole and Throssell 2008). This is because the social activist academic can become other to themselves, in that they have to discuss in intellectual terms their passions and motivating forces, thereby causing tension between subjectivity and the objectification of this subjectivity.

The War on Terror: *Taqiyya*

It could be argued that a new global 'plateau' has been reached after the events of 11 September 2001 in the United States. The 'war on terror' had started before 9/11, but after the attacks the ways in which the war on terror in Western democracies focused on Islamic extremists (or freedom fighters from the opposite perspective) were intensified globally. We are living through this age of intensification, and it is a macro factor with respect to the Australian voices research project. The war on terror has become a ubiquitous element in everyday life, both from a Western and an Islamic perspective. The infiltration of everyday life by war has also succeeded because 'New modes of disseminating terror threaten the basic notions of survival in general, creating a generalized state of terror where death hangs over, regulates, every moment that is lived' (Negarestani 2007: 54). The four most perspicuous modes of disseminating terror are the internet, television, radio and film. The qualitative analysis theme of 'Media and representation' did include material that addressed issues connected to these modes of dissemination, yet the government report failed in terms of following these issues into more controversial areas, such as the connection between the war on terror and *Taqiyya*, or the Islamic doctrine of deception on the field of battle (see Ibrahim 2010). Rather, the government voices analysis focused on aspects of the war on terror such as the culturally prevalent Islamophobia: 'The research literature, the survey, the interviews and the discussion groups all point to the long-term debilitating effects of what Muslim communities see as Islamophobia' (Collins et al. 2010: 128). The qualitative section of the report took a position on the voices of influence on young Muslims that defended the Muslim community of Australia. In effect, the report expressed empathy with a defensive Muslim position, rather than taking seriously the implications of the doctrine of *Taqiyya* as a coordinated response to the West's global war on terror. The empathy of the report was in line with the perspective of multiculturalism, which normatively determines the harmonisation of different cultural groups within one society. In contrast, nomadic analysis includes the concept of *Taqiyya*, as the nomadic analysis of data is able to move between focal points in order to describe the ways in which voices may be influential and how this connection is changing in the present climate:

> There has been a distortion and alteration of 'Taqiyya' (*Taghieh*) from its original defensive and devout function in the dawn of Islam. Rather than a strategic (dis)simulation – a justified concealment of true beliefs in situations where harm or death will definitely be encountered if the true beliefs are declared (the wider meaning of Taqiyya being to avoid or shun any kind of danger); it is reinterpreted as a silent and fluid military infiltration, a course of action which forms one of the elemental components of fetishized *Jihadism*. (Negarestani 2007: 57–8)

The closest alignment that I found with respect to *Taqiyya*, and its new meanings due to Jihadism, came in the cybercafé in Lakemba and after the incident with the 'man interrupting'. In the transcript, the 'man interrupting' mentions a 'child over there'. I subsequently went and interviewed this 'child', who was in fact a seventeen-year-old male Palestinian from Iraq called Ali (A). He had recently arrived in Australia, and spoke little English. I therefore asked him the prepared questions about the voices that influenced his perspective through a translator (T):

(T): Example.

(A): For example, in Iraq, if someone defends his country, they say about him terrorist. If anyone comes to take your country you have to defend it. It's not about religion. It's about defence about your country about yourself. They say you're gonna make bomb or something like that just about nothing. You defend your family, mother, father, or child if you're married, or wife. You have to defend you have to keep him safe.

Ali was obsessed by war. He argued in Arabic in front of me with the translator about the wars in Iraq and Israel, and kept coming back to the topic during the interview. It was as if war had got behind everything that Ali thought and said. The distortions of *Taqiyya* had spread in a conceptual field through which Ali now saw the world. This is more than ideology, discourse or phenomenology. The 'living out' of Taqiyya through a transcript such as Ali's requires a philosophical approach to data such as immanent materialism and nomadic analysis in order to make sense of the within-ness and disguise of the concepts involved (cf. Deleuze 1994).

(A) (Arabic – translated into English): Yes tell him that. Tell him that the Jews have been occupying Palestine for more than sixty-one years and every day they promise something and they're killing people, destroying people. Tell him they are the only ones who can kill . . .

(T): He's saying that the Jews for hundreds of years have been attacking Palestine and stuff, and all those little countries around there. He doesn't see the purpose, they just go in and kill kill kill, and come back out. Yeah, he's just wondering why.

(A) (Arabic – translated into English): Tell him, they don't want us to do anything. They just want us to sit there quietly. They don't want us to defend ourselves.

(T): He goes they're gonna get up and defend themselves. They're not just gonna sit there taking it. Like say someone came up to you and wanted to fight you. You wouldn't want to fight but if he comes up and throws a punch at you you're gonna defend yourself. You're not just gonna sit there and let him hit you. That's how he feels with the war.

Language gives the agent one way of disguising meaning, here through English-Arabic translation. Another form of disguise is by speaking in general, ambiguous and rhetorical forms. Furthermore, beneath the elements of linguistic deception, the underlying effect of this transcript is that of threat and potential violence. This is due in part to the emotional turmoil of the agent, and the expression of this turmoil when interviewed. In terms of nomadic politics, the material forces flowing through Ali are collected and dispersed in the vague admonishments of war. There is also the level of affect here (see Cole 2011), whereby Ali's desire to do something worthwhile in the world is regulated and formed by continuing global events such as the war on terror and *Taqiyya*. Needless to say, the dialogue above did not make it into the government report, but is included here as part of this nomadic analysis.

Conclusion

This study has shown how performing nomadic analysis creates differences in kind from royal or state science. One's position as a university researcher is put under pressure due to this approach. On one hand, the government funds research and accordingly indicates the outcomes, style of reporting and overall position that is to be taken on the data, in this case, that of social ecology. On the other hand, nomadism reconstructs the research from the inside and through the unconscious, putting pressure on the data field in terms of the rational nature of evidence and the concepts that nomadism implies. One could say that nomadic analysis acts as a kind of magnetism, drawing out the elements of the data with the greatest speeds and potential for transformation that is non-sedentary. The potential for transformation in nomadic analysis relates to the ways in which data affects the researcher and unties them from territorialised notions of information gathering. The skill of the nomadic analyst revolves around working in and through such data magnetism, allowing the data to transform the researcher, or to 'become other than' the normative. This point has been demonstrated in this chapter by the choice of transcript material and the corresponding analysis. Nomadic analysis leaves behind what is normatively bound, sedentary, 'defence-minded' and reactionary in the data. This nomadic form of qualitative research acts to sieve the data, focusing on the flighty, and grasping sometimes miniscule comments, moments and asides that have impact and traction. The researcher is necessarily lost in this process, neither being subjectively placed nor working entirely objectively. The highly volatile middle ground of the nomadic analyst is also a conceptual position, which Deleuze and Guattari (1994) later related to creativity. In their last joint work, they describe conceptual creativity as being the most important job of philosophy. This is because the thinker has to continually reinvent themselves on the conceptual plane in order to avoid the traps of ordered, conformist society and its latest fashions. The nomadic analyst requires a similar conceptual flexibility so they are not drawn towards a type of correlationalism (see Meillassoux 2006) between ideas and data. This correlationalism would reinforce an ideal of the nomad as romantic wanderer; in the case of this study, doing abstract, unrelated intellectual work on voices, young Muslims and their lives in Australia. In contrast, the nomadic analysis of this chapter, which works through immanent materialism, questions the gaps between thought and data, and aims to dissolve power dualisms or the imposition of one mandated perspective. The voices that influence young Muslims in Australia are detangled from their context, and henceforth sent on an unknown journey.

Note

1. All names that appear in this chapter (except mine!) are self-selected pseudonyms.

References

Anyon, J. (2009), *Theory and Educational Research: Towards Critical Social Explanation*, New York and London: Routledge.

Badiou, A. (2003), *On Beckett*, Manchester: Clinamen Press.

Bergson, H. (1965), *Duration and Simultaneity (With Reference to Einstein's Theory)*, Indianapolis: Bobbs-Merrill.

Braidotti, R. (1994), *Nomadic Subjects*, New York: Columbia University Press.

Braidotti, R. (2000), 'Teratologies' in I. Buchanan and C. Colebrook (eds), *Deleuze and Feminist Theory*, Edinburgh: Edinburgh University Press, pp. 156–73.

Brassier, R. (2011), 'Concepts and Objects' in L. Bryant, N. Srnicek and G. Harman (eds), *The Speculative Turn: Continental Materialism and Realism*, Prahan, Victoria: re.press, pp. 47–66.

Cole, D. R. (2007), 'Techno-shamanism and Educational Research', *Ashe! Journal of Experimental Spirituality*, 6: 1–22.

Cole, D. R. (2008), 'Deleuze and the Narrative Forms of Educational Otherness' in Inna Semetsky (ed.), *Nomadic Education: Variations on a Theme by Deleuze and Guattari*, Rotterdam: Sense Publishers, pp. 17–35.

Cole, D. R. (2011), 'The Actions of Affect in Deleuze: Others Using Language and the Language that we Make . . .' in D. R. Cole and L. J. Graham (eds), *The Power in/of Language*, Special Issue, *Educational Philosophy and Theory*, 43(6): 549–61.

Cole, D. R. and P. Throssell (2008), 'Epiphanies in Action: Teaching and learning in synchronous harmony', *The International Journal of Learning*, 15(7): 175–84.

Collins, J., A. Jakubowicz, A. Pennycook, D. Ghosh, D. Cole, A. Kais, J. Hussain and W. Chafic (2010), 'Voices Shaping the Perspectives of Young Muslim Australians', *Cosmopolitan Civil Societies Research Centre*, University of Technology, Sydney.

De Landa, M. (1991), *War in the Age of Intelligent Machines*, New York: Zone Books.

Deleuze, G. (1994), *Difference and Repetition*, trans. P. Patton, London: Athlone.

Deleuze, G. (1997), *Essays Critical and Clinical*, trans. D. W. Smith and M. A. Greco, Minneapolis: University of Minnesota Press.

Deleuze, G. and F. Guattari (1987), *A Thousand Plateaus: Capitalism and Schizophrenia*, trans. B. Massumi, London: Athlone.

Deleuze, G. and F. Guattari (1994), *What is Philosophy?* trans. H. Tomlinson and G. Burchell, London: Verso.

Fisher, M. (2009), *Capitalist Realism: Is there No Alternative?* Winchester: Zero Books.

Foucault, M. (1977), 'Theatrum Philosophicum' in *Language, Counter-memory, Practice*, New York: Cornell University Press.

Hodgson, N. and Standish, P. (2009), 'Uses and Misuses of Poststructuralism in Educational Research', *International Journal of Research and Method in Education*, 32(3): 309–26.

Ibrahim, R. (2010), 'How Taqiyya Alters Islam's Rules of War Defeating Jihadist Terrorism', *Middle East Quarterly* (Winter): 3–13.

Law, J. (2007), 'Making a Mess with Method' in W. Outhwaite and S. P. Turner (eds), *The Sage Handbook of Social Science Methodology*, Beverly Hills and London: Sage, pp. 595–606.

Leclercle, J. J. (2010), *Badiou and Deleuze Read Literature*, Edinburgh: Edinburgh University Press.

McCoy, K. (2010), 'Into the Cracks: A Geology of Encounters with Addiction as Disease and Moral Failing', *International Journal of Qualitative Studies in Education*, 23(5): 615–34.

Masny, D. and D. R. Cole (eds) (2009), *Multiple Literacies Theory: A Deleuzian Perspective*, Rotterdam: Sense Publishers.

Meillassoux, Q. (2006), *Après la finitude: Essai sur la nécessité de la contingence*, Paris: Seuil.

Negarestani, R. (2007), 'The Militarization of Peace: Absence of Terror or Terror of Absence?' in R. Mackay (ed.), *Collapse I*, Oxford: Urbanomic.

Panter-Brick, C., S. E. Clarke, H. Lomas, M. Pinder and S. W. Lindsay (2006), 'Culturally Compelling Strategies for Behaviour Change: A social ecology model and case study in malaria prevention', *Social Science and Medicine*, 62(3): 2813–41.

Schmidt, G. (2004), 'Islamic Identity Formation Among Young Muslims: The case of Denmark, Sweden and the United States', *Journal of Muslim Minority Affairs*, 24(1): 31–45.

St. Pierre, E. A. (1997), 'Nomadic Inquiry in the Smooth Spaces of the Field: A Preface', *International Journal of Qualitative Studies in Education*, 10(3): 365–83.

Tamboukou, M. (2004), 'Nomadic Trails in the Unfolding of the Self', *Spacesofidentity.net*, 4(2), Bazaar Issue/2nd Networks Special.

Whitehead, A. N. (1933), *Adventures of Ideas*, New York: The Free Press.

Notes on Contributors

Mindy Blaise
Mindy Blaise is an Associate Professor in the Department of Early Childhood Education and Co-director of the Centre for Childhood Research and Innovation, at the Hong Kong Institute of Education. Mindy's areas of research interest relate to working with 'postdevelopmental' and post-foundational perspectives to rethink early childhood teaching, research, curriculum and childhood. Her research focuses on gender politics in the early years and encourages the field to engage with, rather than shut-down, difference and diversity. She is currently involved in three research projects that are examining different aspects of childhood in the Asia-Pacific region. These include: Researching postcolonial childhoods across Hong Kong, Australia and Canada; Exploring the cultural politics of gender/sex/uality in early childhood across Hong Kong, Korea and Singapore; and The literacy wall: researching literacy activities in a Hong Kong kindergarten.

David R. Cole
David R. Cole is an Associate Professor in Literacies, English and ESL at the University of Western Sydney, Australia. David has edited four books called, *Surviving Economic Crises though Education* (Peter Lang); *Multiple Literacies Theory: A Deleuzian Perspective* (Sense), with Diana Masny; *Multiliteracies and Technology Enhanced Education: Social Practice and the Global* Classroom (IGI), with Darren Pullen; and *Multiliteracies in Motion: Current Theory and Practice* (Routledge), with Darren Pullen. He published a novel in 2007 called *A Mushroom of Glass* (Sid Harta), and his latest monograph is entitled *Educational Life-forms: Deleuzian Teaching and Learning Practice* (Sense). David uses his knowledge of Deleuze and multiple and affective literacies to investigate areas of educative interest.

Rebecca Coleman

Rebecca Coleman is a Lecturer in the Department of Sociology, Lancaster University. Her research is concerned with theoretical and empirical explorations of the relations between bodies and images, and has a particular focus on the future and affect. Publications include *The Becoming of Bodies: Girls, Images, Experience* (Manchester University Press) which develops a feminist Deleuzian account of empirical research with teenage girls, and *Transforming Images: Screens, Affect, Futures* (Routledge), an analysis of how images of transformation are organised around the potentiality of the future, and are felt and lived out affectively.

Sarah Dyke

Sarah Dyke is a PhD student based at the Education and Social Research Institute, Manchester Metropolitan University. Her research focus is to disrupt common sense notions of the autonomous, bordered, intentional subject whose actions, affects and body are individualised, categorised and fixed. Here, Sarah's particular area of interest is 'disordered eating', linguistic and bodily emissions in the context of the Deleuzian event. Work which Sarah hopes to develop in the future will explore the implications of the reification of anorexia in online and offline spaces. Here, the work of iconoclasm and the paradox that Sarah engages with in this volume will be advanced.

Silvia M. Grinberg

Silvia M. Grinburg is a researcher at the National Committee of Science and Technology in Argentina (CONICET), Professor of Pedagogy and Sociology of Education, Director of the Centre for Contemporary Pedagogical Studies (National University of San Martín, UNSAM), and Coordinator of the socio-pedagogic division, National University of Patagonia, UNPA. Silvia's interests include questions of educational inequality, specifically processes of subjectivation, governmentality, biopolitics and education. In recent years, she has been developing research in the contexts of extreme urban poverty and hyperdegraded territories (shantytowns). She has published extensively on these issues in books and journals including *Gender and Education* and *Emotion, Space and Society*.

Anna Hickey-Moody

Anna Hickey-Moody is a Lecturer in Gender and Cultural Studies at the University of Sydney where she teaches and supervises in the areas of youth culture, masculinity, the cultural politics of schooling and aesthetics. She has developed a philosophically informed cultural studies approach to the arts as a subcultural form of humanities education and is interested in recent theoretical turns to affect and the politics and aesthetics of masculinity. Anna's first book, *Unimaginable Bodies*, explores the implications of theories of affect for cultural studies of education. She argues that aesthetics can teach embodied knowledges of disabled young people, which may constitute counter-discourses to dominant medical and sociological narratives of these youth. She developed this approach in different ways in her second book, *Youth, Arts and Education*. This book rethinks the political significance of young people's art work to better understand the cultural knowledges they utilise in developing aesthetic subjectivities.

Alecia Youngblood Jackson

Alecia Youngblood Jackson is Associate Professor in the Department of Leadership and Educational Studies in the College of Education at Appalachian State University, USA. Her research interests bring feminist and poststructural theories of power, knowledge and subjectivity to bear on deconstructions of narrative, voice, experience, and materiality; and qualitative method in the postmodern. She has publications in *The International Journal of Qualitative Studies in Education, Qualitative Inquiry, The International Review of Qualitative Research*, and the *British Journal of Qualitative Research*. Her books include: *Voice in Qualitative Inquiry* (co-edited with Lisa Mazzei, Routledge) and *Thinking with Theory in Qualitative Research: Viewing Data Across Multiple Perspectives* (co-written with Lisa Mazzei, Routledge).

Jamie Lorimer

Jamie Lorimer is a Lecturer in the Department of Geography at Oxford. His research develops approaches to environmentalism for the Anthropocene. In an era when humans have become an earth-changing force we can no longer have recourse to modern understandings of a pure Nature, removed from Society and revealed through objective Natural Science. Instead, we need new approaches that are sensitive to the hybridity of the environment and the contested nature of claims for environmental knowledge. His research develops a new approach to biogeography that emphasises the dynamic, more-than-human nature of life, the practical and mediated nature of environmental knowledge, and the importance of cosmopolitan approaches to environmental politics.

The majority of his work has examined the history, politics and cultures of wildlife conservation.

Maggie MacLure

Maggie MacLure is Professor of Education in the Education and Social Research Institute (ESRI) at Manchester Metropolitan University. She has a particular interest in the development of theory and methodology in social research. She is the founder-director of the international Summer Institute in Qualitative Research. Her book *Discourse in Education and Social Research* (Open University) received a Critics' Choice Award from the American Educational Studies Association.

Lisa A. Mazzei

Lisa A. Mazzei is Associate Professor in the Department of Education Studies, College of Education, University of Oregon, USA, where she teaches curriculum theory and qualitative research. She is also Visiting Research Fellow at the Education and Social Research Institute, Manchester Metropolitan University, UK. She is co-author with Alecia Y. Jackson of *Thinking with Theory in Qualitative Research* (Routledge), co-editor of *Voice in Qualitative Inquiry*, with Alecia Y. Jackson (Routledge), and author of *Inhabited Silence in Qualitative Research* (Peter Lang).

David Mellor

David Mellor is a Research Assistant in the Graduate School of Education, University of Bristol, UK. He is currently working on the Governance of Educational Trajectories in Europe (GOETE) study. His publications can be found in the journals: *Sexualities, Cambridge Journal of Education, Qualitative Researcher* and *Gender and Education*.

Emma Renold

Emma Renold is Professor of Childhood Studies at the School of Social Sciences, Cardiff University, Wales. She is the author of *Girls, Boys and Junior Sexualities* (Routledge), the co-founder of youngsexualities.org and co-editor of the journal *Gender and Education* (2006–12). Working with feminist poststructuralist and post-humanist/new materialist theories, her research explores young gendered and sexual subjectivities across diverse institutional sites and public spaces. Her latest research project (with Gabrielle Ivinson) applies Deleuzo-Guattarian concepts to re-theorise bodies, affects and subjectivity in a community multimedia ethnography of girls' and boys' negotiations of place and space in a semi-rural post-industrial locale. She is currently working on an edited collection, *Childhood, Sexuality and Sexualisation* (with Jessica Ringrose and Danielle Egan).

Jessica Ringrose

Jessica Ringrose is a Senior Lecturer in the Sociology of Gender and Education at the Institute of Education, University of London. Recent research projects have explored gender and sexual identities among teens in secondary school, considering uses of digital technology, 'sexting' and 'cyberbullying'. She is part of an on-going research project with Emma Renold enacting feminist-research-activism-assemblages with teens and teachers in secondary schools. Theoretically and methodologically her work develops feminist poststructural and psychosocial approaches to understanding subjectivity and affect. Her recent books include *Rethinking Gendered Regulations and Resistances in Education* (edited, Routledge) and *Post-Feminist Education? Girls and the Sexual Politics of Schooling* (research monograph, Routledge).

Carol Taylor

Carol Taylor is a Senior Lecturer at Sheffield Hallam University. Carol's research interests are student engagement, gender, embodiment and subjectivity, 'new' material feminisms, power and spatiality, and student identities. Carol is interested in the development of visual, creative and participatory research methods, narrative theory, and feminist and post-structuralist methodologies. Her recent research projects include the use of videonarratives to promote student reflexivity; exploring student engagement using visual research methods; and a TLRP/BERA Meeting of Minds Fellowship which explored Deleuzian analytics in relation to educational practices. Carol is currently leading a project on student foodscapes.

Index